VW
TRANSPORTER
OWNERS WORKSHOP MANUAL
1954-1967

COVERING MODELS

Volkswagen Van, Pick-up, 1200cc 1954-1964

Volkswagen Kombi, Micro-bus, 1200cc 1954-1964

Volkswagen Van, Pick-up, 1500cc 1963-1967

Volkswagen Kombi, Micro-bus, 1500cc 1963-1967

BROOKLANDS BOOKS LTD.
P.O. BOX 904, AMERSHAM,
BUCKS, HP6 9JA. UK
sales@brooklands-books.com

INTRODUCTION

This do-it-yourself Workshop Manual has been specially written for the owner who wishes to maintain his vehicle in first class condition and to carry out the bulk of his own servicing and repairs. Considerable savings on garage charges can be made, and one can drive in safety and confidence knowing the work has been done properly.

Comprehensive step-by-step instructions and illustrations are given on most dismantling, overhauling and assembling operations. Certain assemblies require the use of expensive special tools, the purchase of which would be unjustified. In these cases information is included but the reader is recommended to hand the unit to the agent for attention.

Throughout the Manual hints and tips are included which will be found invaluable, and there is an easy to follow fault diagnosis at the end of each chapter.

Whilst every care has been taken to ensure correctness of information it is obviously not possible to guarantee complete freedom from errors or omissions or to accept liability arising from such errors or omissions.

Instructions may refer to the righthand or lefthand sides of the vehicle or the components. These are the same as the righthand or lefthand of an observer standing behind the vehicle and looking forward.

OWM834

ISBN   9781855201972

First Edition 1970
Brooklands Edition 1991

© Brooklands Books Ltd. 1993 and 2014

CONTENTS

Newcomer Sets High Standard

German-built 15-cwt. Van has Four-wheel Independent Suspension and Rear-mounted Air-cooled Engine : A Cab Heater and Other Refinements are Provided

by Laurence J. Cotton, M.I.R.T.E.

(Above) Stop-start tests were accomplished on a 1 in 4¼ gradient when carrying part load. The Volkswagen has a smart appearance with modern styling. (Right) The van is seen here approaching Ludgate Circus, with Holborn Viaduct in the background, during its trials in London traffic.

THERE are few power units, for light commercial vehicles, that can compare with the efficient operation of the Volkswagen four-cylindered horizontally opposed petrol engine. In its entirety, the 15-cwt. van is remarkable both in construction and performance, as I found during a series of tests, totalling over 200 miles in one day. Much can be said for the driving comfort in that I felt far from weary at the end of the run.

Having previously driven a Volkswagen in Germany, its liveliness with light load was not surprising, but trying the van with a 15-cwt. payload on home ground confirmed that it is speedy and economical, and well equipped, in its lowest ratio, to soar over the 1-in-4¼ gradient of Succombs Hill with power to spare.

In physical layout it is similar to the Volkswagen car, having the compact, four-stroke, overhead-valve petrol engine housed in a compartment at the rear. It is air cooled by a fan and a constant temperature is maintained by a thermostat which also passes a regulated flow of air over an oil cooler. No difficulties were encountered in cold-start tests after the van had been left out overnight on a parking ground during a period when several degrees of frost were recorded.

The engine is reached by lifting a

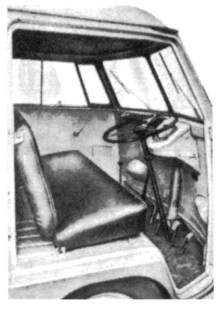

The wide forward-hinged door provides easy access to the cab, which has a bench-type seat. The heater duct is seen attached to the front panel.

hinged panel at the back of the body. In this compartment there are also the 6-v. battery, 8¾-gal. petrol tank and spare wheel, the latter being housed on a shelf above the power unit. Accessibility to the dynamo, coil, distributor, carburetter and petrol pump, is excellent, which is to be expected with the small, flat engine being housed longitudinally in a compartment which is as wide as the body.

As my tests started before daybreak, I appreciated the built-in illumination of the engine bay when connecting the petrol lift pump to an auxiliary supply. This small attention to detail is found in many other parts of the van.

The clutch and four-speed synchromesh gearbox are attached to the front of the engine and the final drive is through a spiral-bevel gear to swinging half axles, and then through a secondary spur reduction gear in the hubs. The Volkswagen power and transmission units are thus compactly grouped and arranged for easy change or major repair. The engine, of 1.192-litres capacity, and a compression ratio of 6.2 to 1, develops 30 b.h.p. at 3,400 r.p.m.

Like the car, the commercial version, which is available as a van, eight-seater bus, ambulance and as a combination of a bus and van, is of semi-integral construction having a basic structure for all models but differing in the assembly of the upper sections.

The commercial versions are all forward-control types with the front axle situated directly below the full-width driving seat. Considering the 8-ft. wheelbase is about the same as many local-delivery electric vehicles, the suspension of the Volkswagen is extraordinarily good.

The independent front suspension units employ trailing links on laminated square-section torsion bars and the independent units at the divided rear axle have round-section torsion bars. Double-acting hydraulic shock absorbers are fitted at all wheels.

Good Suspension

Although tested with varying payloads up to 17 cwt. maximum, I found nothing to criticize in the springing, and even deliberate driving over a 4-in. kerbstone at 15 m.p.h. failed to " bottom " the buffers.

The wide cab doors, hinged at the front, give good access to the driving seat, but the gear and hand-brake levers projecting through the floor obstruct the driver so that he cannot get out on the near side without some difficulty. There is a speedometer-milometer which is the only instrument provided, the head lamp beam, traffic indicators, dynamo charging and oil pressure being indicated by lights on the facia panel.

No fuel gauge is provided, but the tank has a three-way tap affording a one-gallon reserve after the main supply is used. Although austere, the instrument-panel equipment is adequate for a van.

Built-in Heater

With the engine at the back of the body, the cab would be cold in winter without some form of heating. A built-in heater, therefore, forms standard equipment, hot air from the engine being suitably ducted to the cab.

This I found to be most effective within a few minutes of starting the engine, and the only possible fault that could be visualized is that fumes that are prone to emanate from an engine that has seen considerable service might also be forced into the cab. As it is, Volkswagen has provided an effective unit without additional cost.

(Above) The Volkswagen climbed Succombs Hill, carrying full load, without stopping on the 1 in-4¼ section. It is well geared for rapid local delivery and is economical under all conditions of load or duty.

The cab furnishing is severe, a compressed paper-board lining being used to window level, and, as already indicated, the instrumentation costs little. It is surprising, therefore, to find swivelling glass vents and sliding windows in the doors, twin windscreen wipers, and cab and interior lights in the body forming standard equipment.

The low engine position does not prevent rear doors being fitted to the van body, but on the model tested there was a 3-ft. 10-in.-wide opening with two doors at the near side and similar doors can be provided at the off side as an optional extra. For a 15-cwt. van the payload space of 141 cu. ft. in the main section of the body, plus another 21 cu. ft. over the engine bay, might invite overloading. The loading height, when unladen is 1 ft. 7 in.

After taking delivery of the van from V.W. Motors, Ltd., in London, I loaded 15-cwt. of ballast in the body and drove through the busiest part of the city to the suburbs. The engine idled and ran smoothly, but, like other Volkswagen models I have driven, could not always be guaranteed not to stall when pulling up sharply in traffic.

Although its acceleration, with load, could not equal that of the fast newspaper delivery vehicles, the van put up a spirited performance and

Volkswagen Consumption Tests

Load	Non-stop		One stop per mile		Four stops per mile	
	m.p.g.	m.p.h.	m.p.g.	m.p.h.	m.p.g.	m.p.h.
15 cwt.	28.7 at	31.2	25.7 at	31.6	19.1 at	27.1
8 cwt.	32 at	31.6	28.6 at	31.7	21.6 at	27.9
Empty	33.3 at	31.6	30.5 at	31.6	24.6 at	27.9

with reduced payload it kept its place at the head of all other traffic.

Apart from being easy to control in steering and general handling, the gear change was without fault and rapid movements of the lever evoked no protest from the box. It is preferable to pass through all four gears for the best acceleration with full load. On a quiet level stretch of road alongside the Thames I found the acceleration rate to be from rest to 30 m.p.h., 13.2 sec., and to 40 m.p.h., 22.7 sec.

No Wheel Locking

The maximum effort on the pedal failed to lock the wheels during braking, which is unusual for a vehicle of the light-van class. The Volkswagen has hydraulic braking which, when carrying full load, will stop the van in 43 ft., from 30 m.p.h., which corresponds to 0.7g. The excellent distribution of load, 18¼ cwt. on the rear axle and 18 cwt. at the front, may have been contributory to the prevention of wheel locking although the brake frictional area corresponds to 81 sq. in per ton with this load.

Before starting consumption trials from Godstone, I tried the Volkswagen on Succombs Hill to verify the maker's claim that the van will climb a 1 in 4.3 gradient with full load. This it did without faltering, but I could not stage a stop-start trial on the 1 in 4¼ gradient without abusing the clutch. With an 8 cwt. payload, however, the result was quite successful. The van made no fuss when starting from rest on a 1 in 5 gradient with a 15-cwt. load and a passenger. It was well geared for general work.

Extensive fuel consumption trials

5

were made, embracing varying degrees of load and making one- and four-stops-per-mile tests in addition to continuous running. The result of these trials is shown in the accompanying table, the speed for the one- and four-stops-per-mile tests being developed from the time the wheels were turning.

By running these trials early in the morning there were no traffic difficulties, and between 5.30 a.m. and 10 a.m. 18 runs were made with comparable conditions and reasonably equal average speeds. From the results it is apparent that the maker's claim for a consumption rate of 30 m.p.g. is not unreasonable at a steady speed with load. The course chosen was slightly undulating.

As I did not spare the engine or brakes during the local-service trials, the return of 19.1 m.p.g. carrying full load and stopping every ¼ mile is an economical figure. It is upon the results of these trials that I acclaim the Volkswagen engine to be above average in its efficiency. It is especially good for local deliveries because of its rapid " warm up " from cold, no engine heat being lost in a water-cooling jacket.

After 200 miles arduous work there was no increase in pedal travel, neither could the brake adjusters be taken up without binding the wheels. If competition is measured by the performance of the Volkswagen the standard is high.

MODEL : Volkswagen 15-cwt van.

WEIGHTS :

	Tons	cwt.	qr.
Unladen	—	18	0
Payload	—	15	0
Driver, observer, etc. ..	—	3	2
	1	16	2

DISTRIBUTION :

Front axle	—	18	0
Rear axle	—	18	2

ENGINE : V.W. four-cylindered horizontally opposed overhead-valve petrol engine; bore 77 mm. (3.03 in.); stroke 64 mm. (2.52 in.); piston-swept volume 1.192 litres (72.74 cu. in.); maximum output 30 b.h.p. at 3,400 r.p.m.; R.A.C. rating 14 h.p.

TRANSMISSION : Through single-dry-plate clutch to four-speed gearbox, and spiral-bevel drive to open driving shafts with reduction gear in the hubs.

GEAR RATIOS : 3.60, 1.88, 1.23 and 0.8 to 1 forward; reverse 4.63 to 1; rear-axle ratio 6.2 to 1.

BRAKES : Hydraulically operated to all wheels. Hand brake linked mechanically to rear wheels only. Diameter of drums 9 in.; total frictional area 81 sq. in., that is, 44.4 sq. in., per ton gross weight as tested.

FRAME : Integral with body.

STEERING : Worm and cam follower.

SUSPENSION : Two square laminated torsion bars at front, individual solid torsion bars at rear. Double-acting hydraulic shock absorbers at all wheels.

ELECTRICAL : 6v. compensated-voltage-control system with 85-amp.-hr. battery.

FUEL CONSUMPTION : (a) Non-stop, 28.7 m.p.g. at 31.2 m.p.h. average speed; (b) one stop per mile, 25.7 m.p.g.; (c) four stops per mile, 19.1 m.p.g.; that is, 52.4 gross ton-m.p.g. as tested (a), 46.9 gross ton-m.p.g. (b) and 34.8 gross ton-m.p.g. (c) giving a time-load-mileage factor of 1,633.

TANK CAPACITY : 8¾ gallons, range approximately 160-250 miles.

ACCELERATION : Through gears, 0-30 m.p.h., 13.2 sec.; 0-40 m.p.h., 22.7 sec.

BRAKING : From 20 m.p.h., 19 ft. (22.5 ft. per sec. per sec.); from 30 m.p.h., 43 ft. (22.5 ft. per sec. per sec.).

WEIGHT RATIOS : 0.823 b.h.p. per cwt. gross weight as tested. Payload 41 per cent. o gross load.

TURNING CIRCLES : 37 ft. both locks.

MAKERS : Volkswagenwerk, G.m.b.H., Wolfsburg, Brunswick, Germany. Concessionnaire : V. W. Motors, Ltd., 7-9 St. James's Street, London, S.W.1.

ROAD TEST No. 513—VOLKSWAGEN 15-CWT. VAN

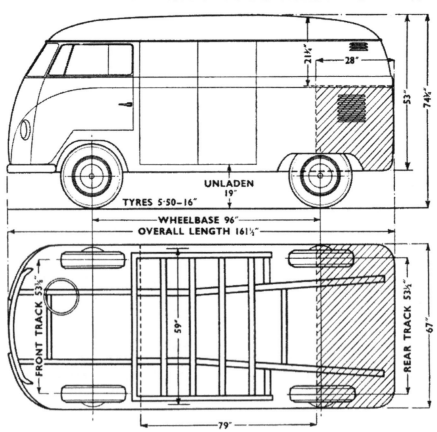

This article first appeared in Commercial Motor in April 1954 and we are indebted to them for allowing us to reprint it.

GENERAL DESCRIPTION

The illustration is a section through a typical Volkswagen Transporter showing the disposition of the various components. The chassis frame is a steel floor stiffened by a deep backbone tunnel down the middle. Outrigger members connect the backbone to a sill round the outer edge to which the body is bolted, the assembly being an extremely rigid structure. The floor carries a front plate to which the front suspension and steering system is bolted, and a fork at the rear supports the engine and transmission unit.

The flat four ohv engine is aircooled by a fan in a housing, the fan being bolted to the front end of the generator shaft. Heated air is ducted to the vehicle interior when required. The engine is bolted to a four-speed transmission unit, the final drive being to the differential. From here the drive passes to axle shafts which are carried inside tubes ball jointed to the transmission casing. The outer ends of the tubes carry the brake mechanisms and radius arms, the arms being secured to the outer ends of torsion bars to provide the rear suspension system. The axle shafts carry the hubs and rear wheels at their outer ends. In order to obtain the required gear reduction the outer ends of the rear axle casings carry double-reduction gearing.

The front suspension consists of transverse torsion bars carried inside tubes bolted to the frame. The outer ends of the bars are coupled to arms which in turn are connected by links to the kingpins and stub axles for the front wheels. Thus, the wheels are all independently sprung and damping is provided by telescopic tubular dampers. The controls and steering are located well forward of the front axle.

Major modifications in design were made on the following dates. It will be noticed that after the initial change of engine capacity in January of 1954 most of the other changes take place in August of each year. This is the result of skilful planning to ensure that any reorganization of the assembly lines is made during the work's shutdown for the annual holiday.

A sectional view of the Transporter

January 1950: The Transporter model introduced with an 1131 cc engine.

January 1954: The '1200' model is introduced, with the engine capacity raised to 1192 cc and the compression ratio to 6.6:1. Power output goes up from the original 25 bhp to 30 bhp at 3400 rev/min. An oil bath air cleaner is fitted, the ignition and starter switches are combined and the lubrication and carburetter systems modified.

May 1959: The Transporter engine completely redesigned. The cylinder head has wedge-type combustion chambers with valves working at an angle. Separate cam followers are substituted for the earlier pushrod and follower assembly. The crankcase is stiffened, a sturdier crankshaft is fitted and the fuel pump location and its drive redesigned. A fully-synchronized gearbox is also fitted to the Transporter.

August 1960: The compression ratio is increased to 7:1, which pushed the power output up to 34 bhp. All models have the four forward gears synchronized. The carburetter is fitted with an automatic choke and the distributor changed from one with centrifugal and vacuum advance mechanisms to one with vacuum advance only.

August 1962: A new fresh-air heating system is introduced. Heat exchangers in the exhaust system ensure that the heated air is free from fumes.

August 1964: A new engine cooling system is fitted. This controls the volume of cooling air by flaps instead of by the original regulator ring. This provides for a larger volume of heated air to the vehicle interior without over-cooling the engine when starting up from cold.

January 1963: The Transporter is fitted with a 1493 cc engine. The compression ratio is 7.8:1 and the power output 42 bhp at 3800 rev/min. On some models the front and rear brake circuits are independently operated by a tandem master cylinder.

August 1967: The engine capacity is increased to 1584 cc with a compression ratio of 7.7:1. The power output of this engine is 47 bhp at 4000 rev/min. A 12-volt electrical system is introduced.

Model identification: It is important to quote this when ordering spare parts, or in correspondence with the manufacturers. The locations of the three sets of numbers are as follows:

The identification plate: On earlier Transporters it is in the cab roof on the righthand side of the air duct. On later Transporters the plate is on the righthand side of the cab rear panel.

The chassis number: This is to be found in the engine compartment on the righthand engine coverplate.

The engine number: On all models this is stamped on the crankcase flange immediately below the generator support bracket.

CHAPTER 1

THE ENGINE

1:1 Description

In such an unconventional vehicle as the Volkswagen Transporter it would be reasonable to expect an engine of equally unconventional design and this is the case. Examination of **FIGS 1:1** and **1:2** will enable the component parts to be identified and it will soon become apparent that there is very little difference between the basic design of the early and late type engines. The flat-four arrangement of the cylinders is such that pairs of cylinders face each other horizontally on either side of the crankshaft. The four finned cylinder barrels are identical and interchangeable and closely resemble their motorcycle counterparts, being cooled by air, flowing over the fins. Cylinder heads are provided by a single aluminium alloy casting to each pair of cylinders, the casting being secured by eight long studs and nuts. To give more durable working surfaces there are pressed-in valve guides and valve seat and sparking plug inserts.

On the early engine the overhead valves are horizontally disposed and are operated by inclined pushrods with integral cam followers. The later design of engine has inclined valves 8 and pushrods 20 in **FIG 1:2**. The inner ends of the rods register in separate bucket-type cam followers 22. Oiltight pushrod covers are ribbed to accommodate changes in length due to expansion and contraction. The slope on the covers enables lubricating oil from the valve gear to drain back into the crankcase.

The two pairs of cylinders 9 are mounted on a crankcase which is split vertically on the centre line. During manufacture the two halves of the crankcase are machined as an assembly and only a complete crankcase can be supplied as a spare part. It is not possible to renew one half of the case by itself.

The crankcase carries the crankshaft 26 in four bearings, No. 1 bearing at the front being a light-alloy bush with flanges to take end thrust. No. 2 bearing is of the split light-alloy type although later engines may have steel-backed lead-alloy shells. Nos. 3 and 4 are light-alloy bushes. The bearing surfaces of the crankshaft are hardened.

The short and very sturdy connecting rods 15 are fitted with thinwall lead-bronze bearing shells in the big-ends and there is a bronze bush for the gudgeon pin in the small-end.

The light-alloy pistons 10 carry fully floating gudgeon pins which are retained by circlips and there are three piston rings, the bottom one being of the oil control type.

On early engines the short, stiff, camshaft 28 runs in bearings machined directly in the crankcase, but on later

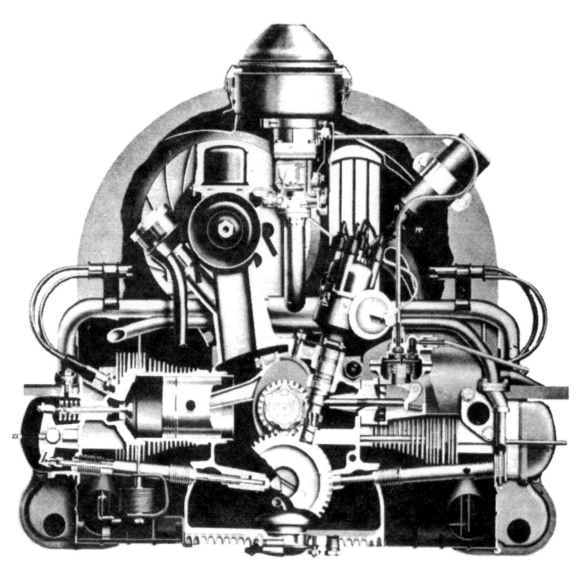

FIG 1:1 A sectioned view of the earlier design of engine showing the horizontal valves and one-piece pushrods and cam followers. Note the horizontal pushrod operating the fuel pump on the lefthand side below the distributor

engines the bearings are fitted with renewable liners. The rearmost bearing liners are flanged to take care of end thrust due to the helical timing gear. There are only four cams because each one operates two valves, one on each side of the engine. The large single helical timing gear is made from light-alloy and is riveted to the camshaft. It engages with a smaller gear which is keyed to the crankshaft between rear bearings 3 and 4. The rear end of the camshaft drives an orthodox gear-type oil pump 27.

The pump draws lubricating oil from a strainer 29 in the ribbed sump and passes it to a vertical oil cooler 3 positioned in the air flow from the cooling fan. From here the cooled oil passes through drilled passages to the main and big-end bearings, to the camshaft bearings and up the hollow pushrods to the rockers and valve gear. From here the oil drains down the inclined pushrod covers back to the sump. The cylinder walls, pistons and gudgeon pins are lubricated by splash. In cold weather, when the oil is of high viscosity a pressure relief valve 11 allows oil to pass directly to the engine without passing through the cooler.

The distributor 6 is driven by a spiral gear keyed to the crankshaft just in front of the rear bearing.

The generator 24 is belt-driven from a pulley on the rear end of the crankshaft. The forward end of the generator shaft carries a fan 12 which supplies the large volume of cooling air required. Some of this air, when heated by the exhaust system is used for interior heating. On the early engine the amount of cooling air was automatically controlled by a thermostat and a throttle ring, but as this often restricted the amount of air for heating the interior, the system was changed to one where the volume of air is not restricted. The flow of air through the engine cooling ducts is then thermostatically controlled by flaps instead. On the later engines heated air for the interior is obtained by passing air over finned heat exchangers 21. This replaces the original system in which it was possible for fumes to contaminated the heating air.

The complete engine is not attached to the chassis but is secured by four bolts to the transmission flange which is in-line with the rear face of the flywheel 25. The transmission and final drive case is flexibly mounted in a

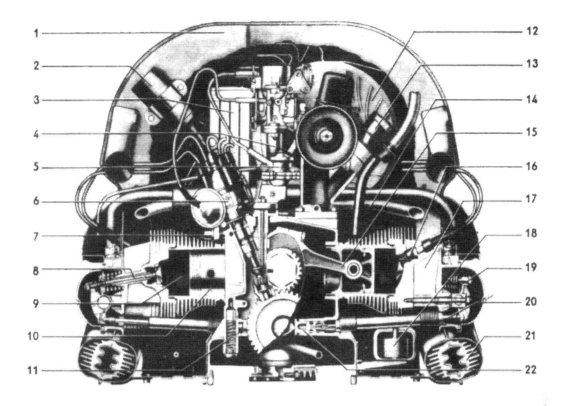

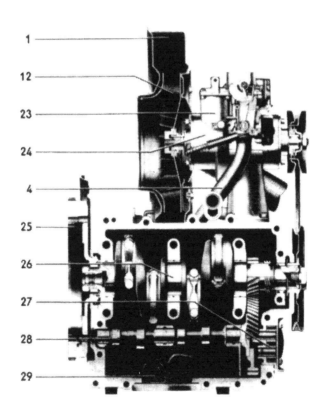

FIG 1:2 The redesigned engine introduced in May 1959. Note the inclined valves, the separate cam followers and the new position for the fuel pump, with vertical pushrod operation

Key to Fig 1:2   1 Fan housing   2 Ignition coil   3 Oil cooler   4 Intake manifold   5 Fuel pump   6 Distributor
7 Oil pressure switch   8 Valve   9 Cylinder   10 Piston   11 Oil pressure relief valve   12 Fan   13 Oil filter and breather
14 Preheating pipe   15 Connecting rod   16 Spark plug   17 Cylinder head   18 Thermostat   19 Rocker arm
20 Pushrod   21 Heat exchanger   22 Cam follower   23 Carburetter   24 Generator   25 Flywheel   26 Crankshaft
27 Oil pump   28 Camshaft   29 Oil strainer

FIG 1:3 Using feeler gauges to adjust the valve rocker clearance

FIG 1:4 Finding TDC when adjusting valve clearances. Pulley notch in-line with crankcase joint (righthand dotted line), and rotor arm in-line with notch on distributor body (lefthand dotted line)

cradle formed at the rear end of the chassis backbone. The engine is thus cantilever mounted and can be withdrawn from the transmission simply by detaching the wiring, the carburetter controls and the fuel pipe and undoing the four bolts. It will be noted that the sump is part of the crankcase so that it is impossible to service the camshaft and crankshaft components without removing the engine and splitting the crankcase.

It is proposed to use not only the designations '1200' and '1500' throughout this Manual but to append the bhp figures as well. This will enable us to cover engines of the same capacity but of different design, the most important change being in May 1959 when a completely redesigned engine was introduced.

1:2 Servicing without engine removal

Apart from adjustments to the fuel and ignition systems, and these will be found in the appropriate chapters, the most likely operation to be tackled without removing the engine is that of adjusting the rocker clearance. Adjustment of fan belt tension is covered in **Chapter 4, Section 4:6**.

Adjusting the rocker clearance:

Valve clearance increases when the engine is hot, so all adjustments must be made with the engine cold. Excessive clearance leads to noisy operation and performance suffers because the timing will be wrong. Insufficient clearance will also affect the timing. If the clearance is very small the valves will not be seating when they are supposed to be closed and this will cause burning of both valves and seats. The reduced compression will then lead to poor performance.

FIG 1:3 shows the method of making clearance adjustments. Before removing the covers to gain access to the rockers it is essential to clean all dirt from the covers and surrounding parts. Then prise off each spring clip and remove the covers. If the gasket sticks firmly to one surface, leave it in position, but if there has been obvious leakage from the cover joint be prepared to renew the gasket.

Adjustment should be made in a cylinder sequence of 1, 2, 3 and 4. Viewing the cylinders from the rear of the car, No. 1 is right front, No. 2 is right rear, No. 3 is left front and No. 4 is left rear. Start with No. 1 cylinder. The two valves will be fully closed on the compression stroke when the piston is at TDC. This position is found quite simply by turning the engine over by pulling on the fan belt. Alternatively use a spanner on either of the pulley nuts. Remove the distributor cap and turn the engine anticlockwise. Watch the front rim of the crankshaft pulley for a notch, and when this is in-line with the vertical joint between the crankcase halves, the rotor arm of the distributor should be in the position shown in **FIG 1:4**. Note that the righthand notch in the pulley is used as a datum and the rotor is in-line with a small nick on the face of the distributor body. In this position the rotor indicates TDC for No. 1 cylinder on the compression stroke. To arrive at the same position for No. 2 cylinder turn the engine anticlockwise 180 deg. so that the rotor arm turns through 90 deg. Two further rotor movements of 90 deg. each will give the TDC positions for cylinders 3 and 4.

With No. 1 cylinder correctly set, check the clearances between No. 1 rocker arms and valve stems with feeler gauges. If incorrect, adjust as shown by loosening the locknut and turning the adjuster until the correct feeler just slides between the surfaces. Hold the adjuster with the screwdriver and tighten the locknut, then check the clearance again. With all clearances adjusted, see that the cover joint faces and gaskets are clean and dry and fit the covers, renewing the gaskets if there has been leakage. This is important on early engines as otherwise oily fumes may enter the vehicle through the heating system.

Correct valve clearance with cold engine:

Transporters from August 1954 to May 1959: Inlet and exhaust, .004 inch.
Transporters from May 1959 to June 1960: Inlet .004 inch, exhaust .008 inch.
Transporters from June 1960 until August 1965: Inlet .008 inch, exhaust .008 or .012 inch.
Transporters after August 1965: Inlet and exhaust, .004 inch.

Due to design changes there may be confusion over clearances. Usually there is a 'sticker' label on the fan housing which indicates the correct clearance.

Lubrication servicing:

Renew the engine lubricating oil every 3000 miles. Drain the sump and remove the strainer cover (see **FIG 1:5**). Clean the strainer gauze with a brush and petrol, not a fluffy rag. Install with new gaskets and new copper washers. Do not overtighten the nuts. With the vehicle standing on level ground put in 4⅜ pints of fresh oil of the correct grade.

1:3 Removing and replacing the engine

With the exception of valve clearance adjustment, and removal of the oil pump, all further engine overhauling must be done with the engine out of the vehicle. Fortunately the engine is light enough for two men to be able to remove it providing they have adequate clearance under the vehicle. This can be arranged by working over a pit. The alternative is to raise the vehicle on a hoist, or jack up and support the rear of the vehicle until it is about three feet off the floor. **At this point we must emphasize the great importance of ensuring the safety of operators by arranging suitable supports under the car in the absence of a pit or hoist.** These supports must be capable of remaining firm under all stresses.

Remove the engine as follows:

1 Disconnect the battery earthing strap. Remove rear crossmember. Take off air cleaner complete with elbow. Disconnect leads from generator, coil and oil pressure switch.
2 Disconnect the accelerator cable from the carburetter, remove spring and withdraw cable. Remove flexible fuel pipe at front cover plate and seal pipe with a suitable clamp.
3 Disconnect both heater control cables and detach flexible pipes from the heat exchanger. Take off the sound neutralizing pipe and tail pipe as a unit.
4 Unscrew the two lower nuts from the engine mounting. Two more will be found on the top behind the fan housing, the nuts facing the rear. Do not remove these until the weight of the engine has been taken on a jack, preferably a trolley jack which can be trundled about. With the jack in position unscrew the nuts from the two upper mounting bolts behind the fan housing. An assistant will be required to stop the bolts from turning while the nuts are removed.
5 The next operation needs great care to avoid damaging the drive shaft or the clutch driven plate and release bearing. Whilst being withdrawn rearwards a matter of 4 inches, the engine must be kept perfectly square with

FIG 1:5 Oil strainer cover removed from underside of sump to reveal strainer gauze and gaskets

FIG 1:6 Removing the screws securing the rear cover plate

the transmission casing and its weight completely supported until the clutch driven plate and the release plate are clear of the drive shaft (see **Chapter 5**). **Serious damage can be caused by allowing the engine to tilt or by letting its weight hang on these components.** When the parts are clear of the drive shaft the engine can be tilted down at the rear and lowered away. Keep an eye on the distributor while doing this.

Refit the engine as follows:

These operations are described on the assumption that the clutch has not been disturbed. If the clutch has been dismantled, refer to **Chapter 5** for instructions on centring the clutch driven plate. This is essential because

FIG 1:7 Early rocker shaft mounting showing half-round recesses in mounting brackets

FIG 1:8 Later rocker shaft mounting showing the split mounting block

the splined hub of the driven plate must accept the splined drive shaft and allow the spigot of the shaft to enter the central bearing in the flywheel retaining nut as can be seen in the section in **FIG 1:23**.

1 Put $\frac{1}{3}$ oz. of Universal grease in the bearing in the flywheel retaining nut. Lubricate the starter shaft bush, the starter drive gear and the flywheel ring gear. Use heavy-duty grease on the splines of the drive shaft or dust with molybdenum disulphide powder applied with a brush or piece of clean cloth.

2 Clean the mating flanges of the engine and transmission. Engage a gear to stop the drive shaft from turning.

3 Pay particular attention to the warnings in preceding Operation 5 and proceed to fit the engine. **Never at any time let the weight of the engine hang on the drive shaft.** To engage the splines of the clutch plate and the drive shaft turn the engine by

means of the fan belt. Push the engine home, guiding the lower mounting studs into the corresponding holes in the transmission flange. Partly tighten the upper mounting nuts, fully tighten the lower nuts and then return to the upper nuts. Replace the rear cross-member.

4 Adjust the accelerator cable at full throttle, refit the cables and pipes and adjust the ignition timing as instructed in **Chapter 3**. Check the sump oil.

1:4 Dismantling the engine

On vehicles made before August 1964 which have the original type of heating arrangements shown in FIG 4:4, proceed as follows:

1 Remove the coverplate in front of the engine, take off the fan belt and disconnect the wire between the coil and distributor.

2 Remove the fan housing and the generator. Pull off the crankshaft pulley with an extractor. Disconnect the fuel pipe.

3 Remove the induction manifold and the preheater pipe, the silencer and heater assembly. Remove the heating channels and the cylinder coverplates, also the plate under the fan pulley.

4 Remove the clutch. Remove the cylinder head covers and the rocker shafts.

5 Remove the cylinder heads, the pushrod tubes and the pushrods.

6 Remove the deflector plates and then the cylinders, followed by the pistons. Remove the oil cooler and the oil pump. Remove the fuel pump.

7 Remove the distributor and lift out the drive gear. Remove the flywheel.

On vehicles after August 1964 with the later type of heater arrangements:

1 Repeat the preceding instructions but note the following differences when dealing with the sheet metalwork.

2 Take off the two large hoses between the fan housing and the heat exchangers. Remove the preheater pipe sealing plate. Remove the generator with fan housing and control flaps.

3 Remove the rear air deflecting plate and the lower part of the warm air duct.

Finish dismantling by splitting the crankcase for access to the camshaft and crankshaft.

More detailed instructions on the various operations will follow. For those which concern the engine cooling and heating system refer to **Chapter 4**.

1:5 Servicing cylinder heads

If necessary, the rocker gear can be removed from the heads without detaching the heads from the cylinders. There are two types of rocker shaft mounting, the early one being shown in **FIG 1:7** and the later type in **FIG 1:8**. In each case the removal of two nuts will enable the shaft to be lifted off. Note the split mounting blocks which fit over the studs on the later type, together with the oil seals on the studs.

Before removing the cylinder heads devise some means of stopping the cylinder barrels from lifting off the crankcase. Loops of wire or rope attached to some convenient point could be arranged or make up a clamp to fit between the fins. Care must be taken however not to stress the fins, which are brittle. Remove the cylinder head nuts and tap the head fins with a soft-faced hammer used squarely on the edges of the fins to avoid breakage. This should loosen the heads and they can then be lifted off. Note that there is no gasket between the head and barrel mating faces.

Removing the valves:

Use a valve spring compressor to compress the valve springs and so release the two split collets from each valve stem (see item 6 in **FIG 1:9**). Remove the compressor and lift off the spring cap 5 and spring 8. Later models from early 1964 have an oil deflector ring 7 on the valve stem below the cap. Remove any burr from the cotter grooves in the valve stems and push out the valves, keeping them in the correct order for reassembly or mark them on the head. Note that since 1962 the springs have close-wound coils at one end. This end is always fitted adjacent to the cylinder head.

Servicing valves, seats and springs:

If decarbonization is intended, scrape the carbon from the head before removing the valves. This will protect the valve seats. Use a piece of wood or a soft tool when cleaning the carbon from the alloy head to prevent scratching. Remove the valves and check the stems and seats. Renew the valves if the stems are worn or bent, or if the seats are deeply pitted and burnt. Light marking can be removed by grinding-in but heavier defects should be removed by a garage equipped with a valve-refacer. Clean and polish the valve heads before grinding.

Clean all carbon from the ports and have the valve seatings reground by a VW agent if they are deeply pitted or burnt. Remove the carbon from the counterbore at the inner end of the valve guide. It is not possible to renew the valve guides or the seat inserts because of the high interference fits in the head. **Any serious defects are best overcome by exchanging heads for factory-reconditioned parts.** Clearances between valve stems and guides should be, inlet .002 to .003 inch and exhaust .0032 to .0045 inch. Clearances should not exceed .0065 inch for either valve. Valve seat widths should be, inlet .05 to .06 inch and exhaust .06 to .08 inch. Seat widths can be reduced by a VW agent using special grinding tools.

Grind in the valves with a suction cup tool, putting a light spring under the valve head so that the valve will lift off the seat when pressure is released. Use coarse paste if the seats are fairly deeply pitted and finish off with fine. Spread the paste lightly round the valve seat and use a semi-rotary grinding action, letting the valve rise off the seat now and then to help the distribution of the paste.

When the seats are a smooth matt grey without any signs of pitting, clean every trace of grinding paste from both head and valves. A useful check of the accuracy of the grinding can be made by marking the valve seat with several pencil lines across the face. If the valve is then rotated on the head seating all the lines should disappear.

On engines made after May 1959, valves that have worn stem ends can be salvaged by using valve caps, Part No. 113109621. The cap is placed on the valve stem before refitting the rocker arms.

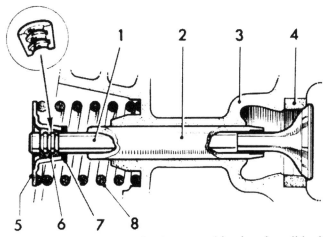

FIG 1:9 Later type of valve assembly showing ribbed collets **6**. Earlier collets had an internal taper instead. Note oil seal **7**

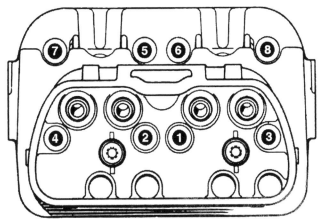

FIG 1:10 Sequence for preliminary tightening of cylinder head nuts

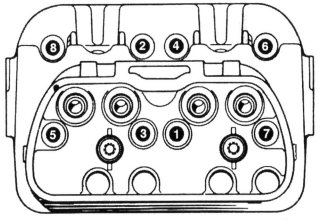

FIG 1:11 Sequence for final tightening of cylinder head nuts

Before refitting the valves examine the springs for cracks and check the length against the figures given in Technical Data. Coat the valve stems with oil or molybdenum-disulphide paste and insert in the guides. If fitted, replace the oil deflector rings on the stems and install the springs and caps. Remember to fit springs with close-coiled ends so that the close coils are adjacent to the cylinder head. Compress the springs and replace the

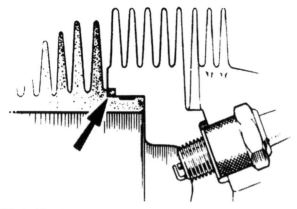

FIG 1:12 Position of gasket ring between cylinder head and barrel on earlier engines. Split in ring faces outwards

FIG 1:13 Check pushrod tube length at **A**. Dimension should be $7\frac{1}{8}$ inches on early engines and $7\frac{1}{2}$ inches on subsequent engines

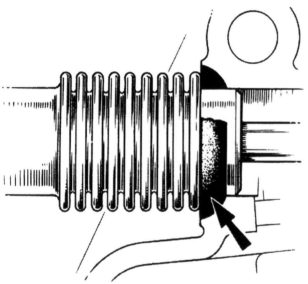

FIG 1:14 Sealing washers on pushrod tube ends must be in good condition and seated correctly

cotters, using a little grease to hold the cotters in place while the compressor is released. Press down on the valve stem to check that the assembly is correct.

Refitting cylinder heads:

Before fitting the heads, check the tightness of the securing studs. If they cannot be firmly tightened because of defective threads in the crankcase it is possible for special inserts to be fitted by a VW agent.

When replacing the heads, note that the only gaskets between the head and cylinder barrels are those down the barrels, near the first fin as shown in **FIG 1:12**. These gaskets are not fitted to later engines and were used on earlier engines to ensure that combustion gases could not enter the car through the heating system. There is no

gasket between the top of the barrel and the register in the cylinder head.

Before actually placing the heads on the barrels check the pushrod tubes for length. As shown in **FIG 1:13** the dimension over the corrugations should be $7\frac{1}{8}$ inches on earlier engines and $7\frac{1}{2}$ inches on subsequent engines. Tubes can be stretched carefully if they are not up to length. When fitted, the tube seams must face upwards. Also check that the seals shown in **FIG 1:14** are in good condition and properly seated on the ends of the tubes.

With the head in place and the pushrod tubes correctly seated, fit the washers and nuts, coating the threads with graphite paste, and tighten down in the two sequences given in **FIGS 1:10** and **1:11**. During the first sequence use a torque wrench set to break at 7 lb ft. Final tightening should be to a figure of 22 to 23 lb ft, using the second sequence. Prior to 1961 use a torque of 27 lb ft.

1:6 Servicing the rocker gear

To dismantle the rocker shaft, remove the spring clips at each end. Mark the rockers to ensure correct reassembly and pull off the washers, rockers, spacing tube and spring, or the bearing supports according to model. Check the rocker arms and the shaft for wear. Undue wear of the adjusting screw faces which bear on the valve stems will make accurate clearance setting impossible. Also check the pushrod sockets of the rocker arms for wear.

Reassemble the parts, lubricating the shaft and rockers. Slacken off all the adjusting screws. Before finally tightening the rocker shaft securing nuts, check the point of contact between each adjusting screw and valve stem. A small offset as shown at 1 in **FIG 1:16** is correct and it is possible to move the rocker shaft laterally to achieve this result, due to some clearance on the securing studs. On later assemblies like those shown in **FIG 1:15** ensure that the shaft supports are fitted with the chamfered faces outwards and the slots upwards. The shaft securing nuts are of a special grade, and are copper-plated so that they can be readily recognized. Tighten them to 18 lb ft. If no more work on the engine is intended, adjust the rocker clearances and replace the covers.

1:7 Cylinder barrels and pistons

With the heads off, the cylinders can be removed. The pushrods must be extracted and the deflector plates removed from under the cylinders. Pull off the cylinders and mark the piston crowns for correct reassembly if they are to be removed.

Removing and servicing pistons:

Remove one gudgeon pin circlip and heat the piston to 80°C (176°F). The expansion will free the gudgeon pin which can then be pushed out. Piston rings must be removed with a ring tool, but if removal is not strictly necessary they can be left in the grooves to avoid breakage.

Clean the piston crown and ring grooves free from carbon but use a soft tool and take great care not to damage the alloy surfaces. Rough treatment of the ring grooves will result in increased oil consumption. When the pistons are clean, check them for clearance in their respective cylinder barrels, but first look on the piston sides for unbalanced wear indications. Carbon or wear at the top on one side of the piston and at the bottom of the skirt on the other side is a sign that the connecting rod is bent.

Piston clearance cannot be checked with feelers, but only by measurement with precision instruments. The clearance between piston and cylinder bore should be .001 to .002 inch. On the latest '1500' engine the clearances should be .0015 to .0024 inch measured at right angles to the gudgeon pin about $\frac{1}{2}$ inch below the piston crown. If the clearance reaches the figure of .008 inch replace both piston and cylinder by a pair of the same size and weight grading. If the cylinder of a damaged piston shows no signs of wear it is sufficient to renew the piston alone, making sure that it is of the correct grade. The four pistons must not differ in weight by more than 10 grammes (.35 oz). If the oil consumption has reached one pint in 300 miles the cylinders and pistons need renewal. Measure the cylinder bore $\frac{1}{2}$ inch below the top edge. Measure the piston at the bottom of the skirt, at right angles to the gudgeon pin axis.

Piston crowns are marked in various ways to indicate size and weight grading (see **FIG 1:17**). They are also stamped with an arrow which should point to the flywheel when installed. Paint spots are used to indicate both size grading (blue, pink and green) and weight grading (brown for —weight and grey for +weight). In this way it is possible for the VW Spares Department to match pistons and cylinders exactly.

Gudgeon pins should normally be a tight push fit in the piston bosses but it may be found that the pin is only a light push fit even when the piston is cold. The pin may slide out of the piston under its own weight but this does not mean that it is necessarily due for replacement. The two standard sizes of pins are colour-coded black and white. If the piston holes exceed a diameter of .7874 inch then use oversize pins which are colour-marked green. Clearance between the pin and the connecting rod bush should lie between .0001 and .0006 inch. If the clearance reaches the wear limit of .0016 inch renew the pin and the connecting rod bush. **Do not try to install an oversize pin in a worn bush.** When fitting gudgeon pins, oil them and push them into the heated pistons without stopping. The temperature for heating the pistons is given in the instructions for removing gudgeon pins. A third size of pin colour-coded green, is available for 1500 pistons with a bore in excess of 22.001 mm.

Piston rings:

When fitting new rings check the gaps and file the ring ends if necessary. Use a piston to push the ring about $\frac{1}{4}$ inch up the cylinder bore from the bottom. Using feeler gauges the gap should be .012 to .018 inch for compression rings and .010 to .016 inch for the oil control ring which is fitted in the bottom groove. The wear limit is .037 inch. Also check the side clearance in the grooves. For the top compression ring this should be .003 to .004 inch with a wear limit of .005 inch. For the lower compression ring the figures are .002 to .003 inch with a wear limit of .004 inch. For the oil control ring the clearance should be .001 to .002 inch with a wear limit of .004 inch. Note that the two compression rings are marked 'TOP' or 'OBEN' for correct fitting.

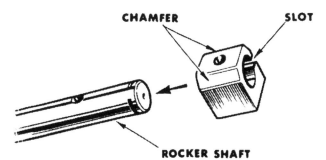

FIG 1:15 Fit mounting blocks to rocker shaft with chamfer outwards and slot facing upwards

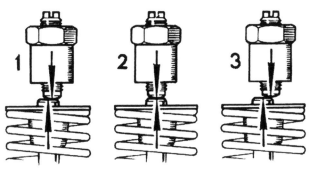

FIG 1:16 Rocker adjusting screw should contact valve stem slightly off-centre as at **1**. Positions **2** and **3** are incorrect

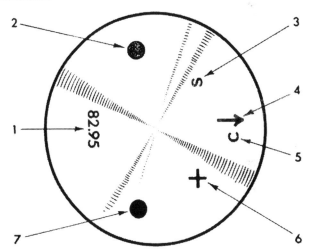

FIG 1:17 Grading marks on a piston crown. Position may vary on earlier models

Key to Fig 1:17 1 Piston size in mm indicating matching size (pink, blue or green) 2 Paint spot 3 Gudgeon pin bore size grading (S = black, W = white) 4 Arrow must point towards flywheel when piston is fitted 5 Index letter for piston Part No. 6 + or — indicates weight grading 7 Weight grading by paint spot. Brown = —weight, grey = +weight

Fitting pistons and cylinders:

Insert the gudgeon pin circlip at the flywheel end of the piston boss. If the pin is tighter than a light push fit, heat the piston. Fit the lubricated pin in one steady movement. Fit the second circlip. **Make sure that the arrow or the word 'VORN' on the piston crown points towards the flywheel.**

The cylinder flange, the gasket, and the mating surface of the crankcase must be perfectly clean. Remove all traces of the old gasket and use a new one for each

FIG 1:18 Operation of lubricating system. On left, engine cold, oil thick, relief valve plunger right back against spring. Oil goes direct to engine but excess pressure relieved by oil return to sump. Centre, oil thining, plunger partially returned to block relief to sump. Some of main supply to engine goes by way of cooler. Right, oil at running temperature and much thinner. Plunger returned by spring, all oil to engine goes through cooler

cylinder. Oil the piston and set the rings so that the gap in the oil ring is uppermost. The gaps in the other two rings should be evenly spaced 120 deg. apart. Oil the cylinder bore, compress the rings and slide the cylinder into place. The head studs must not contact the cylinder fins. When installing the deflector plates seat them correctly and ensure that they cannot rattle by bending them until they bear tightly on the studs.

1:8 The lubricating system

We propose to deal with the lubricating system before discussing the crankcase because the component parts can all be serviced with the engine in situ.

The system:

The gear-type oil pump is bolted to the rear of the crankcase below the fan pulley and is driven from the rear end of the camshaft. It lifts oil from a strainer in the sump and pumps it under pressure to the oil passages, to an oil pressure relief valve and to an oil cooler bolted on top of the engine where it is cooled by ducted air from the fan.

When the oil is cold and thick, pressure is high and to avoid restricting the flow to the bearings by passing it through the oil cooler, the oil is bypassed direct to them. This is done by the relief valve plunger lifting as shown on the left in FIG 1:18. As the oil warms up the pressure drops so that the relief valve plunger moves to the left to allow oil to pass both through the cooler and direct to the engine. When the oil has reached operating temperature the pressure has dropped. The relief valve plunger then routes all the oil through the cooler. At all times any excess pressure of oil will pass the relief valve and fall back into the sump.

The strainer:

The strainer is illustrated in FIG 1:5. On early types the drain plug is not in the cover plate, and the strainer assembly is deeper. When servicing the strainer, clean off all old gasket material from the joint faces and scrub the gauze clean with a brush and fuel. **Do not use fluffy rag as fibres may adhere to the gauze.** When refitting the strainer make sure that the suction pipe in

the sump enters the strainer and is a snug fit. The bottom end of the pipe must be clear of the domed base of the strainer. On recent models with the squat type of strainer, measure the distance between the crankcase face and the tip of the suction pipe. The dimension should be .39 ± .040 inch. On this type it is also necessary to check the measurement from the strainer flange to the bottom domed face of the strainer to ensure clearance for the drain plug. The dimension should be .236 ± .040 inch.

Check the joint faces for flatness, use a new gasket and fit new washers under the securing nuts. Do not overtighten.

The oil pressure relief valve:

This will be found under the rear of the engine on the lefthand side (see item 11 in FIG 1:2). Always check this valve first if there are oil circulation problems, such as a leaking oil cooler or oil starvation causing engine seizure, as these might be due to a sticking plunger in the valve.

Remove the plug and gasket and withdraw the spring and plunger. If the plunger sticks, pull it out with a 10 mm metric tap, which can be lightly screwed into place. Check the surface of the plunger for signs of seizure. If these are evident, also check the bore in the crankcase. Polish out the scores but do not remove any metal otherwise. Renew the plunger if its condition is doubtful. Check the spring for wear and settling. A new spring in the free position should measure, on engines made before the 1961 models were introduced, 2.04 to 2.08 inches. On engines from 1961 the free length of the spring should be 2.44 to 2.52 inches. Renew a spring if it is curved along its length and shows signs of the coils rubbing in the bore. Renew the plug gasket when re-installing.

The oil cooler:

This can be removed, as shown in FIG 1:19 but note that it can also be taken off with the engine in the vehicle by removing the fan housing. The two outer nuts are best unscrewed with the type of cranked spanner shown. If the cooler has been leaking first check the oil pressure relief valve and then, if necessary, subject the cooler to a test pressure of 85 lb/sq in. The ribs of the cooler must not touch each other and the partition plate must not be loose. Renew the two gaskets when re-installing the cooler and make sure the retaining nuts and the bracket are tight.

The oil pump:

The location of the pump can be seen as item 27 below the crankshaft pulley in **FIG 1:2**. To remove the pump:

1 Remove the engine rear coverplate as indicated in **FIG 1:6**.
2 Remove the fan pulley with an extractor, using the slots provided.
3 Remove the sheet metal pulley cover. Remove the oil pump cover nuts and take off the cover and gasket. Lift out the gears. The parts are shown in **FIG 1:20**.
4 To withdraw the pump housing make up a bridge piece from flat steel so that the two ends are bent down at right angles and straddle the pump flange. Make a threaded bolt with prongs which fit inside the pump housing passages and have the bolt long enough to protrude through a central hole in the bridge piece to take a nut. Tighten the nut and draw the pump housing out of the crankcase.

Wear will result in loss of pressure. Check the backlash between the gear teeth with feeler gauges. The permissible backlash is .001 to .003 inch. With the gears in position and the housing face free from old gasket material, place a straightedge across the face and measure the clearance between the straightedge and the gear faces. This should not exceed .004 inch. Wear of the coverplate face will make this clearance excessive so renew all the parts needed to reduce the clearances. The idler gear pin must not be loose in the housing. If peening will not lock it in place, renew the housing and also the pin if worn. The outer end of the pin must be .02 to .04 inch below the housing face.

To install the pump turn the engine until the pump driving slot in the end of the camshaft is vertical. Fit the pump housing and gears, using a genuine .003 inch gasket without jointing compound. Fit the cover with a similar gasket without compound. Run up the cover nuts finger tight. Turn the engine over for two complete revolutions. This will centre the driving slot and tongue. Make sure the housing does not move and tighten the cover nuts.

1:9 The distributor drive shaft

The location of the drive shaft is indicated by the arrow in **FIG 1:21**. Note the offset driving dogs on the distributor shaft. Assuming that the distributor has already been removed, remove the fuel pump. Remove the pushrod housing **after** the pushrod has been lifted out. In this case blank off the hole so that nothing can be dropped into the crankcase. Adhesive tape will do.

1 Extract the small spring 3 from the top of the drive shaft (see **FIG 1:22**).
2 Set No. 1 cylinder to the firing point on the compression stroke and devise an expanding tool which will grip the bore of the shaft and enable it to be turned to the left and lifted out at the same time. It might be possible to tap a piece of hardwood into the slot and use it to lift out the shaft.
3 There is one or possibly two washers under the drive shaft pinion. Hook these out or use a magnet if the

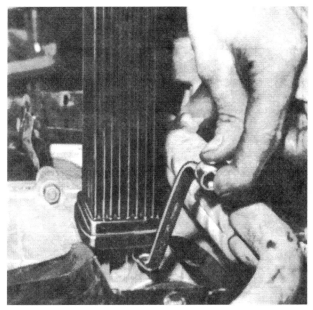

FIG 1:19   Removing oil cooler with cranked spanner

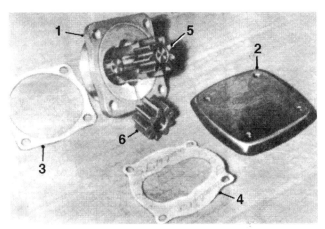

FIG 1:20   Component parts of oil pump

Key to Fig 1:20   1 Pump housing   2 Cover
3 Gasket for housing   4 Gasket for cover   5 Driving gear
6 Idler gear

FIG 1:21   Location of distributor drive shaft arrowed. Note offset driving dogs on end of distributor shaft

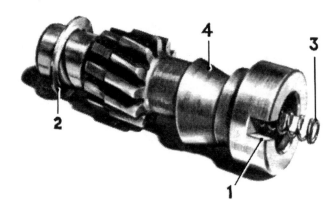

FIG 1:22 Distributor drive shaft

Key to Fig 1:22 1 Offset dogs driving distributor 2 Thrust washer(s) 3 Spring 4 Fuel pump operating eccentric

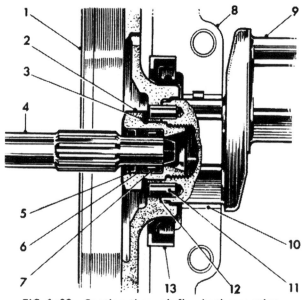

FIG 1:23 Section through flywheel mounting

Key to Fig 1:23 1 Flywheel 2 Gland nut, securing flywheel 3 Gland nut lockwasher 4 Main drive shaft 5 Retainer 6 Felt sealing ring 7 Needle roller bearing 8 Crankcase 9 Crankshaft 10 Crankshaft bearing 11 Flywheel locating dowels 12 Flywheel gasket 13 Crankshaft oil seal

engine is installed. If the engine is out of the vehicle turn the crankcase upside down so that the washers fall out. Be very careful not to drop these washers into the crankcase. During reassembly a piece of rod is used as a guide to ensure that this cannot happen.

4 Check the drive gear and fuel pump eccentric for wear. If the gear teeth are worn it will be advisable to check the drive gear on the crankshaft as well. Renew the washers under the drive shaft gear if they are worn.

Set the pulley notch in-line with the crankcase joint as shown in **FIG 1:4**. No. 1 piston will then be at the top of its compression stroke and both valves will be closed. Fit the washer(s) by sliding them down a piece of rod which locates in the housing. Install the driving shaft in the position shown in **Chapter 3, FIG 3:4**. Looking down on the end of the shaft the large offset should be

at the front and the slot should be at right angles to the crankcase joint line. Insert the small spring, guiding it down a piece of rod to ensure that it locates in the shaft recess. Install the distributor and set the ignition timing as instructed in **Chapter 3**. Refit the fuel pump.

Remember that if the engine is completely dismantled, the oil pump, the coverplate under the pulley and the crankshaft pulley itself must be fitted before the distributor shaft.

1:10 Removing and refitting the flywheel

Refer to **FIG 1:23** for details of the flywheel assembly. The flywheel is located on crankshaft 9 by four dowel pins 11 and secured by the large central gland nut 2. Inside the nut is a needle roller bearing 7 which supports the rear end of the transmission drive shaft. An oil seal 13 is fitted into a recess in the crankcase 8 and has a lip which seals on the flywheel flange.

Before removing the flywheel it is a good plan to check the crankshaft end float so that adjustment can be made if necessary. Set up a dial gauge so that the plunger bears on the flywheel face. Drive the crankshaft backwards and forwards to the limit of its movement, using a soft-faced hammer, and record the total float indicated. Adjustment is needed if the float exceeds .006 inch. The correct figure is between .003 and .005 inch. The flywheel must be removed to gain access to the adjusting shims 12.

Removing the flywheel:

Remove the clutch and clutch driven plate. Prevent the flywheel from turning. The official VW tool spans several starter gear teeth and is bolted to the casing, and a similar device could be fabricated. Remove the nut, which is extremely tight, and pull off the flywheel.

Check the starter gear teeth for damage. A VW Service Station can have the teeth re-machined by removing up to .08 inch on the clutch side of the teeth and re-chamfering them. Check the dowels for wear and looseness. Wear in the dowel holes can be cured by having new holes drilled by a Service Station. Check the needle bearings in the gland nut for wear. A section through the nut is shown in **FIG 1:23**. Prior to 1955 a bronze bush was used in the gland nut and this cannot be replaced by the needle bearing type.

Adjusting the end float:

On removing the flywheel, note that there is a sealing gasket 12 fitted over the dowels on most models. Early engines had a paper gasket which compressed to .006 inch. The gasket and dowels are clearly shown in **FIG 1:24**.

Always use a genuine replacement gasket. Later engines had a metal gasket and recent models have a sealing ring and no gasket. Note also the adjusting shims for end float, usually three in number. Shims are available in various thicknesses and, knowing the dial indicator reading for excessive end float and using a micrometer on the shims it is possible to calculate the thickness required to bring the end float to the correct figure. Subtract the required end float from the measured float. Do not use more than three adjusting shims and never use more than one gasket. Remember that the thickness of the gasket will affect the end float.

Renewing crankcase to flywheel oil seal:

While the flywheel is off, examine the seal and the flywheel flange for signs of damage and leakage. Polish the flywheel flange if there is any roughness where the seal lip contacts it. To renew the seal, prise out the old one and clean out the crankcase recess. It helps to chamfer the outer edge of the recess with a scraper to facilitate fitting the new seal.

Coat the recess with sealing compound and press the seal into place with the lip facing inwards. **FIG 1:25** shows the operation, the centre bolt of the VW tool being screwed into the crankshaft. The seal must bed down squarely in the recess.

Replacing the flywheel:

Clean the mating surfaces thoroughly and smear the oil seal contact surface with oil. Fit a new gasket over the dowels. Look for the out-of-balance marks on the crankshaft, flywheel and clutch. The crankshaft mark is a paint dot on the side of the hole for the gland nut. The flywheel has a paint dot and a small hole on the clutch face. The clutch has a paint line on the outer edge of the pressure plate. Not all three components need have out-of-balance marks. Using the crankshaft mark as a datum, fit the flywheel and clutch with their marks spaced out 120 deg. apart. If only two components are marked space them 180 deg. apart.

Before fitting the gland nut smear 10 gram (.35 oz) of universal grease in the roller bearing. If a check of the bearing and the spigot on the end of the transmission shaft reveals excessive clearance it is possible to obtain undersize bearings which have a bore .0032 inch smaller than standard. Excessive clearance may be responsible for chatter on clutch take-up. Tighten the nut with a torque wrench set at 217 lb ft.

Check the flywheel for runout. Maximum runout of the face when measured on the greatest diameter should not exceed .012 inch.

It may be of interest to owners to know that on some models a thrust piece and spring were fitted between the crankshaft and the rear end of the transmission shaft to eliminate noise when idling. These parts can be fitted to Transporters after 1959. The cone-shaped spring has its large coil against the crankshaft, in the bore for the gland nut. The thrust piece seats on the small end of the spring and in the recess in the end of the transmission shaft.

1:11 Dismantling the crankcase

According to model, do the following:
1 Remove the oil strainer, the oil pressure switch and the oil pressure relief valve if not already removed.
2 Remove the oil filler.
3 Unscrew the crankcase nuts and tap on the righthand half of the case with a rubber hammer. **Do not attempt to drive a screwdriver between the joint faces.** Before parting the case it will be necessary to remove the throttle ring bearing shaft of the air regulator on earlier models. It will also be helpful at this point to indicate the differences between the models. Before the engine was redesigned, through-bolts held the halves together, whereas studs are now used. There are six 12 mm and twelve 8 mm studs, two

FIG 1:24 Flywheel removed, showing dowels and gasket

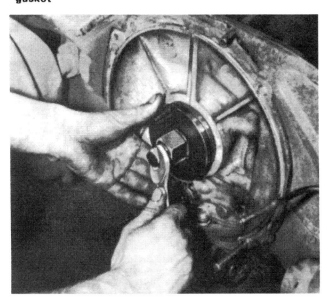

FIG 1:25 Fitting a new crankshaft oil seal

8 mm through-bolts and a third which also acts as a hinge pin for the original type of air regulator valve. On either side of the front camshaft bearing are two 8 mm studs with nuts tightened on the outside. Here lies the major difference between this and the earlier engine which had two short bolts hidden behind the flywheel, so that the flywheel had to be taken off to get at them.

Before parting the crankcase halves it will also be useful to consider making some spring clips to hold the cam followers in place on later engines. This will stop the followers from falling out and will be particularly useful when reassembling. The clips are coiled up from stout wire like the spring end of a safety pin and the two legs span a pair of followers to grip and hold them in place.

4 Lift out the camshaft and crankshaft, the crankshaft oil seal and the blanking plug at the flywheel end of the camshaft. Lift out the cam followers. On early engines

FIG 1:26 Top view shows original type of one-piece pushrod and cam follower with arrow indicating the flat. Lower view is of the later type of separate pushrod and cam follower

FIG 1:27 Early connecting rod on left, showing securing bolts. Later type on right uses fixed bolts and nuts. Arrows indicate the marks which must be upwards on installation

with integral pushrods and followers, remove the guide plates from the crankcase if necessary. These plates prevent rotation of the cam followers and can be seen in **FIG 1:28**. Both types of pushrods and followers are shown in **FIG 1:26**.

5 Lift out the camshaft bearing shells and the main bearing shells for No. 2 crankshaft bearing, which is the second from the flywheel end. Lightly mark the backs of the shells so that they can be restored to their original positions if they are not renewed. Do not mark in such a way that burrs are raised. Note that early engines had camshafts which ran directly in the crankcase, but when the 1966 models were introduced, renewable bearing shells were fitted instead. End thrust was then taken by flanged shells next to the timing gear. The camshaft remains unchanged.

6 Clean the crankcase halves, removing old jointing compound with a solvent. Be particularly careful not to raise burrs on the mating faces through careless handling. These faces must be absolutely flat and true. Examine the halves for cracks or damage and the

camshaft bearings in early engines for scoring and excessive wear. On all types of engines the bores of the camshaft and crankshaft bearing housings can be measured with precision instruments to check for wear. The 'crush' on the main bearing shells should be about .002 inch to ensure that they are tightly gripped when the crankcase is assembled. It is possible to obtain factory-reconditioned crankcases fitted with main bearing shells which are oversize on the outside diameter. These crankcases are stamped 'P' when the mating surfaces have been planed to bring them closer together. Crankcases with oversize bores for the main bearings are stamped 'O'. Further checks on the crankcase would include the condition of the bores for the cam followers, and the tightness of studs. The tapped holes for studs can be restored by fitting Helicoil inserts. Also check the fit of the main bearing locating dowels. If the suction pipe to the oil pump is loose, peen round the hole to tighten it. Finally, clean out all oilways with compressed air. If any bearing metal has 'run' it is essential to clean out all particles of alloy from every oil passage. Finish off by injecting clean engine oil before reassembling. The operation of reassembling the crankcase is covered later, after the crankshaft and camshaft have received attention.

1:12 The crankshaft and connecting rods

Checking crankshaft end float has been covered in **Section 1:10**. When the crankshaft is lifted out complete with connecting rods, it can be seen that, counting from front or flywheel end, Nos. 1, 3 and 4 main bearings are one-piece bushes, the flanges on No. 1 bearing taking end thrust No. 2 bearing is of the split type. A limited number of engines were made with all the bearings of the split type, and some with No. 2 bearing taking crankshaft end thrust. At the rear end the shaft carries a concave oil thrower, No. 4 main bearing, a retaining ring for the distributor drive gear, which is keyed to the shaft with a Woodruff key and then a spacing ring followed by the small timing gear also keyed with a Woodruff key. Lastly comes No. 3 main bearing bush. Remove all these parts after prising out the fan pulley key from the extreme rear of the crankshaft. Observe the fit of the gears, as these should be a press fit on the shaft. To facilitate removal, heat the gears to about 176°F. Remove the front main bearing bush.

Removing and servicing connecting rods:

Refer to **FIG 1:27** which shows the original type of rod having bolts to secure the cap. The latest type of rod uses bolts which are captive in the cap, together with securing nuts. Note that identification numbers are stamped on both rod and cap. If in doubt, mark the rods lightly so that they can be restored to their original positions on reassembly. Remove as follows:

1 Unscrew the clamping bolts or nuts and remove the caps. Lift out the bearing shells, noting the locating tags and notches. If it is likely that the same shells will be used on reassembly, mark them very lightly on the back for correct location.

2 Check the weight of the rods. Any variation should not exceed 10 grams. Any rod which is outside the weight limit should be taken to an authorized VW agent for

attention, as metal should only be removed at precise locations.

3 Check the fit of the gudgeon pin. It should be a light push fit at room temperature. Normally the clearance should be between .0004 and .0008 inch, with a wear limit of .0016 inch. Do not try to fit an oversize pin to overcome excessive clearance but have a new bush fitted and reamed to suit.

4 Check the connecting rod alignment. One of the signs of a bent rod is offset marking of the piston skirt. If there is bright wear above the gudgeon pin hole on one side and similar marking below the hole on the other side the piston has been tilted in the bore due to a bent connecting rod. In expert hands a bent rod can be straightened, but the alignment check needs very accurate mandrels and gauging equipment.

5 Assemble each rod in turn on its crankpin, tightening the bolts to a torque of 36 lb ft, using Plastigage for checking the running clearance. While assembled, check the end float, which should be .004 to .016 inch. Dismantle the rod and measure the thickness of the Plastigage. The running clearance should be .0008 to .003 inch. Worn shells can be renewed, but it is also essential to check the crankpins for wear and ovality if clearance is excessive. Nominal diameter of Nos. 1 to 3 crankpins is 2.1654 inch, and of No. 4 crankpin 1.5748 inch.

6 Maximum permissible ovality of the crankpins is .0012 inch. The same figure also applies to the main bearing journals. Anything in excess of this calls for a new or reground crankshaft and bearings. Regrind undersizes are approximately the equivalent of —.010, —.020 and —.030 inch.

7 Renew all bearing shells which are scored or have bearing metal breaking away. **Never try to adjust the running clearance by filing the caps or the shells.** It is not necessary to scrape the bearing surfaces of the shells. Make sure the tags on the shells fit into the notches in the connecting rod and cap.

8 When refitting connecting rods, oil the bearing surfaces liberally. When the bolts or nuts are tightened to the correct torque figure the rods should fall from the horizontal position under their own weight. **Light taps with a hammer** on the outer faces of the cap will help to settle the parts into their correct relationship and may help to ease a tight bearing. Refer to **FIG 1:27** and note the forged marks arrowed on the shank of each rod. These marks must face upwards in an assembled engine.

The crankshaft and main bearings:

At one time all the main bearings were of aluminium-alloy but recent engines have a No. 2 main bearing of steel-backed lead-alloy. This is the one which is split. Check journals and bearings as follows:

1 Look for scored journals on the crankshaft and check that ovality does not exceed .0012 inch. If the shaft can be supported in V-blocks for a check on runout, this must not exceed .001 inch at the 2nd and 4th journals with the other two supported in the blocks.

2 Measure the bores of the bearing bushes and the corresponding journals. Running clearance when new is .001 to .004 inch **after** allowing for the .002 inch by which the crankcase halves 'crush' the bearings.

The wear limit is .0072 inch. The most effective way to measure the bores is to assemble the bearings in the crankcase with the nuts fully tightened.

3 Worn crankshafts can be reground as indicated in the preceding notes on worn crankpins. It is best to fit a factory reground shaft as the dimensions for the fillet radii joining the journals to the crank webs are very important. The crankshaft will also be carefully tested for cracks.

4 It may be of interest to some owners to know that the journal diameters were increased in May 1959. Before this, the standard connecting rod journal diameters and those of main bearings 1 to 3 were 1.9681 inch and No. 4 was 1.5748 inch. After that date the diameters of the connecting rod journals and main bearings 1 to 3 were 2.1650 inches and that for No. 4 was 1.5748 inch.

5 Before refitting a crankshaft, check the following points. Make sure the bearing shell dowel pins are tight. If they are loose, new holes can be drilled by a VW Service Station. Any foreign matter embedded in the working surfaces of the bearing shells should be carefully scraped out without removing any bearing metal. Radius the sharp edges of the oil holes in the crankshaft, especially after a regrind. If it was obvious when removing the drive gears that they would not be a tight press-fit on the crankshaft when they were replaced it will be necessary to check whether new gears would be a cure or whether the crankshaft ought to be built up and ground to the correct size. Clean out all oilways with compressed air or by forcing paraffin through under pressure and then inject clean engine oil. Reassembling the crankshaft in the case will be covered in **Section 1:14**.

1:13 The camshaft and followers

When the crankcase was split, removal of the camshaft was possible. Note that the camshaft journals ran directly in the crankcase on early engines, as in **FIG 1:28**. Later engines from August 1965 are provided with replaceable bearing liners located by tags and notches. No. 3 liner has flanges to take camshaft end thrust. The large timing gear is riveted to the camshaft permanently.

FIG 1:26 shows the two designs of pushrods and cam followers. The early type had an integral pushrod and follower, the latter having a flat on one side which prevented rotation, being guided by a D-shaped hole in a guide plate bolted to the crankcase. When the re-designed engine was introduced on the Transporter in May 1959, the original type was superseded by separate pushrods and cam followers. The followers were larger in diameter and did not need guide plates, being free to rotate. With the change from the 30 to the 34 bhp engine the camshaft bearings were increased in diameter.

Service the camshaft and bearings as follows:

1 Check the riveting of the timing gear to the camshaft. Check the cams and bearing surfaces for excessive wear. The cam faces must be smooth and square, but light scoring can be smoothed down with a very fine oilstone.

2 If the camshaft can be mounted between centres, check the runout of the centre journal, which should not exceed .0008 inch. When installed, the end float of

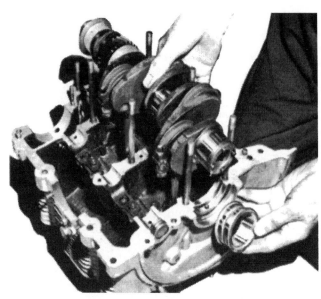

FIG 1:28 Crankshaft removed, showing front bearing drilled for dowel

the camshaft should lie between .0024 and .0045 inch with a wear limit of .0055 inch. For engines before No. 5067818 the end float is .0012 to .0033 inch, and early 30 bhp engines should have a float of .0008 to .0029 inch. Renewal of the rear bearing liner may effect a cure for excessive float providing the thrust faces of the camshaft are not worn. When installed, bearing running clearance should lie between .0008 and .002 inch with a wear limit of .005 inch. Remember that there is a 'crush' on the bearing liners when assembled in the crankcase and this affects running clearance by reducing it.

3 Examine the bearing shells for wear and scoring. It is a good plan when renewing the shells to lightly chamfer the edges of the crankcase bores at the crankcase mating surfaces to prevent pressure on the shells causing seizure. Be careful to fit the tag on the shells into the notches in the crankcase.

4 The backlash between the timing gears can only be checked while the crankshaft is installed, so refer to the reassembly operations. With the crankshaft serviced and fitted into one half of the crankcase, fit the camshaft and rock the timing gears back and forth with both hands, at all points during a complete revolution of the large gear. The minimum backlash is desirable, the clearance lying between .0004 and .002 inch. Excessive backlash due to wear can be cured by fitting a new camshaft with an oversize gear. The pitch radius of the teeth is increased from standard in steps of $\frac{1}{100}$ mm and the gear is marked on the camshaft side with +1, +2 and so on. There are also undersizes marked —1 and so on, with a standard gear marked 'O'. Do not confuse the 'O' to indicate size, with the timing mark which is stamped near a tooth on the rear face of the gear.

Camshaft modifications:

From Chassis No. 624263 and Engine No. 5009585 a modified camshaft was fitted to the 34 bhp Transporter

engine, and the base of the follower was changed in diameter to 1.162 inch. The earlier type of camshaft and followers should not be fitted to the 34 bhp engine. However, the modified camshaft can be fitted from Engine No. 3400000 (May 1959) but the modified cam followers must also be fitted.

Servicing camshaft followers:

First we will consider the original type of one-piece pushrod and follower. This can be seen in FIG 1:26. The follower has a flat on it and a guide is bolted to the crankcase with a D-shaped hole in it through which the follower is assembled and which stops it from rotating.

Unlocking a tabwasher and removing one nut will permit the removal of each of the four guides from inside the crankcase halves. Renew if worn. When correctly fitted, the clearance between the flat on the follower and the guide plate should lie between .0004 and .0008 inch and slight setting of the plate is possible, but be careful that the plate does not shift when the nut is tightened. Excessive wear can be cured by fitting oversize cam followers. Adjustment is correct when an oiled follower and pushrod assembly will fall through under its own weight without perceptible side clearance. As the rod is part of the assembly, checking for wear should also include an examination of the ball end which fits in the rocker. Check the faces of the cam followers where they bear on the cams. Deep scoring calls for renewal.

Separate cam followers should be checked for wear on the face. Deep scores and breakdown of the surface will also probably be accompanied by excessive clearance in the crankcase bores, so that renewal is indicated. When new the clearance is between .001 and .002 inch. If it exceeds .005 inch the cam followers may be worn, but there is also the possibility that the crankcase halves will need renewal too. While checking the followers, examine the pushrod ends for signs of undue wear.

1:14 Reassembling the engine

Assuming that all servicing of the individual parts has been done according to the instructions in the preceding sections, it is now possible to proceed with the assembling. Do the following, observing absolute cleanliness and lubricating all working surfaces liberally:

1 Insert the cam followers in the lefthand case. Insert the bearing shell dowel pins for the main bearings, if they were removed. FIG 1:28 shows the dowels and the drilled bearing at the front end.

2 Assemble the connecting rods to the crankshaft as instructed in Section 1:12 and lower the shaft into place. Make quite sure that the shells are properly seated in the main bearing housings. The oil thrower at the fan pulley end must have its concave face to the rear.

3 Install the camshaft with the timing gears correctly meshed. The 'O' mark on the large wheel should mesh between the dots on the two crankshaft gear teeth as shown in FIG 1:29. Fit the sealing plug at the flywheel end of the camshaft, coating it with jointing compound first (see FIG 1:30). Fit the oil seal at the flywheel end of the crankshaft.

4 Prepare the righthand half of the crankcase by fitting the cam followers. These will need holding in place with the spring clips mentioned during dismantling. This will not, of course, apply to the early engines which have combined pushrods and cam followers.

5 Check that the mating surfaces of the crankcase halves are perfectly clean and free from burrs. Smear a thin and even film of jointing compound on the faces, being careful to keep it well away from the oil passages in the main and camshaft bearings. Join the halves together and fit the nuts. If, with moderate tightening, the crankshaft cannot be turned, split the case again and determine what is wrong. Start to tighten the securing nuts in the correct sequence. First do the 8 mm nut adjacent to the 12 mm nut for No. 1 main bearing at the flywheel end of the case. Tighten this nut to 14 lb ft and then do the remaining nuts part of a turn at a time until they are all tight. The torque figure for the 12 mm nuts is 24 to 26 lb ft.

6 On early engines do not forget that there are two 6 mm bolts and nuts near the front camshaft bearing and that these must be fitted before the flywheel. Of the remaining nuts, the six 10 mm nuts must be tightened to 22 lb ft and the ten 8 mm nuts to 15 lb ft.

7 Fit the oil relief valve and the oil pressure switch. Remove the spring clips from the cam followers in the righthand half of the case.

Continue with reassembling in the reverse sequence to dismantling. Fit the oil pump and the coverplate under the fan pulley. Fit the pulley, tightening the bolt to a torque of 40 to 47 lb ft. Fit the oil strainer and coverplate. Fit the flywheel, tightening the retaining nut to a torque of 217 lb ft. A long steel bar or piece of angle iron bolted to the flywheel face by two bolts in widely-spaced clutch fixing holes will hold the assembly while the central nut is tightened. Assemble the pistons to the connecting rods and fit the cylinder barrels. Hold these down with some temporary clamps if the crankshaft is to be turned before the heads are put on. Fit the pushrods and tubes and replace the cylinder heads, referring to **Section 1:5** for details of gaskets required. Note that on engines fitted with the original type of heater installation without the later type of heat exchangers in the exhaust system, must have a gasket between the head and the spigot down the barrel near the first fin, as shown in **FIG 1:12**. This is intended to ensure that combustion gases cannot enter the air cooling system and so contaminate the hot air to the car interior. The actual sealing between the head and barrel is made without a gasket. It will be found much easier to fit the cylinder heads if the crankcase is set so that each pair of cylinders is vertical and upright in turn. Remember to fit the air deflector plates. Also make quite sure that the pushrods are correctly located when reassembling the rocker gear. Adjust to the correct clearance.

It will probably be as well to wait until after the engine is refitted before fitting the distributor and its drive and the fuel pump. Details of correct ignition timing are given in **Chapter 3**.

Take extreme care when fitting the clutch cover, using a mandrel to centre the driven plate. This is not necessary if the clutch was not removed from the flywheel. Refer to **Chapter 5** for details of centring the driven plate. Keep the engine square with the transmission shaft and proceed

FIG 1:29 Setting the camshaft timing. Tooth marked '0' on large gear meshes between two teeth on smaller gear marked with dots

FIG 1:30 Camshaft lifted out, showing early-type crankcase without camshaft bearing liners. Note plates which prevent rotation of cam followers. Arrow indicates sealing plug

with the operation after referring to the instructions in **Section 1:3**.

Fill the sump with oil of the correct grade. In cases of difficulty with the silencing and air cooling arrangements, refer to **Chapter 4**. The instructions will cover the setting of the air regulating ring on vehicles with the original type of air cooling and heating system, and also the adjustment of the fan belt.

Adjust the accelerator cable correctly according to the notes in **Chapter 2** and carry out final adjustment of the slow-running after the engine has reached normal running temperature.

1:15 Fault diagnosis

(a) Engine will not start

1 Defective ignition coil, but check that carbon brush in distributor cap contacts rotor arm
2 Faulty distributor capacitor (condenser)
3 Dirty, pitted or incorrectly set contact breaker points
4 Ignition wires loose, insulation faulty
5 Water on sparking plug leads
6 Battery discharged, corrosion of terminals
7 Faulty or jammed starter
8 Sparking plug leads wrongly connected
9 Vapour lock in fuel pipes
10 Defective fuel pump
11 Overchoking or underchoking. Check automatic choke
12 Blocked pump filter or carburetter jets
13 Leaking valves
14 Sticking valves
15 Valve timing incorrect
16 Ignition timing incorrect

(b) Engine stalls after starting

1 Check 1, 2, 3, 4, 5, 10, 11, 12, 13 and 14 in (a)
2 Sparking plugs defective or gaps incorrect
3 Retarded ignition
4 Mixture too weak
5 Water in fuel system
6 Fuel tank breather pipe blocked
7 Incorrect valve clearances

(c) Engine idles badly

1 Check 2 and 7 in (b)
2 Air leaks at manifold joints
3 Carburetter idling adjustment wrong, pilot jet blocked
4 If fast-idle, automatic choke not switching off
5 Over-rich mixture
6 Worn piston rings
7 Worn valve stems or guides
8 Weak exhaust valve springs

(d) Engine misfires

1 Check 1, 2, 3, 4, 5, 8, 10, 12, 13, 14, 15 and 16 in (a); 2, 3, 4 and 7 in (b)
2 Weak or broken valve springs

(e) Engine overheats

1 Weak mixture, ignition over-advanced
2 Fan belt slipping
3 Thermostat defective or wrongly set
4 Control flaps inoperative, regulating ring incorrectly adjusted
5 Loss of cooling air through badly fitted fan housing, ducts and coverplates
6 Oil cooling system not working

(f) Compression low

1 Check 13 and 14 in (a); 6 and 7 in (c); and 2 in (d)
2 Worn piston ring grooves
3 Scored or worn cylinder bores

(g) Engine lacks power

1 Check 3, 10, 12, 13, 14, 15 and 16 in (a); 2, 3, 4 and 7 in (b); 6 and 7 in (c); and 2 in (d). Also check (e) and (f)
2 Leaking joints and gaskets
3 Fouled sparking plugs
4 Automatic ignition advance not operating
5 Exhaust system blocked

(h) Burnt valves or seats

1 Check 13 and 14 in (a); 7 in (b); and 2 in (d). Also check (e)
2 Excessive carbon round valve seats and head

(j) Sticking valves

1 Check 2 in (d)
2 Bent valve stems
3 Scored valve stems or guides
4 Incorrect valve clearance

(k) Excessive cylinder wear

1 Check 11 in (a) and check (e)
2 Lack of oil
3 Dirty oil
4 Piston rings gummed up or broken
5 Badly fitting piston rings
6 Bent connecting rods
7 Dirt under cylinder mounting flanges

(l) Excessive oil consumption

1 Check 6 and 7 in (c) and check (k)
2 Ring gaps too wide
3 Oil return holes in pistons choked with carbon
4 Scored cylinders
5 Oil level too high
6 External oil leaks, check oil cooler
7 Incorrect grade of oil

(m) Crankshaft and connecting rod bearing failure

1 Check 2 in (k)
2 Restricted oilways
3 Worn journals or crankpins
4 Failure of oil pump, oil cooler, relief valve or strainer
5 Loose bearings, loose connecting rod caps
6 Bent connecting rods or crankshaft

(n) High fuel consumption

1 Vehicle in poor mechanical condition
2 Bad driving habits, excessive acceleration in low gears
3 Incorrectly adjusted ignition and carburation
4 Flooding of float chamber
5 Automatic choke not working properly
6 Fuel leakage
7 Incorrect jet sizes

(o) Engine vibration

1 Loose generator mounting
2 Fan out of balance
3 Clutch and flywheel out of balance
4 Misfiring due to mixture, ignition or mechanical faults

CHAPTER 2

THE FUEL SYSTEM

2:1 Description

On Transporters the fuel tank is fitted in the rear compartment. Until 1960 there was a three-position fuel tap which was fixed to the tank and which had a manual control inside the car. This arrangement was superseded by a fuel gauge with a mechanical connection to a float in the tank.

Pipelines carry the fuel to a mechanical pump mounted on the engine and driven by an eccentric cam on the distributor drive shaft. Up to 1960 the pump was of the type shown in **FIG 2:1**. This was followed, in August 1960, by the type shown in **FIG 2:2**. **FIG 2:4** shows the most recent type with the filter fitted in the side.

The pump delivers fuel to a downdraught carburetter fitted with an air cleaner. Carburetter types range from early models with manual choke control to later types with automatic choke control. Diaphragm-operated accelerator pumps are fitted to all models to give a richer mixture when sudden demands are made on the engine.

2:2 Maintenance of tanks and gauges

Removing fuel tank:

1 On all vehicles except the Pick-up it is necessary to remove the engine to reach the tank in the engine compartment. On the Pick-up the tank is behind a partition panel and it is removed by taking off the corresponding coverplates in the lower deck locker.

2 Close the fuel tap if fitted and pull off the flexible hose. Drain the fuel. Remove the rubber seal from the filler tube. Disconnect the tap control cable, if fitted, and disconnect fuel gauge lead.

3 Remove the two tank fixing screws, lift off retaining straps and take out the tank.

When working on the tank and fuel tap in situ, always disconnect the battery as there is a risk of fire due to spilled fuel and a shortcircuit. This can happen if a spanner touches terminal 30 on the starter.

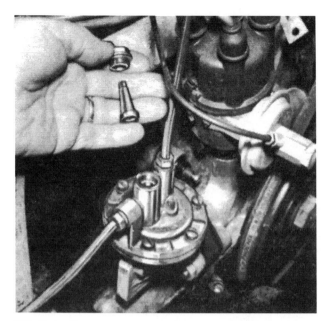

FIG 2:1 The fuel pump fitted prior to 1960. The tubular gauze filter is removed by unscrewing the top hexagon plug

FIG 2:2 A fairly recent fuel pump with a disc-type gauze filter under the top cover. The most recent type is shown in FIG 2:4

Servicing fuel tap:

1 Remove the stopscrew and the lockscrew for the ring screw on early models. On more recent three-way taps, press down the ring with a piece of tubing and remove the circlip. Pull out the tap and rubber seal.

2 Clean the filter with fuel and a brush. Do not use rag. Clean all the parts and dry them with compressed air, not rag. Renew the rubber seal if defective. Always use a genuine factory replacement which is proof against all kinds of fuel.

3 Reassemble in the reverse order.

Re-installing fuel tank:

The tank must be cleaned by blowing out with compressed air. When refitting the tank in the reverse order to dismantling, renew the anti-squeak packing if it is damaged.

If fitted, check the operation of the fuel tap control, especially if it has been stiff or even immovable. The cable sleeve is secured to the seat bench to the right of the heater control knob. It then passes through the tool compartment along the heating cable tube.

The cable must not be kinked. Before trying to straighten it, disconnect the cable sleeve from the guide bracket in front of the tap. Check that the bracket enables the cable to work the tap properly. Lubricate the cable with universal grease and check the tap, lubricating it by rubbing in some molybdenum paste or graphite grease with a piece of rag.

When the cable sleeve is free from kinks, attach it to the guide bracket for the tap. Push the control knob right in. Turn the fuel tap to the stop in the fully open position and secure the cable to the lever.

Adjusting mechanical fuel gauge:

If the tank has been disturbed it will be necessary to reset the fuel gauge. This is best done with an empty tank. First remove the luggage compartment lining to reach the rear of the instrument panel and the sender unit in the top of the tank. Remove the unit cover. Examine the back of the gauge where a knurled screw will be found and an arrow marked on the case.

Enlist the aid of someone to watch the gauge needle inside the car. Press on the sender unit lever to which the cable is attached to ensure that the float inside the tank is at its lowest position. Turn the knurled screw on the back of the gauge in the direction of the arrow until the needle is at zero. In this position there is about one gallon of fuel left in the tank when the needle is on the 'R' mark. If the sender unit is removed from the tank at any time, renew the cork gasket under the flange on replacement, and adjust the gauge.

2:3 Fuel pump description

The principle of operation is the same for all types and FIG 2:3 should be used for reference. This is a section of the pump shown in FIG 2:2, as fitted to later vehicles. Note, however, that the most recent models are fitted with a tubular filter in the side of the pump. Under the top cover of this latest pump there is a diaphragm-operated valve which stops the flow of fuel when the engine is not running. On starting up, pressure of fuel opens the valve.

Pushrod 10 in the sectioned illustration is driven to and fro by an eccentric on the distributor drive shaft. This operates lever 9 which flexes diaphragm 5 through a pull-rod. The diaphragm is pressed upwards by spring 6. Suction valve 3 takes fuel from the clean side of filter 11 and delivery valve 12 passes fuel to the carburetter.

When the diaphragm moves downwards the partial vacuum in the chamber above it causes valve 3 to open and fuel is drawn in. On the upward stroke of the diaphragm, aided by spring 6, the suction valve closes and delivery valve 12 lifts off its seat to allow fuel to be pumped through outlet 13 to the carburetter.

The fuel pump fitted to the '1500' Transporter uses different suction and delivery valves in order to pump fuel at a slightly higher rate.

2:4 Fuel pump servicing

Routine maintenance is confined to filter cleaning. Do this every 3000 miles on vehicles up to 1965 and every 6000 miles on models after August 1965. Shut off the fuel supply on later models by fitting a clamp to the flexible hose. Remove cover 2 and lift out the disc-type filter 11. On other models remove the hexagon-headed plug, as shown in **FIGS 2:1** and **2:4** to reach the tubular filter. Clean filter gauzes with fuel and a brush, never a fluffy rag. When refitting the filter, renew the gasket if it is hard or damaged. In the case of the pump with the circular filter, do not overdo tightening of the screw.

After completing this operation, run the engine and check that there is no fuel leakage from the cover or hexagon plug.

Removing and dismantling fuel pump:

Disconnect the pipes from the pump, unscrew the two flange nuts and lift off the pump. **It is important to remove the pushrod next,** followed by the intermediate flange and gaskets. These parts are all shown in **FIG 2:5.**

Remove the filter. On early models like that shown in **FIG 2:1**, remove the pump cover (six screws), press down on the diaphragm and disconnect it from the rocker arm. On all models remove the rocker fulcrum pin by driving it out after removing a spring ring, if fitted. On later models remove the inspection cover (two screws), and use a screwdriver to remove the rocker return spring. On the early pump the spring is removed after unscrewing a slotted plug at the bottom. On later models the six flange screws can now be removed, the diaphragm pressed down and the rocker arm removed.

Check the operation of the valve by sucking and blowing at the inlet and outlet ports. The valves on the early pump can be removed after three screws have been taken out of the retaining plate. Note that the smooth lapped faces of the valves contact the seats. If the valves do not seat effectively and corrosion of the seats is suspected, renew the top half of the pump.

Inspect the diaphragm and reject it if it is cracked or has hardened. Excessive wear of the rocker arm and fulcrum pin will also call for renewal.

Reassembling the fuel pump:

On early pumps assemble the valves and retainer plate and check that the valves operate. Assemble the rocker arm and pin, securing the latter with punch marks on the body. Fit the rocker arm spring and plug. Replace the diaphragm with the spring underneath and engage the pullrod with the rocker arm. Nip the pump flange in a vice and press the rocker arm .55 inch inwards measured from the flange joint face. Fit the pump cover and tighten the screws evenly and diagonally, making sure the diaphragm is not creased.

On later pumps, reassemble in the reverse order to dismantling, using the preceding method to position the diaphragm before tightening the cover flange screws. Note that the inlet and outlet pipes should be above the

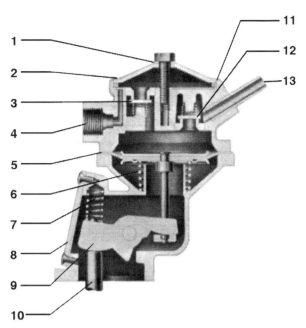

FIG 2:3 Cross-section of the fuel pump fitted after 1960

Key to Fig 2:3   1 Gasket   2 Fuel pump cover
3 Suction valve   4 Fuel intake   5 Diaphragm
6 Diaphragm spring   7 Spring   8 Inspection cover
9 Rocker arm   10 Pushrod   11 Filter   12 Delivery valve
13 Fuel outlet

FIG 2:4 The latest type of fuel pump with tubular gauze filter removable after unscrewing a hexagon plug from the side

side coverplate, and the diaphragm should be flat while the screws are tightened. Replace filter flat side downwards and check that the sealing washer is correctly positioned in the cover. Fill the lower pump chamber containing the rocker arm with universal grease.

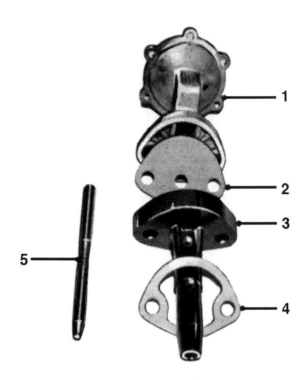

FIG 2:5 Components of the pushrod drive to the fuel pump

Key to Fig 2:5   1 Pump body   2 Gasket—pump to flange
3 Moulded plastic intermediate flange   4 Gasket—flange to
crankcase   5 Pushrod

Adjusting fuel pump stroke:

Pumping pressure is determined by correct adjustment of the pushrod stroke and also by the strength of the spring 6 under the diaphragm, as shown in **FIG 2:3**. If stroke adjustment is correct and there is carburetter flooding the spring must be weakened or renewed. If the spring is already weak, giving fuel starvation, it can be stretched or renewed.

To adjust the pushrod stroke, fit the intermediate flange and gaskets over the pump fixing studs. The oil passage in the intermediate flange faces upwards on early models. **Always install the intermediate flange before inserting the pushrod as there might be a chance that the rod could slide through into the crankcase.** The rounded end of the rod should contact the eccentric on the distributor drive shaft.

On early models the stroke of the rod is .16 inch. Turn the engine over and measure the amount the rod protrudes from the intermediate pump mounting flange with gaskets in place underneath the flange. When right in, the measurement should be 1.14 inch and when the rod is at full stroke the measurement should be 1.34 inch. To adjust the stroke fit the appropriate gaskets under the intermediate flange. Never use fewer gaskets than are actually required or damage to the diaphragm may result.

On later models carry out the preceding operation but note that, although the stroke is still .16 inch the amount of pushrod protruding at minimum and maximum stroke is .3 and .5 inch respectively.

Re-installing fuel pump:

Fit the later type of pump so that the coverplate faces left. Retighten the flange nuts when the engine has reached running temperature but do not overtighten. Check that the rubber grommet carrying the fuel pipe is correctly fitted in the engine front coverplate.

2:5 Carburetter descriptions

There are three types of Solex downdraught carburetters to be covered in this section and the following are brief descriptions:

Type 28 PCI:

This was fitted to models up to May 1959 and can be readily identified because it has a manually-operated choke control (see **FIG 2:6**).

Type 28 PICT:

This was fitted from May 1959 to 1963. The manual choke control was dropped and an automatic choke incorporated, using a bi-metallic spring. Further control over the automatic choke was made by a vaccum piston.

Type 28 PICT-1:

This was fitted in 1963 and was similar to the 28 PICT but the vacuum piston was changed to a diaphragm control (see item 5, **FIG 2:7**).

Operation of 28 PCI carburetter:

A section through the carburetter is shown in **FIG 2:8** and the salient features can be identified. The volume of fuel carried in the float chamber is controlled by a float and needle valve. When the level of fuel is correct the float will close the valve and prevent fuel entering until the level falls again. Air is drawn down through the carburetter body past the strangler butterfly. This movement of air is due to a depression in the inlet manifold caused by the suction of descending pistons on their inlet strokes.

To obtain a rich mixture for starting from cold, the strangler butterfly can be closed manually by operating the control knob. At idling speeds, fuel and air passing down from the pilot jet are fed to the inlet manifold past the volume control screw, which can be adjusted to give even slow-running. With the engine running hotter and an increased demand for mixture following on the opening of the throttle butterfly by the accelerator pedal, an emulsified mixture of fuel and air leaves the main spraying assembly and passes down into the inlet manifold. Sudden demands for extra performance from the engine are met by increasing the richness of the mixture through the action of a pump connected to the throttle spindle. A diaphragm is flexed to draw in fuel through a non-return valve and, on the pressure stroke, to pump it to a jet past a second non-return valve. This fuel then enters the main choke tube as a rich emulsion to give the mixture required for powerful acceleration.

Operation of 28 PICT and PICT-1 carburetters:

The section shown in **FIG 2:9** is representative of both these types but the following differences should be noted. The change from PICT to PICT-1 types means that

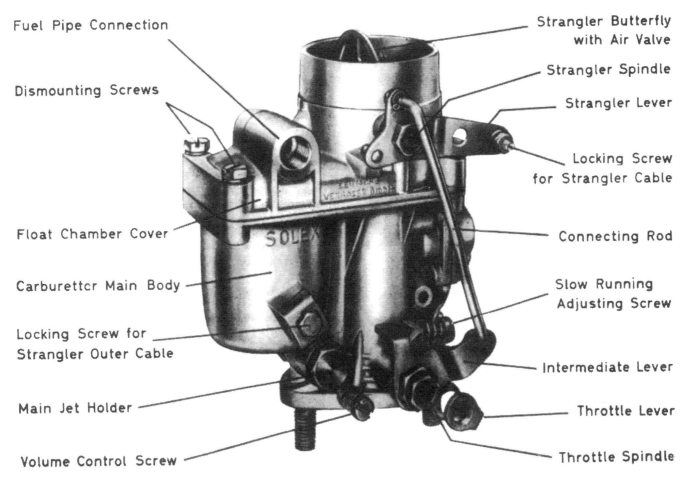

Fuel Pipe Connection

Dismounting Screws

Float Chamber Cover

Carburetter Main Body

Locking Screw for
Strangler Outer Cable

Main Jet Holder

Volume Control Screw

Strangler Butterfly
with Air Valve

Strangler Spindle

Strangler Lever

Locking Screw
for Strangler Cable

Connecting Rod

Slow Running
Adjusting Screw

Intermediate Lever

Throttle Lever

Throttle Spindle

FIG 2:6   Early Solex carburetter, type 28 PCI. Note cable-operated strangler

the vacuum piston 34 is replaced by a spring-loaded diaphragm, as shown in **FIG 2:10**. Note also the absence of the power fuel tube 39. This power fuel system is fitted to later Transporters to obtain maximum output from the engine. It provides extra mixture at high engine speeds and high manifold depression but does not operate at low engine speeds.

The automatic choke provides a cold engine with the necessary rich mixture and weakens the mixture automatically as the engine warms up. The device can be seen on the righthand side of both **FIGS 2:10** and **2:11**. It consists of a bi-metallic spring and heater coil contained in a ceramic body. The moving end of the spring engages a lever on the choke valve shaft. The choke valve is closed on a cold engine. When the ignition is switched on, current flows through the heater element, which takes two or three minutes to heat up fully. When the engine starts a rich mixture is drawn from discharge arm 32 under the influence of manifold depression caused by descending pistons creating a partial vacuum on their inlet strokes. To prevent the mixture from becoming excessively rich, a very high degree of vacuum will operate vacuum piston 34 or the equivalent diaphragm on later models so that the choke valve is opened slightly to admit more air. The choke valve also flutters between closed and open positions because it is mounted on its shaft with a larger flap hanging downwards and this is pressed open by the incoming flow of air.

A further refinement is the provision for setting the throttle position at various openings of the choke valve. The principal can be seen in **FIG 2:10** on the right. The lever attached to the throttle spindle carries an adjustment screw which abuts on a stepped cam at the upper end of the carburetter. The cam is secured to the choke valve shaft. When the valve is closed for cold starting the cam is in such a position that the screw is on the highest step and is held back in the dotted position to give an open throttle which prevents the engine from stalling. As the engine warms up and the choke valve spindle turns, it also turns the stepped cam. This allows the stopscrew and lever to move inwards in a series of steps, under the pull of a spring, and reduce the throttle opening until, with a hot engine, normal slow-running speed is reached.

Slow-running mixture is provided by pilot jet 45 and volume control screw 25, the latter being adjustable for setting the mixture correctly. The main mixture supply is provided by jet 24. It is emulsified in tube 41 which also incorporates an air correction jet to prevent excessive richness at high speeds. The mixture then issues from discharge arm 32 to mingle with the incoming air.

A rod 22 connects a lever on the throttle spindle to pump lever 20. Sudden opening of the accelerator for brisk demands on engine power causes the pump lever to flex diaphragm 19. This will pump fuel through passages to non-return valve 30 and so to discharge tube 33. The squirt of fuel provides the enriched mixture needed.

31

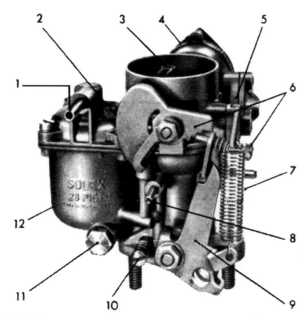

FIG 2:7   Later type of Solex carburetter, type 28 PICT-1

Key to Fig 2:7   1 Fuel inlet   2 Float chamber cover
3 Float chamber vent tube   4 Automatic choke (strangler)
5 Vacuum control for automatic choke   6 Stepped cam on
choke valve shaft with idling adjustment screw   7 Throttle
valve lever return spring   8 Vacuum connection to distributor
9 Throttle valve lever   10 Volume control screw
11 Main jet plug   12 Float chamber

2:6 Carburetter cleaning and adjustment, type 28 PCI

On this type of carburetter having the manual choke
control it is recommended to clean it every 3000 miles.
To make a thorough job of this it is best to remove the
float chamber cover complete. Refer to **FIG 2:6**.

1 Remove the air cleaner and disconnect the fuel pipe.
2 Remove the four dismounting screws. Disconnect the
   choke or strangler cable by undoing the locking screw
   at the outer end of the strangler lever. Disconnect the
   connecting rod from the same lever.
3 Lift away the top cover complete. Remove the float 52
   in **FIG 2:12**. Remove the main jet holder 66 to be
   found just below the strangler cable clamp. Note main
   jet 68. Remove the pilot jet 69 and the pilot jet air-
   bleed 70. Remove the air correction jet 65 and emulsion
   tube 64. From the cover 151 remove screw 151a.
   Remove screw 1a from the body 1. Remove the float
   needle valve 156 from the cover.
4 Blow out all passages with compressed air and clean
   out the float chamber. Clean the needle valve and the
   jets with compressed air or use a tyre pump if compressed air is not available. Never use wire to clean jets
   as it may alter the size and shape of the hole. Check the
   jet sizes against those given in Technical Data at the
   end of this book. Do not fit different jets from those
   specified as nothing will be gained by the modification.
   The screws 1a and 151a enable passages and a jet to
   be cleaned. These can be seen in **FIG 2:8**, the lower
   passage being marked 'Fuel supply to pump' and the
   jet shown as the 'Pump jet'. If the volume control
   screw seems to be inoperative when it is turned for
   slow-running adjustment, remove it and clean both

valve and passages. Check that the tip is not bent or
broken off due to excessive tightening.
5 When refitting the top cover, renew the gasket 152.
   The word 'OBEN' on the float toggle lever must face
   upwards. Connect up the disconnected controls and
   check the action of the strangler control, lubricating
   the cable if necessary. The choke or strangler valve
   must be fully open with the operating knob pushed in.

The only adjustment which is needed is to the slow-
running. Before making any alterations to the tuning,
make sure that the engine is at normal running temperature and satisfy yourself that the rest of the engine is in
good mechanical condition, with the valves seating
properly, with clearances correctly set, with no leaking
gaskets, particularly in the inlet manifold, and with the
sparking plugs and ignition system correctly adjusted.
It is never safe to assume that the carburetter is at fault
until every other part of an engine and its auxiliaries is
known to be in good condition and correctly set. To
adjust the slow-running, refer to **FIG 2:6** and proceed as
follows:

With the engine at normal running temperature turn
the slow-running adjustment screw in or out to get a fast
idling speed slightly above the usual setting. Slacken off
the volume control screw until the engine starts to hunt
and then screw it in slowly until the engine is running
smoothly. The volume control screw must never be
tightened right down. The engine will now be running too
fast to adjust the slow-running screw for correct idling
speed. Return to the volume control screw and try turning
it part of a turn in and out. If there is no improvement in
smooth idling the adjustment is correct. A final check is to
snap open the throttle and then close it suddenly with the
clutch pedal depressed to apply the extra load of the
release bearing. If the engine then stalls, increase the
idling speed.

2:7 Carburetter removal and servicing, type 28 PCI

To remove the carburetter proceed as follows:
1 Remove the air cleaner and disconnect the fuel line.
2 Disconnect the accelerator cable at the throttle lever
   (see **FIG 2:6**), then remove the swivel pin from the
   lever.
3 Unscrew the nuts from the mounting studs and lift off
   the carburetter.

To dismantle the carburetter use **FIG 2:12** for reference.
Follow the sequence covered in preceding **Section 2:6**
and in addition remove the pump cover 99 and the associated parts. The venturi or choke tube 61 can be extracted
by unscrewing a retaining screw. If the throttle and choke
or strangler butterflies and spindles are worn, remove
screws 4 and 173 to release the plates and allow the
spindles to be pushed out. Excessive wear of the spindles
and bearings leads to air leaks which make it impossible
to tune the carburetter correctly. The cure is to renew
the spindles and the body or cover. Check with Technical
Data that the jets are of the correct sizes.

Service all the parts by careful examination for wear.
To test the float if flooding has been troublesome,
immerse it in hot water. The expanding air inside the
float will issue as bubbles from any perforation. As
soldering will increase the weight of the float it is best to

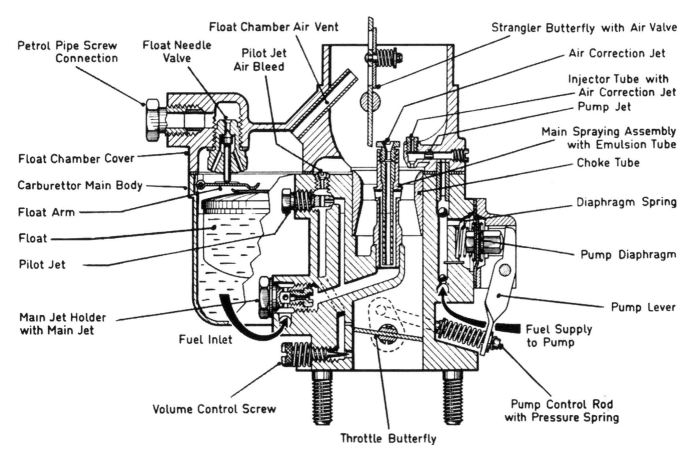

FIG 2:8 Section through early Solex carburetter, type 28 PCI

Labels (clockwise from top left):
Petrol Pipe Screw Connection
Float Needle Valve
Float Chamber Air Vent
Pilot Jet Air Bleed
Strangler Butterfly with Air Valve
Air Correction Jet
Injector Tube with Air Correction Jet
Pump Jet
Main Spraying Assembly with Emulsion Tube
Choke Tube
Diaphragm Spring
Pump Diaphragm
Pump Lever
Fuel Supply to Pump
Pump Control Rod with Pressure Spring
Throttle Butterfly
Volume Control Screw
Fuel Inlet
Main Jet Holder with Main Jet
Pilot Jet
Float
Float Arm
Carburettor Main Body
Float Chamber Cover

renew a punctured one. Trouble from flooding or starvation may be due to a faulty float needle valve 156. This must also be renewed.

Check the springs 94, 113 and 174. Check the pump diaphragm 93 and renew it if faulty. Carburetter hesitation or a 'flat spot' when opening the throttle suddenly is usually a sign of a defective diaphragm. Check the valve in the strangler butterfly 172 for proper sealing and make sure it opens easily. Make certain that the tip of volume control screw 26 has not been broken off in the body of the carburetter through overtightening.

Reassembling, type 28 PCI:

Reassemble the carburetter in the reverse order to dismantling, renewing the cover gasket 152. Also renew gaskets 67 and 157. Any leakage at the main jet plug 66 must be cured. As assembly proceeds, check that the choke or strangler spindle is free and effectively returned by spring 174. Fit the venturi 61 so that the radiused end is uppermost. This will also bring the smallest part of the bore of the venturi nearer the top. The word 'OBEN' on the float toggle lever must face upwards.

Finally re-install the carburetter and connect the controls, making sure that the strangler valve is fully open with the operating knob pushed right in when connecting the cable. Put a touch of grease on both cables. To connect the accelerator cable so that it puts no strain on the cable at full throttle, open the throttle valve so that there is a clearance of about .04 inch between the throttle lever and the stop on the carburetter body. Fully depress the accelerator pedal and connect the cable to the throttle lever on the carburetter. See **Section 2:13** for information on the removal and installation of the cables.

2:8 Carburetter adjustment, type 28 PICT

Use **FIG 2:9** for reference purposes. Adjust the idling as follows:

Run the engine up to normal running temperature and refer to the points raised at the beginning of the same instructions in **Section 2:6**. Having checked that the engine is in sound mechanical condition and that the sparking plugs and ignition system are correctly adjusted, set the idling screw for a fast-idle as shown in **FIG 2:13**. Make quite sure that the screw is not in contact with any of the steps on the cam, which will indicate that the choke valve is not fully open.

Turn the volume control screw as shown in **FIG 2:14**. Screw in clockwise until the engine speed begins to drop and then turn it back $\frac{1}{4}$ to $\frac{1}{3}$ of a turn in an anticlockwise direction. Readjust the idling screw to give the desired idling speed. Check by opening and shutting the throttle suddenly. If the engine stalls, increase the idling speed slightly. It is not uncommon for engines to stall when the clutch is disengaged, due to the extra load of the clutch release bearing, so try the idling speed under those conditions too. Poor idling may be caused by leaking gaskets, loose inlet manifold flanges, leaking valves or faulty ignition.

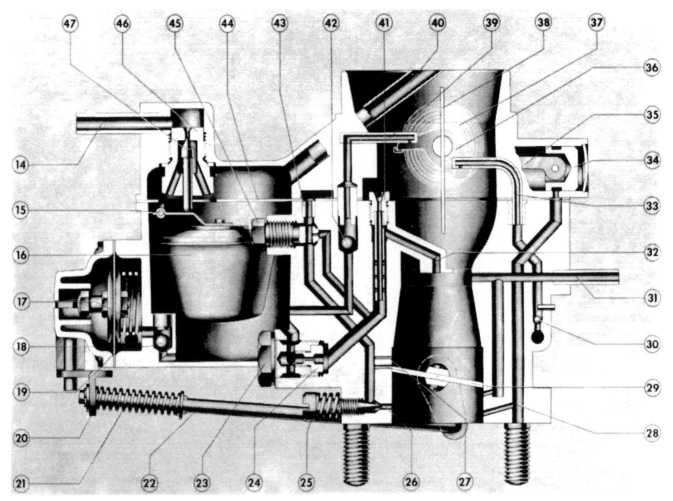

FIG 2:9   Solex carburetter, type 28 PICT with vacuum piston and automatic choke

Key to Fig 2:9   14 Fuel line   15 Float toggle   16 Float   17 Pump spring   18 Ball check valve for accelerator pump
19 Pump diaphragm   20 Pump lever   21 Spring   22 Pump connector rod   23 Main jet carrier   24 Main jet
25 Volume control screw   26 Idle port   27 Bypass ports   28 Vacuum drilling   29 Throttle valve
30 Ball check valve in accelerator pump drilling   31 Vacuum connection   32 Discharge arm   33 Accelerator pump discharge tube
34 Vacuum piston   35 Piston rod   36 Operating lever   37 Bimetal spring   38 Choke valve   39 Power fuel tube
40 Float chamber vent tube   41 Air correction jet with emulsion tube   42 Ball check valve in power fuel system
43 Pilot air drilling   44 Gasket   45 Pilot jet   46 Float needle valve   47 Float needle

2:9 Carburetter removal and servicing, type 28 PICT

Remove the carburetter as follows:

1 Detach the preheater connection to the air cleaner and remove the air cleaner. Disconnect the fuel pipe.
2 Pull off the electrical lead to the heater element on the righthand side. Pull the vacuum hose off the carburetter.
3 Disconnect the throttle cable from the lever and remove the spring, washer and lever swivel pin. Undo the two nuts under the mounting flange and lift off the carburetter.

Servicing the carburetter, type 28 PICT:

Use **FIG 2:9** for reference. It will also be found useful to refer to the exploded parts illustration of the 28 PICT-1 in **FIG 2:18** as many of the items are similar. Dismantle as follows:

1 Remove the five screws and lift off the cover shown in **FIG 2:15**.
2 From inside the cover unscrew the float needle valve 46.

3 The automatic choke device can be seen facing right in **FIG 2:15**. Remove the three flange ring screws and lift out the ceramic plate, the bi-metal spring 37 and the heater element.
4 Lift out the float 16. Remove the main jet carrier 23 and the volume control screw 25. Remove the air correction jet and emulsion tube 41. Remove the pilot jet 45. These parts can be seen in **FIG 2:16**.
5 Remove the four screws and lift off the pump cover, diaphragm 19 and spring 17, as shown in **FIG 2:17**.

Clean all parts in fuel with the exception of the ceramic plate, the bi-metal spring and the heater element. Blow out all passages and jets with compressed air or a tyre pump. Do not try to clear jets with wire or holes may be damaged or enlarged. Check the sizes against the correct ones given in Technical Data at the end of this manual. Check all gaskets and renew if damaged. Check the fit of the throttle and choke valve spindles. Excessive clearance, particularly of the throttle spindle can lead to air leaks which make accurate tuning impossible. Remove

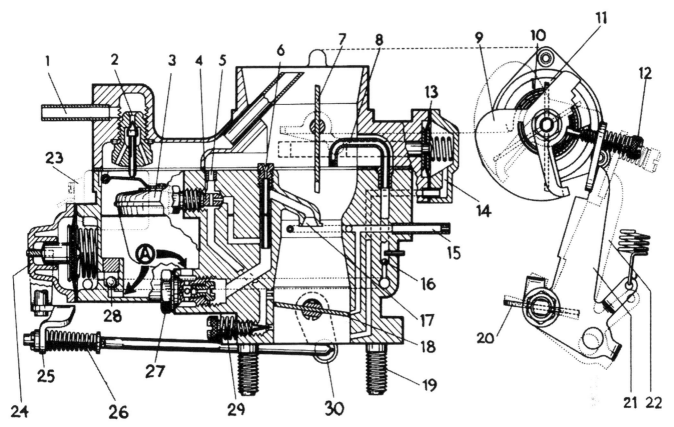

FIG 2:10 Section through Solex carburetter, type 28 PICT-1. Cam and lever fast-idle control on right

Key to Fig 2:10 1 Fuel inlet   2 Float needle valve   3 Float   4 Pilot jet   5 Pilot jet air inlet   6 Air correction jet
with emulsion tube   7 Choke valve (strangler)   8 Accelerator discharge tube   9 Fast-idle cam   10 Bimetal spring
11 Ceramic plate   12 Idling adjustment screw   13 Vacuum diaphragm—choke control   14 Vacuum passage
15 Vacuum connection for distributor   16 Accelerator pump check valve   17 Emulsion discharge arm   18 Throttle valve
19 Mounting stud   20 Throttle valve   21 Throttle lever   22 Throttle lever in fast-idle position   23 Electromagnetic pilot jet
24 Diaphragm accelerator pump   25 Accelerator pump operating lever   26 Spring on accelerator pump rod   27 Main jet plug
28 Check valve for accelerator pump   29 Volume control screw   30 Intermediate lever for accelerator pump   A Fuel entry
to main jet and accelerator pump

the butterfly screws and butterfly plates to extract worn spindles. Wear in the body and cover bearings calls for renewal.

Renew the needle valve if there has been flooding, but also check the float by immersing it in hot water. A stream of bubbles will issue from any puncture. Do not try to solder over the hole but renew the float. Solder will increase the weight of the float and raise the fuel level.

Check the parts of the heater element and bi-metal spring. Renew the complete ceramic plate if any part is damaged. Check the pump diaphragm for damage which can lead to inefficient pumping. Hesitation of the engine or spitting back through the carburetter on sudden acceleration is usually a sign that the pump is not working properly. Check that the vacuum piston 34 is not seized.

Make sure that the tip of the volume control screw is not bent or broken off. Overtightening may break off the tip and leave it jammed in the body.

Reassembling the carburetter, type 28 PICT:

Use new gaskets when reassembling. When fitting the ceramic plate with bi-metal spring and heater element, see that the mark on the plate corresponds with the one on the housing as arrowed in **FIG 2:15**. Put a few drops of oil on the steps of the fast-idle cam. Connect the throttle cable as instructed at the end of **Section 2:7**. When installing the air inlet elbow, do not overtighten the clamping screw or the carburetter cover may be distorted.

2:10 Carburetter adjustment, type 28 PICT-1

The essential difference between these and the preceding models is the use of a diaphragm vacuum control for the automatic choke, as can be seen in **FIG 2:10**. The control can also be seen as parts 35 to 38 in **FIG 2:18**. Note also that the 28 PICT-1 carburetter is fitted with the power fuel system to be seen above ball valve 42 in **FIG 2:9**. This gives a richer mixture at full load and high engine speeds, when a high degree of vacuum will draw fuel from the tube positioned in the carburetter cover. Refer to **Section 2:12** for instructions concerning the electromagnetic pilot jet, if one is fitted. This is the device indicated by the lower righthand arrow in **FIG 2:11** which illustrates a Transporter installation incorporating a governor. This governor is sealed and must not be tampered with.

Adjustment for correct idling is the same as that covered in **Section 2:8**.

FIG 2:11 Transporter carburetter, showing governor, bottom left. Arrow, top right, indicates the automatic choke and arrow, bottom right, the electromagnetic pilot jet

2:11 Carburetter removal and servicing, type 28 PICT

Use the instructions in **Section 2:9** to remove a carburetter, remembering to detach the electrical lead to the electromagnetic pilot jet if such a jet is fitted.

Dismantle and service the carburetter by following the instructions in **Section 2:9**. Refer to **FIG 2:18** which shows the parts of the diaphragm vacuum control 35 to 38 and the electromagnetic pilot jet 17. Unscrew the pilot jet complete and hold the body by hand to unscrew the jet proper, using a second spanner on the large hexagon. Do not grip the body in a vice as consequent distortion may make the needle stick. Clean the jet. Reassemble and check as instructed in **Section 2:12**.

When reassembling the pump diaphragm cover 22, press lever 23 away from the float chamber so that the diaphragm is secured in the pumping position. Fit circlips 31 to pump rod 27 so that there is about $\frac{1}{64}$ inch of play, and insert the cotterpin in the inner hole.

When reassembling the automatic choke, after checking that diaphragm 35 is in good condition, make sure the lug on part 41 engages the notch in the choke housing. Ensure that the ceramic rod between the heater element and the bi-metal spring is correctly located. The operating lever in the housing must engage the hooked end of the spring when the parts are installed. Turn the cap until the mark on the ceramic cover 42 is in-line with the centre mark on the housing before tightening the three screws 45. Do not overtighten. The righthand arrow in **FIG 2:15** shows the marks.

Check the position of the accelerator pump discharge tube 2. When the throttle butterfly is opened, the jet of fuel must spray straight down past the butterfly. Align the tube if necessary.

Refer to Technical Data for details of the correct jet sizes. Connect the accelerator cable as instructed in **Section 2:7**.

2:12 The electromagnetic pilot jet

Recent models are fitted with this device as standard with the object of preventing 'running-on' when the ignition is switched off, see lower righthand arrow in **FIG 2:11**. The electromagnetic operation of a needle opens the pilot when the ignition is switched on. When the ignition is switched off the needle shuts off fuel to the jet. Earlier 1200 engines can be fitted with an electromagnetic pilot jet.

To check the action, unscrew the device and pull the lead off the terminal. Switch on the ignition after checking that the pilot jet grubscrew is screwed right in. Touch the lead to the terminal. The needle should move in and out with a tick, each time contact is made and broken. The needle should move towards the carburetter to close the pilot jet with the lead detached, and away from it to open the jet with the lead in contact. If the valve does not work when tested in this way, or if the engine shows a tendency to run-on, renew the valve. However, failure can be temporarily cured by turning the grubscrew as far to the left as possible to open the valve. Turning the screw in the opposite direction will close the valve and shut off fuel to the pilot jet.

2:13 The accelerator cable

Refer to **FIG 2:19** which shows how the cable is secured to the throttle lever on the carburetter and how the return spring is assembled. The cable passes inside guide tubes through the fan housing and under the body. At the front end it is hooked over a rod connected to the accelerator pedal.

To remove the cable, disconnect it from the throttle lever on the carburetter. Press on the outer sleeve to compress the spring and remove the spring seat shown in the inset to the illustration. Take off the sleeve and spring. Detach the rod from the accelerator pedal and disconnect the cable from the rod. It will be easier to pull the cable out if the rear of the vehicle is lifted. From underneath, pull the cable out of the fan housing guide tube. Pull the plastic hose off the cable and take off the rubber boot at the end of the guide tubes in the frame. Pull the cable towards the front out of the guide tube.

When installing the cable, grease it with universal grease. Take care that it is laid straight between the guide tubes, with rubber boot and plastic hose carefully seated to prevent the ingress of water. Also make sure that the run of the cable is quite free from kinks. To attach it to the throttle lever, reassemble the spring, sleeve and spring seat and thread the cable into the swivel pin in the throttle lever. With the front end hooked to the accelerator pedal rod, open the carburetter throttle valve by the lever until there is about .04 inch clearance between the lever and the stop on the carburetter body. With an assistant to fully depress the accelerator pedal, connect the cable to the throttle lever. This will ensure that there is no excessive tension on the cable which might lead to breakage.

2:14 The air cleaner

This is of the oil bath type which collects dust in an oil-filled reservoir. There must always be free oil above the sludge which is collected, so that servicing periods depend upon conditions. In moist climates on good roads it may be enough to look at the air cleaner every 3000 miles, but a daily check may be needed in very dusty conditions.

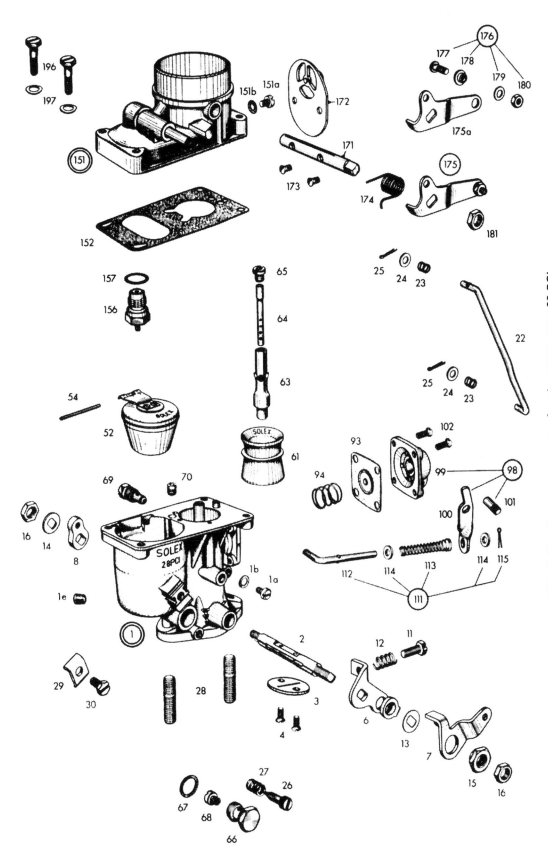

FIG 2:12   Component parts of carburetter, type 28 PCI

FIG 2:13 Idling screw adjustment on carburetters with automatic choke

FIG 2:14 Volume screw adjustment

To clean the filter, detach it from the carburetter after removing the hoses fitted on some models. Keep the cleaner level and do not turn it upside down. Release the two spring clips and lift off the element. Again, do not turn the element upside down. Clean the sludge out of the bowl and fill to the mark with fresh SAE.20 engine oil. If the element is unusually dirty due to neglect, wash it in paraffin or petrol and let it dry before attempting to fit it. Make sure that the gasket is in good condition. At regular intervals, check the oil level in the bowl and top it up if necessary, unless the sludge deposit is heavy enough to justify cleaning. Do not overtighten the cleaner clamping screw when refitting.

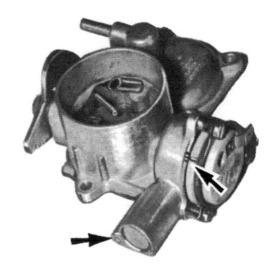

FIG 2:15 Carburetter cover, showing automatic choke. The piston-type vacuum control is indicated by the bottom arrow. Righthand arrow indicates locating marks for ceramic plate

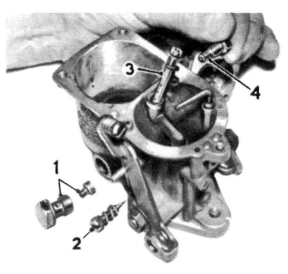

FIG 2:16 Later carburetter, showing jets. 1 Main jet and carrier, 2 Volume control screw, 3 Emulsion tube and air correction jet, 4 Pilot jet

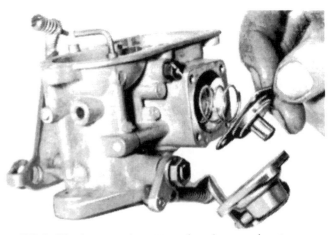

FIG 2:17 Later carburetter, showing accelerator pump dismantled. The fingers are holding the diaphragm

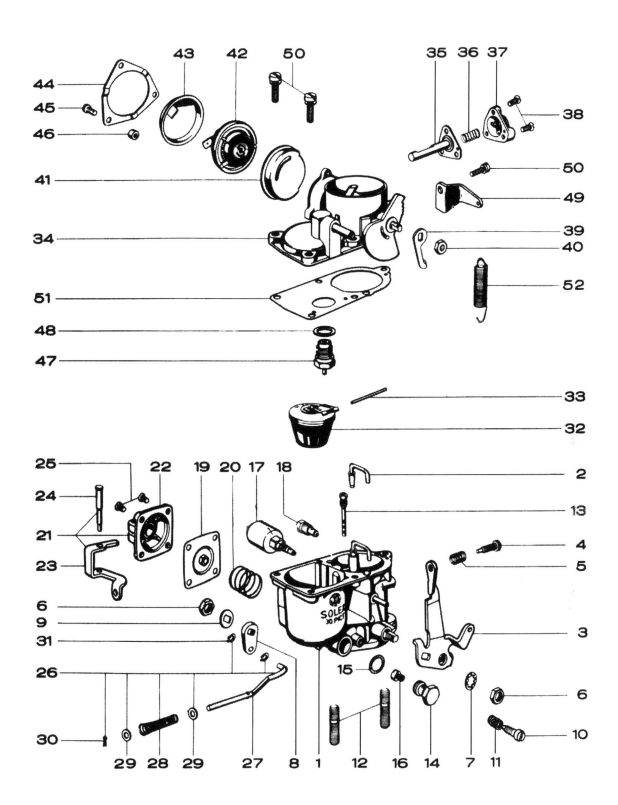

FIG 2:18   Carburetter, type 28 PICT-1

Key to Fig 2:18   1 Body   2 Accelerator pump discharge tube   3 Throttle lever   4 Volume control screw   5 Spring
6 Throttle spindle nut   7 Lockwasher   8 Intermediate lever   9 Washer   10 Volume control screw   11 Spring
12 Mounting studs   13 Emulsion tube   14 Main jet carrier   15 Washer   16 Main jet   17 Electromagnetic pilot jet
18 Pilot jet   19 Accelerator pump diaphragm   20 Pump spring   21 Pump cover assembly   22 Pump cover
23 Pump lever   24 Lever pivot pin   25 Cover screws   26 Pump rod assembly   27 Rod   28 Rod spring
29 Washer   30 Splitpin   31 Circlip   32 Float   33 Float fulcrum pin   34 Carburetter cover
35 Vacuum control diaphragm   36 Spring   37 Cover   38 Cover screws   39 Choke relay lever   40 Choke spindle nut
41 Protecting cover   42 Automatic choke control (heater, bi-metal spring)   43 Cover   44 Securing ring   45 Ring screw
46 Nut   47 Float needle valve   48 Gasket   49 Spring anchor   50 Screw   51 Cover gasket   52 Throttle lever return spring

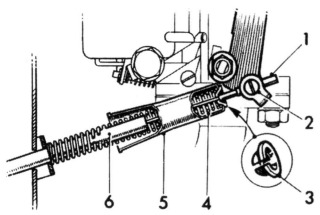

FIG 2:19 Throttle cable to lever fixing

Key to Fig 2:19 1 Throttle cable 2 Cable clamping screw
3 Spring seat 4 Spring 5 Spring sleeve 6 Cable guide tube

FIG 2:20 Later type of air cleaner with weighted flap to control air intake

On more recent models the air intake to the cleaner is fitted with a weight-controlled flap as shown in **FIG 2:20**. This keeps the intake closed against cold air at low speeds so that warm air prevents carburetter icing. This warm air is drawn through a hose adjacent to the exhaust system and into the air cleaner intake. With increasing engine speed the flap is pressed down against the effect of the balance weight and cold air is drawn in. Check the action of the flap to see that it works freely. The flap should only be fixed in the open position if the engine tends to pink when accelerating from low speeds due to using low octane fuel.

2:15 Fault diagnosis

If there is no fuel at the carburetter check that there is plenty in the tank. If satisfactory, disconnect the fuel pipe at the carburetter and operate the starter. If fuel is delivered, check the carburetter float needle valve and jets for blockage.

If no fuel is delivered, disconnect the fuel feed to the pump. If fuel pours out, check the fuel pump filter, valves and diaphragm. If no fuel comes out of the fuel feed pipe it is blocked. Remove the tank and clean with compressed air. Blow through the fuel pipe with compressed air. Other faults are covered as follows:

(a) Leakage or insufficient fuel delivered

1 Air leaks at pipe connections
2 Pump diaphragm screws loose, diaphragm defective
3 Diaphragm spring weak, gasket too thick
4 Pump valves leaking or sticking

(b) Excessive fuel consumption

1 Carburetter out of adjustment or worn
2 Wrong jets fitted, automatic choke defective, manual choke sticking
3 Float needle valve stuck open, float punctured
4 Excessive fuel pump pressure, diaphragm spring too strong, gasket too thin
5 Air cleaner choked
6 Brakes binding, tyres under-inflated

(c) Engine will not start with fuel supply and ignition working

1 Automatic choke not working, manual choke stuck open
2 Bi-metal spring in automatic choke unhooked or broken
3 Ceramic plate broken, heater element not working
4 Float needle stuck, carburetter flooding
5 Jets blocked

(d) Idling speed too high

1 Automatic choke not switching off
2 Heater element defective
3 Slow-running screws incorrectly adjusted
4 Worn throttle butterfly valve

(e) Engine 'runs-on' after ignition is switched off

1 Idling mixture too rich
2 Idling speed too fast
3 Electromagnetic pilot jet valve not working

(f) Engine runs unevenly

1 At idling speed, pilot jet blocked or wrongly adjusted
2 With black exhaust smoke, float chamber flooding through stuck needle valve or punctured float. Pressure from pump may be excessive.
3 At full throttle, fuel starvation

(g) Banging in exhaust on overrun

1 Idling mixture on weak side

CHAPTER 3

THE IGNITION SYSTEM

3:1 Description

There have been several variations in distributor design during the lifetime of the Transporter. At first the distributor was fitted with a centrifugal advance mechanism. This was followed by one which incorporated a vacuum control as well. Later, the centrifugal control was dropped altogether and every subsequent distributor from May 1959 on Transporters, has had vacuum control only. In addition, it is possible for a vehicle to be fitted with a distributor made either by Bosch or by VW. This, fortunately, will not seriously affect the servicing instructions, the chief difference being in the method of adjusting the contact breaker points. The VW distributor is recognizable because the capacitor (condenser) is mounted outside.

The only other point of interest is that, since August 1967, the system has been operating on 12 volts instead of the original 6.

3:2 Operation

The function of the ignition coil is to transform the low voltage of the vehicle's electrical system into a high voltage capable of producing a spark at the plug points.

The high voltage is induced by a current surge produced at the moment when the contact breaker points open. The points are part of the low-tension circuit and are opened by a four-lobed cam mounted on the distributor shaft. These parts can be seen in **FIGS 3:1** and **3:2**. At two revolutions of the engine and one of the distributor, the points open four times and four surges of high-tension electricity are sent out by the coil. These are fed to the respective sparking plugs in the correct firing order by a rotor arm which coincides with a segment and plug lead in the distributor cap at the precise moment when ignition is required. The current is passed to the rotor arm by way of a carbon brush connected to the coil lead. Note that there is a small gap between the rotor arm electrode and the segment in the cap, so that there is no mechanical contact. The high-tension current jumps this gap on its way to the sparking plug.

Automatic control of the moment of ignition is necessary, due to varying loads and speeds of the engine. On early distributors fitted with the centrifugal control, rising speed of the engine causes weights to fly out under the restraint of springs, to advance the ignition. The weights 21, springs 24 and assembly with cams and rotor arm 15, 29 and 70, are shown in **FIG 3:1**. As this control

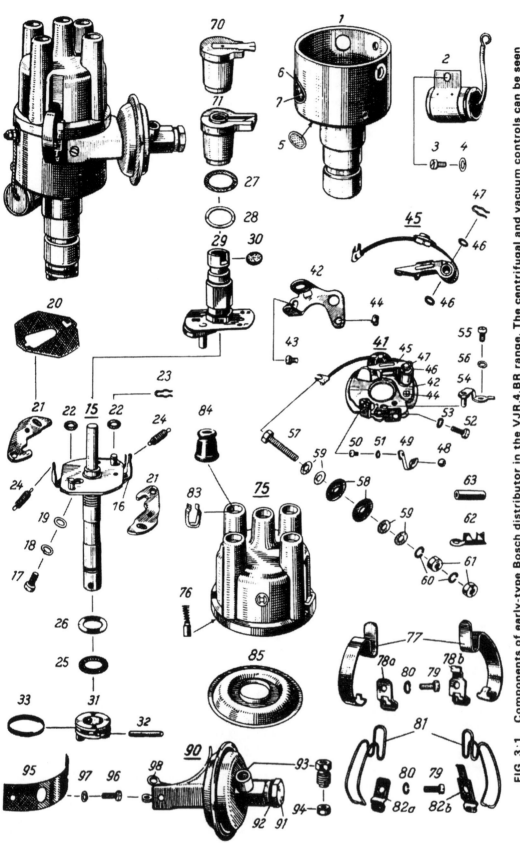

FIG 3:1 Components of early-type Bosch distributor in the VJR.4.BR range. The centrifugal and vacuum controls can be seen

Key to Fig 3:1
1 Body with bush and lubricating felt   2 Capacitor   3 Screw   4 Lockwasher   5 Dust filter   6 Nameplate   7 Rivet
15 Shaft   16 Bracket for spring   17 Screw   18 Lockwasher   19 Washer   20 Screw   21 Centrifugal weights   22 Washers under weights
23 Weight retainer   24 Springs   25 Fibre washer   26 Shim washer   27 Fibre washer on cam   28 Shim washer on cam   29 Camshaft
30 Lubricating felt   31 Driving dog   32 Pin for dog   33 Retaining clip   41 Contact plate and breaker assembly   42 Fixed contact bracket   43 Screw
44 Eccentric adjusting screw   45 Moving contact assembly   46 Washers   47 Retaining clip   48 Ball   49 Ball holder   50 Screw   51 Lockwasher
52 Screws   53 Lockwasher   54 Moving contact assembly   55 Bracket and earth cable screw   56 Lockwasher   57 Terminal 1   58 Insulating washers
59 Washers   60 Lockwashers   61 Nuts   62 Cable terminal   63 Sleeve for terminal   70 Rotor arm   71 Rotor arm with suppressor   75 Cap
76 Brush with spring   77 Retaining clip for cap   78 Shackle for clip   79 Screw   80 Lockwasher   81 Early-type clip   82 Shackle for early clip
83 Cable sleeve   84 Rubber ferrule for cable   90 Vacuum unit assembly   91 Locknut   92 Washer for nut   93 Thread bush   94 Bush packing
95 Packing strip   96 Screw   97 Lockwasher   98 Earthing cable

42

had no effect on the ignition point when there was a varying load on the engine, a vacuum control was introduced. This was connected by small-bore pipe to a port adjacent to the closed position of the throttle valve in the carburetter. The vacuum control is shown as assembly 90 in **FIG 3 : 1** and 60 in **FIG 3 : 2**. The casing contains a diaphragm, one side of which is subjected to atmospheric pressure when there is a depression on the other side due to the connection with the carburetter. Movement of the diaphragm is transmitted to the contact breaker plate by a rod which can be seen facing left. When the vehicle is cruising along with the throttle only partially opened, there is a strong depression in the bore of the carburetter, the diaphragm is deflected and this advances the ignition even more than the centrifugal weights have done. Wide opening of the throttle, particularly under conditions of heavy load and low engine speed means a considerable reduction in the degree of depression in the carburetter. The diaphragm will tend to return to its unflexed position under the influence of an internal spring and will retard the ignition accordingly. This method of controlling the point of ignition is now used without the centrifugal weights.

Models from early in 1960 will be fitted with red plug leads which incorporate radio suppressors. In **FIG 3 : 1**, item 71 is a rotor arm with suppressor, and item 45 in **FIG 3 : 2** is the same part as fitted to Bosch distributor ZV.PAU.R4.

3 : 3 Maintenance and adjustment

The coil :

Keep the insulating cap of the coil clean and dry to prevent current leakage. If the coil is removed during an overhaul, upon replacement the connections are—terminal 15 to ignition switch, terminal 1 to the distributor (contact breaker) and terminal 4 to the distributor cap.

To test whether a coil is defective or not, check the length of spark it will deliver. Before doing this, make certain that the battery and the distributor are in good order. Disconnect lead 4 from the centre socket in the distributor cap. Make sure the lead is not damp, and hold it with a piece of dry rag, keeping well away from the exposed metal end. Hold the end about $\frac{3}{8}$ inch away from the crankcase and crank the engine over. A spark should jump from the lead to the crankcase if the coil is working properly. If the coil is not satisfactory, first check that the capacitor in the distributor is not defective.

The distributor :

Maintenance of the VW distributor is similar to that described for the Bosch distributor.

Release the spring clips and lift off the distributor cap complete with plug leads. Clean the inside and outside of the cap with a dry cloth and examine for cracks or 'tracking'. The latter will show up as a thin black line between adjacent metal parts and the cure for both defects is a new cap. The electrodes in the cap and on the rotor arm are subject to some erosion due to the sparking which takes place over the gap between them. This is not detrimental unless it is obviously excessive. The rotor arm is readily pulled off. Observe the condition of the carbon brush in the centre of the cap. This bears on the metal part

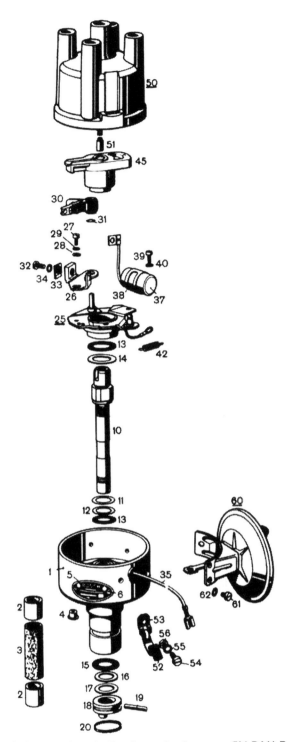

FIG 3 : 2 Later bosch distributor in the range ZV.PAU.R4. This type has a vacuum control unit only

Key to Fig 3 : 2   1 Body   2 Bearing bushes
3 Lubricating felt   4 Dust protector   5 Nameplate
6 Rivet   10 Camshaft   11 Shim washer   12 Washer
13 Fibre washer   14 Shim washer   15 Fibre washer
16 Washer   17 Shim washer   18 Driving dog
19 Pin for dog   20 Retaining clip   25 Contact breaker plate
26 Fixed contact bracket   27 Screw   28 Washer
29 Lockwasher   30 Moving contact   31 Washer
32 Terminal 1   33 Plate   34 Lockwasher
35 Connecting cable   37 Capacitor   38 Clip   39 Screw
40 Lockwasher   42 Return spring   45 Rotor arm   50 Cap
51 Brush   52 Clip for cap   53 Shackle for clip
54 Screw   55 Lockwasher   56 Nut
60 Vacuum unit complete   61 Screw   62 Lockwasher

of the rotor arm. The face should be polished and the brush should be capable of being pressed in and should spring out again quite freely.

Lubrication of the distributor:

This varies in the different models, but one feature is common to them all. **It is essential to be sparing with lubricant and it must not reach the contact breaker points.** Add two or three drops of thin oil into the recess in the top of the shaft after the rotor is removed.

When the centrifugal advance mechanism is known to be fitted, squirt a few drops of thin oil downwards in the space between the contact mounting plate and the shaft. The effect of the centrifugal mechanism can be felt by turning the rotor clockwise until a stop is reached. The rotor should return to the stop in the opposite direction when released. If it does not, the springs are probably faulty.

Add a tiny smear of universal grease to the cam on the shaft below the rotor arm, and put one drop of oil on the top of the pivot pin for the moving contact breaker point. The drive shaft runs in a self-lubricating bush.

The contact breaker points:

Examine the condition of the points by opening them with a finger. They should both have a clean, frosted look. After several thousand miles, it is common for a 'pip' to form on one point and a corresponding hollow to appear in the opposite point. This will not necessarily affect the performance of the ignition system, but if there has been trouble, the points can be removed and finished to a smooth flat surface. This must be done with a measure of skill because the surfaces must be flat and square so that they meet perfectly. To remove the points proceed as follows:

On early distributors:

1 Remove the cap and rotor arm.
2 Disconnect the low-tension lead from the distributor body. Loosen the nut on the terminal and take off the contact breaker arm pin.
3 Disconnect the moving contact spring and insulation from the terminal, taking careful note of the position of the insulation.
4 Remove the fixed point by unscrewing the fixing screw and also the screw attaching the vacuum unit pullrod bracket. Lift off the fixed contact.

On later distributors:

1 Remove the cap and rotor arm.
2 The low-tension lead and the one from the capacitor (condenser) are connected to an insulator. Loosen the hexagon screw clamping the leads, remove the low-tension lead and lift off the moving contact and spring.
3 Remove the screw to the right of the contacts and lift off the fixed contact.
4 Keep a note of the position of the washers for the breaker arm for correct replacement

On the latest distributors:

1 Remove the cap and rotor arm.
2 Pull off the low-tension cable connection.

3 Remove the fixed contact securing screw just above the contacts
4 Remove the circlip from the moving contact pivot pin.
5 Lift off both contacts. Note the breaker arm washers so that they will be replaced correctly.

Cleaning the points:

While in situ they can be cleaned with a cloth moistened in fuel. They may also be held together while a piece of cardboard is drawn between them. When the points have been removed they may have any serious roughness removed with a magneto file. If the tungsten tips to the points are badly worn it is hardly worth trying to restore them, as replacement points are not expensive. The points must be polished with a fine oilstone. This must be done with great care so that the faces are flat and meet squarely when they are re-installed.

Reassembling the contact breaker:

In every case this is simply a reversal of the dismantling instructions, but it is important to ensure the correct replacement of the insulating washers used on the terminal screw on early models, and those for the breaker arm on later models. After reassembly the gap must be adjusted.

Adjusting the contact breaker gap:

The correct gap is .016 inch when the points are fully opened by one of the cam lobes. If there is evidently only a few thousandths of an inch difference between the actual and the recommended gap it is not worth making an alteration to it.

To set the gap, remove the sparking plugs and turn the engine over with a spanner on the crankshaft pulley nut. Stop when the gap between the points is at its maximum. Use feeler gauges to check the gap. If there is considerable variation from the recommended gap slacken the fixed contact locking screw adjacent to the contacts.

There are three methods of adjustment according to the model and year of manufacture of the distributor. The three methods are shown in simple form in **FIG 3:3**. The one which uses an eccentric screw is an early type. Turn this screw to adjust the gap. The Bosch method of adjustment on later models is to place a screwdriver blade between two pips and twist the blade where it engages in the slot in the fixed contact plate. On VW distributors with the type of adjustment shown in the third illustration the screwdriver is twisted while it engages the two slots in the plates at the opposite end to the contacts. After locking the fixed contact plate, check the gap again, and on well-used vehicles it is sensible to check the gap on all four cam lobes. Serious variation may be due to a worn shaft and bushes and renewal is necessary.

It is important when adjusting the breaker gap to refrain from moving the contact breaker mounting plate from its basic position, or the gap will be altered.

After making adjustments to contact breakers it is advisable to check the ignition timing. This must also be done if the distributor is removed and replaced.

3:4 Checking the ignition timing:

This must be done with the engine cold. Examine the front flange of the crankshaft pulley for a notch or notches according to model (see **FIG 3:4**). Where there is only one notch, when this lines up with the joint between the two crankcase halves, the crankshaft will be $7\frac{1}{2}$ deg. before top dead centre (BTDC). When there are two notches, the righthand notch indicates a position 10 deg. BTDC and the lefthand notch $7\frac{1}{2}$ deg. BTDC. Anyone wishing to make the second notch on engines with only a single one can file another 4 mm to the right when viewed from above. Ignition timing figures are given in Technical Data.

If the specified timing for an engine is 10 deg. BTDC and it is necessary to use a low grade of fuel which makes the engine 'pink', set the timing on the lefthand or $7\frac{1}{2}$ deg. notch.

Before checking or setting the ignition timing, always set the contact breaker points to the correct gap. Variations from this will affect the timing. Now turn the engine over until the appropriate mark on the pulley is in-line with the crankshaft joint and the distributor rotor arm lines up with the No. 1 cylinder notch on the rim of the distributor body, as shown in **FIG 3:4**. In this position No. 1 piston is at TDC on the firing stroke.

The following is the best method of ensuring an accurate setting. Do not use a stroboscopic lamp. Fix up a test lamp and leads, using a 6-volt or 12-volt lamp. Connect one lead to No. 1 terminal on the coil and earth the other one, as in **FIG 3:5**. Loosen the screw in the distributor retaining clamp and switch on the ignition. Turn the distributor body clockwise until the contact points are seen to close. Now turn the body anticlockwise very slowly until the lamp lights up and stop turning at once. This is the point when the contacts have opened. Tighten the clamp. The ignition will now be correctly timed on all four cylinders when the righthand notch on the pulley is on top or directly below and in-line with the crankcase joint as the engine is turned over two revolutions.

It is not possible to carry out an accurate setting with the engine warm. The method of setting the ignition timing is suitable for both Bosch and VW distributors.

3:5 Distributor removal and refitting

Remove the distributor as follows:

1 Remove the vacuum pipe at the distributor and disconnect lead 1 from the coil.
2 Take off the distributor cap.
3 Remove the screw holding the distributor retaining bracket to the crankcase. Lift out the distributor.

Refit the distributor as follows:

1 Set the appropriate mark on the crankshaft pulley in-line with the crankcase flange, as shown in **FIG 3:4**. No. 1 piston will now be at TDC on its firing stroke.
2 Look down into the distributor housing in the crankcase and observe the position of the slot in the distributor drive shaft. Note that it is offset. The largest offset must be to the front, away from the crankshaft pulley and the slot must be parallel to the pulley flanges, that is, at right angles to the crankcase joint line, as shown in **FIG 3:4**. Details of the slotted drive shaft

FIG 3:3 Three types of contact breaker gap adjustment. **A** is the locking screw and **B** the adjusting device.. A variation of the first method, using an eccentric screw, can be seen as parts 42 to 44 in **FIG 3:1**. A screwdriver is used in the notches indicated in the other two illustrations

FIG 3:4 Timing ignition by aligning rotor with notch in body rim (top), and pulley notch with crankcase joint (right). Inset shows correct position for distributor drive shaft with slot at right angles to joint and large offset facing forward

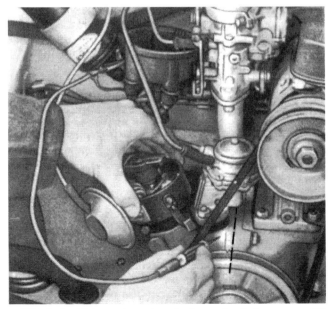

FIG 3:5 Using the electrical method for accurate ignition timing

can be seen in **Chapter 1, FIG 1:22.** Make sure the distance spring is properly seated in the drive shaft head. If the drive shaft has been taken out for any reason, use the instructions in **Chapter 1, Section 1:9** to replace it correctly.

3 Insert the distributor and turn the rotor arm until it points to the notch on the distributor body rim as indicated in **FIG 3:4.** Move the arm slightly backwards and forwards until the driving dogs engage and the distributor can be pressed right home. Fix the clamping plate and then check the ignition timing as instructed in **Section 3:4.** Always remember, when checking the timing, to turn the engine backwards about a quarter of a revolution to take up the play in the drive before turning it forwards to line up the pulley mark.

3:6 Dismantling and reassembling distributor

These instructions, together with **FIGS 3:1** and **3:2** will help in dismantling all types of distributor, bearing in mind the variations mentioned at the beginning of this Chapter. One important point must always be considered before attempting to dismantle the vacuum unit. **The adjustment of the threaded rod and the spring must not be altered.** The adjustment of the spring affects the advance curve of the distributor and if anything is done to upset this adjustment the distributor must be returned to a Service Station for correction.

To dismantle the distributor:

1 Remove the cap and rotor arm. Remove the nut from terminal 1 and take off the low-tension cable and washers. Pull out the connecting cable to the breaker plate.

2 Remove the capacitor 37 in **FIG 3:2.** Remove the contacts 26 and 30.

3 Disconnect the vacuum unit pullrod. On early models remove the pullrod from the ball joint by inserting a hook made of bent wire in the hole in the rod. Remove the vacuum unit.

4 Remove the retaining screw and bracket (if fitted) and lift out the breaker plate. Pull out the low-tension cable.

5 Knock out pin 19 after removing spring clip 20. Pull off driving dog 18 which will permit removal of the shaft 10, or in the case of a distributor with centrifugal timing device, assembly 15 in **FIG 3:1.** Note the position of fibre washers 13 and 15 in **FIG 3:2** and any washers and shims 16 and 17 or 11 and 12. If necessary remove the rubber ring and clamp from the body.

Clean all the parts with a solvent such as petrol but do not immerse the body 1 in it or get solvent on the bushes 2 or lubricating felt 3, or the self-lubricating qualities will be lost. Check the shaft for wear in the body bushes. If excessive renew the distributor. End play can be eliminated by shimming. Check the condition of the contact points, the breaker spring and the action of the vacuum unit pullrod. If the breaker spring is pitted with rust it must be renewed as breakage is very likely. Renew the rubber ring which forms an oil seal on the body spigot.

To reassemble the distributor:

1 Oil the shaft and fill the space between the bushes in the body with grease if there is no felt. Fit the washers correctly and insert the shaft. Turn the shaft so that the rotor arm slot is in-line with the notch in the rim of the body which denotes the position for No. 1 cylinder.

2 Assemble the fibre and steel washers on the bottom end of the shaft and fit the driving dog so that the driving lugs are offset towards the notch in the body rim. Insert the pin and peen over the edges of the hole on both sides to prevent the pin coming out accidentally.

3 When assembling the earlier type of terminal screw, make sure the washers are correctly fitted, as shown in **FIG 3:1.** There is a large insulating washer inside and outside the body and there may be an insulating bush to prevent contact between the screw and the body.

4 On early models lubricate the ball socket for the vacuum unit under the breaker plate. Fit the plate and stop bracket and secure with the screw.

5 On later models, fit the plate and connect up the return spring and the low-tension lead. On both types, fit the vacuum unit. Install the capacitor and adjust the contact points to the correct gap.

3:7 Checking the capacitor (condenser)

A defective capacitor can lead to starting troubles, burned contact breaker points and even a complete failure of the ignition system. To test a suspected capacitor, remove the distributor cap. Turn the engine until the contact points are fully open. Disconnect cable 1 from the ignition coil. Make up a 6- or 12-volt test lamp according to the system fitted to the vehicle, and connect one lead to terminal 1 on the coil and the other lead to the low-tension distributor cable. Switch on the ignition. If the test lamp lights up, the capacitor is earthed and it must be renewed. To continue the test, remove the lamp and reconnect cable 1 to the coil. Remove the central high-tension cable from the distributor cap and hold it carefully by the insulation so that the metal end is about $\frac{1}{4}$ inch from a good earth. Switch on the ignition and open and close the contact points quickly, using a small screwdriver. A spark should jump the gap. If there is no spark try a new capacitor. Substitution is always the easiest way to check for a defective capacitor. It is most important to obtain the correct value of capacitor from the manufacturer or Service Station as an incorrect type will adversely affect the life of the contact points.

3:8 Sparking plugs and leads

The sparking plugs should be removed, cleaned and tested every 3000 miles, and more frequently if there is known to be excessive oil consumption or trouble with starting and misfiring. The preliminary examination of the plugs will be most helpful in assessing the working conditions. A plug which has been fitted to a worn engine which uses oil will be fouled by a wet black deposit or the plug itself may be faulty. If the deposit is black and soft the fuel mixture is too rich. A light grey or brown deposit, if almost white, is a sign of a weak mixture, but if of a darker colour it can be taken as a sign that the plug is firing properly and the mixture strength is correct.

The best way to clean and test plugs is to have them shot-blasted on an official machine and tested under pressure. A sparking plug may spark quite well in the open and yet fail under cylinder pressures. If the plug must be cleaned by hand, go over the threads and the electrodes with a wire brush. Clean the plug interior with a pointed piece of wood, not a sharp metal object. File the electrodes to a bright metallic surface and set them to the correct gap **by bending the outer electrode only. FIG 3:6** shows the method of checking the gap, which should lie between .024 and .028 inch.

It is always advisable to renew the sealing washers when replacing the plugs in the engine. Do not overtighten.

The earlier type of black lead should be checked for chafed insulation, cracks and other defects. Running an engine in the dark will often show where leakage is occurring, particularly in proximity to earthed metal objects. Renew all faulty leads and thus avoid constant trouble from difficult starting and erratic running.

Later leads were initially coloured light red and were fitted to the Transporter until 1960. These had a graphited synthetic core which might result in a very high resistance if broken. Misfiring would then be troublesome. Late in 1960 these cables were replaced by an orange-red type. The most likely cable to be defective when the light red type is installed is the one from the distributor to the coil. A break in the core will eventually damage the outer insulation, particularly at a bend. If an ohmmeter is available, all the leads or cables can be tested for resistance to prove whether a break is present. Remove them complete with connectors and join to the ohmmeter, ensuring good contact with the ends. Move the cable and stretch it slightly during the test.

At approximately 20°C (68°F) the following readings should not be exceeded:

Ignition coil cable 6000 ohms. Cables to cylinders 1 and 2, 25,000 ohms and cables to cylinders 3 and 4, 15,000 ohms.

If the reading is not steady and the needle flicks to higher readings the core is defective.

Interference on radio and television is eliminated by the use of these synthetic core cables, but fitting them demands the use of the gland-type connectors instead of the standard internal-screw type. If, for example, a VHF radio is to be installed it is necessary to fit a suppressed distributor rotor arm and four suppressor adaptors in the sparking plug connectors. To fit the connectors to the cables, care is needed to ensure perfect contact. The method is as follows:

It is possible for the synthetic core to be pushed out of the cable by the gland screw. Therefore, squeeze the cable with a pair of pliers at the place where the connector fits. Incorrect assembly will lead to faulty contact and the cable may be burned through.

The gland-type connectors are only suitable for cables with synthetic cores, that is, those which are coloured red or orange-red. Do not use them on cables with a copper wire core.

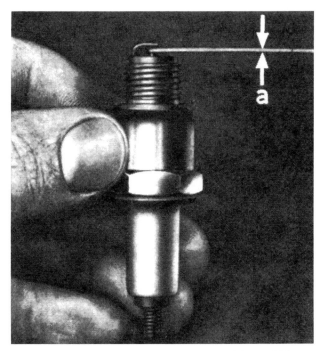

FIG 3:6 Gauge thickness (a) should be .024 to .028 inch when setting the sparking plug gap

3:9 Fault diagnosis

(a) Engine will not fire

1 Battery discharged
2 Contact breaker points dirty, pitted or out of adjustment
3 Distributor cap dirty, cracked or 'tracking'
4 Carbon brush inside distributor cap not in contact with rotor arm
5 Faulty cables or loose connections in the low-tension circuit
6 Distributor rotor arm cracked
7 Faulty coil or coil lead to distributor
8 Broken contact breaker spring
9 Contact points stuck open
10 Faulty capacitor
11 Faulty ignition switch

(b) Engine misfires

1 Check 2, 3, 5 and 7 in (a)
2 Weak contact breaker spring
3 Plug and coil high-tension leads cracked or perished
4 Loose sparking plugs
5 Sparking plug insulation cracked
6 Sparking plug gap incorrect
7 Ignition timing too far advanced or retarded

Inches	Decimals	Milli-metres	Inches to Millimetres — Inches	Inches to Millimetres — mm	Millimetres to Inches — mm	Millimetres to Inches — Inches
1/64	.015625	.3969	.001	.0254	.01	.00039
1/32	.03125	.7937	.002	.0508	.02	.00079
3/64	.046875	1.1906	.003	.0762	.03	.00118
1/16	.0625	1.5875	.004	.1016	.04	.00157
5/64	.078125	1.9844	.005	.1270	.05	.00197
3/32	.09375	2.3812	.006	.1524	.06	.00236
7/64	.109375	2.7781	.007	.1778	.07	.00276
1/8	.125	3.1750	.008	.2032	.08	.00315
9/64	.140625	3.5719	.009	.2286	.09	.00354
5/32	.15625	3.9687	.01	.254	.1	.00394
11/64	.171875	4.3656	.02	.508	.2	.00787
3/16	.1875	4.7625	.03	.762	.3	.01181
13/64	.203125	5.1594	.04	1.016	.4	.01575
7/32	.21875	5.5562	.05	1.270	.5	.01969
15/64	.234375	5.9531	.06	1.524	.6	.02362
1/4	.25	6.3500	.07	1.778	.7	.02756
17/64	.265625	6.7469	.08	2.032	.8	.03150
9/32	.28125	7.1437	.09	2.286	.9	.03543
19/64	.296875	7.5406	.1	2.54	1	.03937
5/16	.3125	7.9375	.2	5.08	2	.07874
21/64	.328125	8.3344	.3	7.62	3	.11811
11/32	.34375	8.7312	.4	10.16	4	.15748
23/64	.359375	9.1281	.5	12.70	5	.19685
3/8	.375	9.5250	.6	15.24	6	.23622
25/64	.390625	9.9219	.7	17.78	7	.27559
13/32	.40625	10.3187	.8	20.32	8	.31496
27/64	.421875	10.7156	.9	22.86	9	.35433
7/16	.4375	11.1125	1	25.4	10	.39370
29/64	.453125	11.5094	2	50.8	11	.43307
15/32	.46875	11.9062	3	76.2	12	.47244
31/64	.484375	12.3031	4	101.6	13	.51181
1/2	.5	12.7000	5	127.0	14	.55118
33/64	.515625	13.0969	6	152.4	15	.59055
17/32	.53125	13.4937	7	177.8	16	.62992
35/64	.546875	13.8906	8	203.2	17	.66929
9/16	.5625	14.2875	9	228.6	18	.70866
37/64	.578125	14.6844	10	254.0	19	.74803
19/32	.59375	15.0812	11	279.4	20	.78740
39/64	.609375	15.4781	12	304.8	21	.82677
5/8	.625	15.8750	13	330.2	22	.86614
41/64	.640625	16.2719	14	355.6	23	.90551
21/32	.65625	16.6687	15	381.0	24	.94488
43/64	.671875	17.0656	16	406.4	25	.98425
11/16	.6875	17.4625	17	431.8	26	1.02362
45/64	.703125	17.8594	18	457.2	27	1.06299
23/32	.71875	18.2562	19	482.6	28	1.10236
47/64	.734375	18.6531	20	508.0	29	1.14173
3/4	.75	19.0500	21	533.4	30	1.18110
49/64	.765625	19.4469	22	558.8	31	1.22047
25/32	.78125	19.8437	23	584.2	32	1.25984
51/64	.796875	20.2406	24	609.6	33	1.29921
13/16	.8125	20.6375	25	635.0	34	1.33858
53/64	.828125	21.0344	26	660.4	35	1.37795
27/32	.84375	21.4312	27	685.8	36	1.41732
55/64	.859375	21.8281	28	711.2	37	1.4567
7/8	.875	22.2250	29	736.6	38	1.4961
57/64	.890625	22.6219	30	762.0	39	1.5354
29/32	.90625	23.0187	31	787.4	40	1.5748
59/64	.921875	23.4156	32	812.8	41	1.6142
15/16	.9375	23.8125	33	838.2	42	1.6535
61/64	.953125	24.2094	34	863.6	43	1.6929
31/32	.96875	24.6062	35	889.0	44	1.7323
63/64	.984375	25.0031	36	914.4	45	1.7717

UNITS	Pints to Litres	Gallons to Litres	Litres to Pints	Litres to Gallons	Miles to Kilometres	Kilometres to Miles	Lbs. per sq. In. to Kg. per sq. Cm.	Kg. per sq. Cm. to Lbs. per sq. In.
1	.57	4.55	1.76	.22	1.61	.62	.07	14.22
2	1.14	9.09	3.52	.44	3.22	1.24	.14	28.50
3	1.70	13.64	5.28	.66	4.83	1.86	.21	42.67
4	2.27	18.18	7.04	.88	6.44	2.49	.28	56.89
5	2.84	22.73	8.80	1.10	8.05	3.11	.35	71.12
6	3.41	27.28	10.56	1.32	9.66	3.73	.42	85.34
7	3.98	31.82	12.32	1.54	11.27	4.35	.49	99.56
8	4.55	36.37	14.08	1.76	12.88	4.97	.56	113.79
9		40.91	15.84	1.98	14.48	5.59	.63	128.00
10		45.46	17.60	2.20	16.09	6.21	.70	142.23
20				4.40	32.19	12.43	1.41	284.47
30				6.60	48.28	18.64	2.11	426.70
40				8.80	64.37	24.85		
50					80.47	31.07		
60					96.56	37.28		
70					112.65	43.50		
80					128.75	49.71		
90					144.84	55.92		
100					160.93	62.14		

UNITS	Lb ft to kgm	Kgm to lb ft	UNITS	Lb ft to kgm	Kgm to lb ft
1	.138	7.233	7	.967	50.631
2	.276	14.466	8	1.106	57.864
3	.414	21.699	9	1.244	65.097
4	.553	28.932	10	1.382	72.330
5	.691	36.165	20	2.765	144.660
6	.829	43.398	30	4.147	216.990

CHAPTER 4

COOLING AND HEATING SYSTEM

4:1 Description

The original cooling and heating system is illustrated in **Chapter 1, FIG 1:1**. The curved blades of the fan can be seen behind the filler cap. The fan is mounted on the front end of the generator shaft, the rear end of the shaft carrying a pulley. This is belt-driven from a pulley on the end of the crankshaft and turns at approximately twice engine speed.

The fan revolves in the top semicircular half of the sheet metal housing in front of the engine, drawing its air from a thermostatically controlled intake in the front face of the housing. This can be clearly seen in **FIG 4:2**. The controlling ring is almost closed when the engine is cold, so restricting the volume of cooling air. When the engine is hot a thermostat tilts the ring to allow more air to reach the fan.

The casing surrounding the fan is extended downwards to enclose the cylinders, and air from the fan is diverted by deflectors to give equal cooling to both sides. The heated air is ejected through ducts facing rearwards under the engine. These apertures can be opened or closed by flaps and a control between the front seats. When they are closed, two more flaps facing forward are opened simultaneously and the heated air is ducted to the vehicle interior.

It will be realised from this description that it is vital that there are no oil or exhaust leaks in the system or they may contaminate the air used to heat the vehicle interior.

The redesigned system:

To overcome the possibility of contamination of the air in the heater system by oil and exhaust fumes, the 1962 models are fitted with a modified air heating arrangement. This consists of finned heat exchangers 21 in **FIG 1:2**. The exhaust gases passing through the inner bore of these devices transmit heat to a large surface area of finning. Some of the cooling air from the fan is diverted to the outside of these heat exchangers, where it is heated and ducted to the vehicle interior if required.

A further modification to this scheme was introduced on the 1965 models. The air intake controlling ring was scrapped and this allowed large volumes of air for interior heating to be available at all times. The engine cooling air is controlled by flaps connected to a thermostat 18. This ensures a rapid warm-up from cold.

FIG 4:1 Locking the back flange of the fan pulley to enable the nut to be unscrewed

4:2 Removing fan and housing

This can be done with the engine in the vehicle as follows:

1 Remove the fan belt. **Do not try to prise the belt over the pulley flanges.** Hold the inner pulley flange by inserting a screwdriver in the hole provided, as shown on **FIG 4:1**. Undo the pulley nut, remove the outer flange, the spacing washers and the belt.

2 Disconnect the battery and remove the rear hood and hinge brackets.

3 On recent models remove the two large heater hoses, one from each side of the fan housing.

4 According to model, remove the generator cables and those for the carburetter choke and oil pressure switch. Remove the cables from the coil. Remove the vacuum pipe and the fuel hose.

5 Disconnect the accelerator cable and pull it out through the front. Remove the carburetter. On recent models, take off the distributor cap and pull off the sparking plug connectors. Also on these models remove the righthand rear part of the lower hot air duct and the thermostat securing screw. Unscrew the thermostat from its rod.

6 Remove the generator securing strap and the two screws, one from each side, indicated at **A** in **FIG 4:2**. On vehicles with the older type of control ring shown in the illustration, unhook the spring **B** and remove screws **C**. Lift off the fan housing together with the generator and fan.

On models fitted with heat exchangers and flap controls, it is possible to check the flaps by removing eight screws from the lower edges of the fan housing. The flaps will come away, complete with a connecting link, after the link return spring has been unhooked. Note that there is a rubber stop in the righthand flap housing.

Removing the fan:

FIG 4:3 shows the fan mounting in section. If the fan housing has not been removed, disconnect the generator cables, remove the driving belt and then unscrew the four setscrews which secure the fan cover to the fan housing. Release the generator strap and lift away the generator complete with fan and cover.

Hold the rim of the fan and unscrew the shaft nut 4. Pull off lockwasher 6, fan 8, spacing washers 7, thrust washer 1, and hub 2. Note Woodruff key 3 in the shaft.

Replacing the fan:

Press the hub right home on the shaft, taking care to ensure that the key is properly seated. Fit the spacing washers, followed by the fan. Tighten the securing nut to a torque of 40 to 47 lb ft. Now check the clearance between the fan and the cover at point **A** in the illustration. The dimension should be .06 to .07 inch and it can be adjusted by means of the spacing washers. If only one washer is needed, place it between the hub and thrust washer 1, putting the other two between the lockwasher 6 and the fan. Spacing washers can only be effective if placed between the hub and the thrust washer. Finally, fit the generator and fan, tighten the cover screws, then the generator strap and reconnect the cables. Fit and adjust the belt as described in **Section 4:6**.

4:3 Servicing heater box, silencer, heat exchanger (prior to August 1962)

On vehicles without the heat exchanger type of installation, the method of directing warm air to the

FIG 4:2 Using a rule to set the top flanges of the fan housing and regulator ring correctly. A is a fan housing securing screw, B is the regulator return spring, and C are the ring securing screws. D is the ring operating lever

interior is shown in **FIG 4:4**. The junction boxes 2 surround the front exhaust pipes on either side, just forward of the engine mounting flange. The boxes are bolted to the lower heating channels 11, the rear ends of which form the exit apertures for engine cooling air. To divert warm air to the vehicle interior, the cable 7 is pulled by the control between the seats and this moves flap 13. At the same time toggle lever 3 will open valve 1. The two operations have the effect of restricting the exit of warm air to the rear and diverting it instead through flexible pipes to the interior.

Removing silencer and heater junction box:

If complete servicing of the system is intended it will be as well to remove the silencer too. This is done by removing the bolts from the preheating pipe flanges, releasing the exhaust pipe clips and removing the bolts from the rear exhaust pipe flanges. Check the silencer and pipes for cracks, corrosion and damage, particularly at the joint between the tail pipe and silencer. Leaking gaskets and cracks can lead to contamination of the heated air to the vehicle interior. The tail pipe must not touch the body and must be heated and set to obtain clearance.

To remove a junction box, detach the flexible heater pipe from the top outlet **A** in **FIG 4:4**. Detach the control cable 7 and release the exhaust pipe flange 4. Release the slotted screw 9, remove the cotterpin from the rear end of rod 12 and unhook the rod from flap 13. Lift away the box and exhaust pipe.

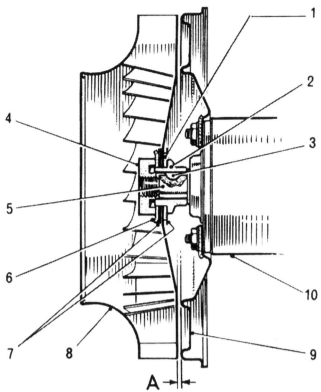

FIG 4:3 Mounting of fan on generator shaft. Dimension **A** should be between .06 and .07 inch

Key to Fig 4:3
1 Thrust washer		2 Fan hub
3 Woodruff key	4 Fan securing nut	5 Generator shaft
6 Lockwasher	7 Spacing washers	8 Fan
9 Fan cover	10 Generator	

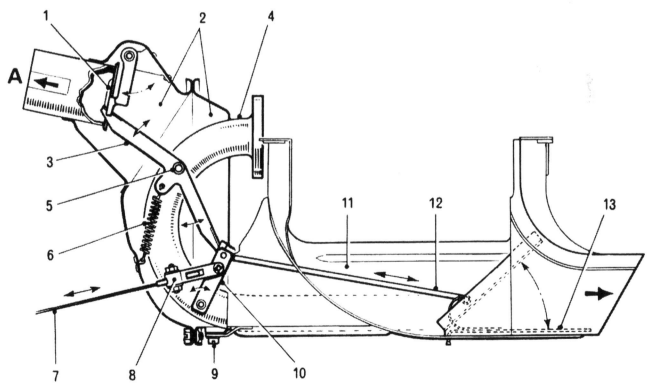

FIG 4:4 Section through heater box and controls prior to 1962

Key to Fig 4:4 1 Exit valve for warm air to vehicle interior   2 Heater junction box   3 Toggle lever   4 Exhaust pipe 5 Toggle lever pivot   6 Lever return spring   7 Heater control cable   8 Cable clamp and link   9 Slotted securing screw 10 Link   11 Lower heating channel   12 Control rod, link to flap   13 Heat control flap

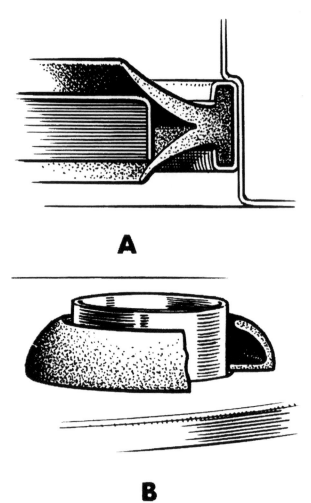

FIG 4:5 Correct fitting of weatherstrip on edge of cover plate at **A**. Correct fitting of rubber grommets round large air hoses to heat exchangers at **B**

The box is readily dismantled by removing the screws from the flanges joining the two halves. Link 8 is attached to lever 10 by a pin and C-washer. Clean the parts and check for damage and corrosion. If the sealing gasket on the outlet valve 1 is faulty, renew the valve complete. Check that this valve is fully closed when the control cable and knob are in the closed position. Lubricate all pivot points with graphite bound with a little grease.

Install the box in the reverse order to removal, but make certain that every point has been checked where fumes could contaminate the heated air. Fit new exhaust pipe gaskets after checking that the flanges are clean and flat.

The heater control cable:

This can be removed by raising the vehicle and slackening the clamp which secures the cable end to the operating link. Remove the rubber grommet from the guide tube and slide it off the cable. Inside the vehicle remove the threaded cap and pull out the knob and cable. Note that the longer end of the cable goes in the righthand guide tube. Drive out the cable pin. Before installing a new cable lubricate it with universal grease. Turn the control knob anticlockwise to the stop and then turn it three turns clockwise. Install the control, making sure that the guide nose enters the slot in the threaded sleeve, which should not project above the edge of the cable guide tube.

Removing the lower heating channel:

The lower heating channel 11 can be removed after the junction box and silencer have been taken off, by releasing the slotted screws. After removal, check it for damage and for free movement of the flap.

Removing silencer and heat exchangers (after August 1962):

To remove the silencer, first remove the rear coverplate (see operation 1 in **Section 4:4**). Remove the heat exchanger clamps at the outer ends of the silencer (two bolts each). Remove the clips from the rising rear ends of the heat exchangers where they connect to the warm air channels on the silencer. Remove the nuts from the silencer-to-cylinder head flange. Take off the preheater adaptor pipe by removing the screw from the left exhaust flange and withdrawing the pipe to the rear. Remove the four screws securing the manifold preheater pipe flanges just outboard of the exhaust flanges. Take off the silencer and remove the old gaskets.

When replacing the silencer, fit new gaskets and check that the flanges are meeting squarely. Check all connections to ensure that they will be leaktight.

To remove the heat exchangers, remove the rear cover as described in operation 1 of **Section 4:4**. Remove the exhaust flange nuts at the front ends of the cylinder heads. Remove the clips connecting the rising rear ends of the heat exchangers to the warm air channels on the silencer ends. From underneath, detach the two brackets on each exchanger from the coverplate (two screws). Remove the exhaust pipe clamps at the extreme outer ends of the silencer and take the exchangers off in a forward direction.

Check the outer shell and exhaust pipes for signs of damage or leaks. If the heat exchangers leak, it is possible for poisonous fumes to enter the vehicle. Make sure all flanges meet squarely and fit new gaskets.

4:4 Removing and replacing cover plates

1 Remove the front and rear cover plates as shown in **Chapter 1, FIG 1:6**. On vehicles with heat exchangers, the rear cover is removed by detaching the two large hoses and the carburetter preheater hose. The fan pulley cover is then removed. Outboard of the large hoses are the small-diameter manifold preheater pipes. Remove the three screws from the sealing plate behind each pipe, noting the asbestos seals. Remove the cover.

2 On earlier vehicles without heat exchangers, remove the front and rear coverplates, the generator and fan housing complete, and the fuel pump coverplate. Remove the exhaust system and then the lower heating channels (see the end of the preceding **Section 4:3**). Remove both cylinder coverplates after removing the sparking plug connectors. Remove the crankshaft pulley and then the pulley coverplate. Take off the pushrod tubes and remove the cylinder deflector plates.

3 On models with heat exchangers, after removing the front and rear coverplates, remove the generator and fan housing complete with control flaps. Remove the carburetter and inlet manifold with preheater pipe. Remove the rear air deflector plate and the lower part of the warm air duct. Remove the adaptor pipe for the

carburetter preheater pipe from the lefthand side. Lift off the cylinder coverplates, take off the fan pulley and remove the pulley cover.

Replacing the coverplates:

Reverse the removal sequence. On early models, the cylinder deflector plates must be fitted before the pushrods and pushrod tubes. Set them slightly so that they press against the cylinder studs to prevent rattling. On all vehicles, check the fit of the cylinder coverplates. They must make complete contact with the fan housing to prevent loss of cooling air. Also check the sealing caps round the sparking plug connectors. When fitting the coverplates make sure that the two lips of the weatherstrip embrace the edges of the plates so that both are sealed as shown at **A** in **FIG 4:5**.

On vehicles with heat exchangers, check the asbestos seals round the manifold preheater pipe. The coverplate must not touch the heat exchanger pipe connections and the two rubber grommets for the large hoses must be fitted with their flat faces in contact with the coverplate, as shown at **B** in **FIG 4:5**.

4:5 Air control adjustment

On vehicles with regulating ring:

The ring is shown in **FIG 4:2** and was finally dropped from the air regulating system in 1964, when the 1965 models were announced. The position of the ring is thermostatically controlled and it must be carefully adjusted or there will be cooling troubles. If it remains permanently open or opens too soon, the engine will warm up too slowly. This will lead to 'spitting back' in the carburetter and excessive fuel consumption. If the ring is slow to open, the engine will get too hot, particularly when working hard in a hot climate. However, the ring will always open fully if the thermostat is faulty, so that the engine cannot then overheat.

To adjust the regulator ring:

The method is shown in **FIG 4:2**. When the engine is cold the ring should rest against the intake flange in a slightly preloaded position. To adjust it correctly with the engine in the vehicle, release the operating lever **D** by slackening the clamp nut. At normal outside temperature, warm up the engine until the upper end of the thermostat touches the upper stop of the support bracket. The thermostat is under the engine on the righthand side and can be seen below the pushrod tube in **Chapter 1, FIG 1:1**. Set the regulator ring so that the top rim is .79 inch away from the fan housing flange as shown in the illustration. On 34 bhp engines with heat exchangers set the flanges apart by 1 to 1.20 inches. Tighten the operating lever in this position.

To adjust the ring if the engine is out of the vehicle and cold, lift the thermostat to the upper stop of its supporting bracket. With the operating lever slack, set the ring as in the preceding paragraph and then tighten the lever. Now secure the thermostat in position. Make sure that the faces machined on the tapped boss of the thermostat fit in the guide hole in the supporting bracket. Turn the thermostat until this is correct and tighten the securing bolt. The regulator ring should now rest against the intake flange in a slightly preloaded condition. Note that there is

FIG 4:6 Outer flange of fan pulley removed to show spacing washers used for adjusting belt tension

a rubber stop fitted to the rim of the regulator ring to prevent actual metallic contact with the fan housing.

Adjusting the air control flaps on models from 1965:

It is assumed that the cylinder coverplates and fan housing have been installed with the control flaps in position in the bottom righthand and lefthand corners of the housing. Screw the thermostat on to its connecting rod from below but do not secure to the bracket. It can be seen in **Chapter 1** as item 18 in **FIG 1:2**. Loosen the nut securing the thermostat bracket, press the control flaps into the open position and move the bracket until the top of the thermostat is touching the upper part of the bracket. Tighten the bracket nut and check the operation of the flaps by moving the thermostat up and down. Tighten the thermostat securing screw after checking that the tapped boss fits snugly in the bracket.

4:6 Adjusting the fan belt

As the belt has to drive both generator and fan it must transmit considerable power at high speeds. It is therefore essential to keep it free from oil and consequent deterioration, and to make sure that it is tensioned correctly. A belt which is too slack will slip and cause engine overheating and undercharging of the battery. A belt which is too tight will be liable to break and may cause damage to the generator bearings.

The method of tensioning the belt can be seen in **FIGS 4:1** and **4:6**. First remove the outer generator flange as shown in the first illustration. The screwdriver is inserted in a hole in the inner flange and supported against the upper generator housing bolt. When the nut is unscrewed the assembly will come part as in the second illustration. The packing washers are used to alter the distance between the two pulley flanges and thus tension the belt. Any spacing washers which are not actually used between the two flanges must be fitted on the outside, under the nut.

If the belt has been running slack, remove a packing washer, reassemble the parts and check the belt tension. Press one section of the belt midway between the pulleys

The belt should yield about $\frac{1}{2}$ inch under firm pressure. If the belt is too slack, remove washers, if it is too tight add washers.

Renew the belt if it has stretched so far that no washers remain between the flanges when the tension is right. Also renew it if it has evidently been running on the spacing washers, or if it has become oily. Be particularly careful when adding oil to the engine to keep it away from the belt. **Do not try to lever the belt over the pulley flanges, or the belt will be ruined and the pulley may be damaged.** Always slacken off the shaft nut.

4:7 Fault diagnosis

(a) Engine runs cool, warms up slowly

1 Regulator ring opens early (first system)
2 Regulator ring stuck in open position

(b) Engine overheats

1 Fan belt slipping
2 Regulator ring not opening (first system)
3 Control flaps not opening (second system)

4 Cooling air leaking out through cover joints and sparking plug covers
5 Sump, oil cooler and cylinder fins caked with dirt
6 Carburetter out of tune, ignition wrongly timed
7 Exhaust system blocked

(c) Heating system ineffective

1 Control cables broken or out of adjustment
2 Heater box valves and flaps not operating
3 Heater pipes disconnected or leaking
4 Engine not warming up properly
5 Air leaks from badly fitting coverplates on early systems

(d) Heating system will not shut off

1 Check 1 in (c)
2 Heater control valves not closing, gaskets faulty

(e) Heater air contaminated by fumes (first system)

1 Oil leaks from engine
2 Leaking exhaust silencer and pipes
3 Leaking exhaust manifold flanges
4 Leaking heat exchangers (second system)
5 Fuel leakage from pump or carburetter
6 Leakage between cylinders and heads

CHAPTER 5

THE CLUTCH

5:1 Description

The VW single-plate clutch is bolted to the front face of the flywheel as shown in the sectioned view in **FIG 5:1**. Flywheel 12 is secured to the crankshaft by a hollow gland nut which carries a needle roller bearing 10. This bearing supports the rear end of the transmission drive shaft 3 which is the connection between the engine and the gearbox when the clutch is engaged. Loosely splined to this shaft is the driven plate 11 which carries a friction lining 13 on each face. The plate is sandwiched between the front face of the flywheel and pressure plate 14. When the clutch is engaged the friction linings are firmly gripped between the flywheel and the pressure plate by the action of compression springs 8. In this position power is transmitted from the engine through the driven plate to the transmission shaft.

When the clutch pedal is depressed, shaft 1 is partially rotated and a fork mounted on the shaft moves release bearing 2 towards the flywheel until it contacts release plate 4 and moves the plate to the right. The release plate then presses on the inner ends of three levers 6 which pivot on fulcrum points. The outer ends of the levers draw the pressure plate away from the driven plate against the pressure of the springs through the agency of bolts and nuts 7. Now released from pressure, the driven plate

slows to a stop and the engine is no longer connected to the gearbox.

5:2 Routine maintenance

The clutch linings wear slowly and this affects the clearances in the operating mechanism. Every 3000 miles on vehicles up to 1965 and every 6000 miles on subsequent models, check the amount of free play at the clutch pedal pad as shown in **FIG 5:2**. The distance **A** should be not less than $\frac{7}{16}$ inch nor more than $\frac{13}{16}$ inch.

To adjust for correct clearance it is necessary to locate the cable end at the clutch operating lever just above and behind the rear axle on the lefthand side, as shown by the top arrow in **FIG 5:3**. On early models, adjustment was made by unlocking and turning a hexagon nut. Later models are fitted with a wingnut. While making the adjustment hold the unthreaded part of the cable end with a pair of pliers. Check the adjustment by depressing the clutch pedal several times and then measure the free movement at the top of the pad as before. It is important to ensure that the stops on the wingnut engage in the recesses in the operating lever. After making the adjustment, smear the nut and thread with grease.

On models before 1960 it is necessary to apply the grease gun to the nipple on the pedal cluster every 3000 miles.

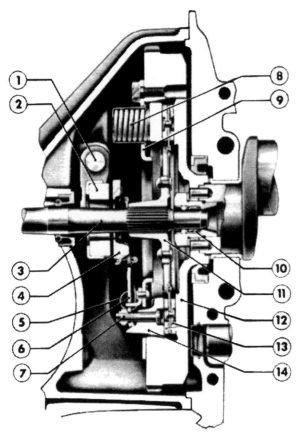

FIG 5:1 Section through typical clutch assembly. Carbon thrust ring **2** is replaced by a ballbearing on later models. Bolt and special nut **7** differ on recent models

Key to Fig 5:1   1 Operating shaft   2 Carbon thrust ring
3 Main drive shaft   4 Release plate   5 Release lever spring
6 Release lever   7 Bolt and special nut   8 Thrust or
pressure spring   9 Cover   10 Needle bearing in gland nut
11 Driven plate   12 Flywheel   13 Clutch friction lining
14 Pressure plate

5:3 Removing and inspecting the clutch

The first operation is to remove the engine as instructed in **Chapter 1**. If it is likely that the same clutch assembly will be replaced, mark the relative positions of the clutch cover and the flywheel to ensure correct balance on reassembly. To prevent distortion of the clutch cover, release the securing bolts a turn or two at a time, working diagonally to avoid tilting. Lift away the clutch assembly and the driven plate.

Examine the contact surfaces of the flywheel and pressure plate. If they are scored or cracked it is possible for them to be reconditioned by grinding and a VW agent should be consulted. Scrap the driven plate if the linings have worn thin, or if they are oily or have a very dark glazed deposit on them. It must be remembered however that a glaze is quite normal providing the lining material is not obscured by a deposit. In any case, if the clutch has been in use for a long mileage it is advisable to replace the driven plate. The minimum permissible thickness is approximately $\frac{3}{32}$ inch. If it is decided to retain the original plate, check the fit of the splined hub on the transmission shaft. The splines should slide freely yet without excessive play. Tight splines will affect clutch operation and gear changing. Maximum permissible lateral runout of the linings is .03 inch.

Check the condition of release bearing 2 in **FIG 5:1**. The illustration shows the earlier type using a carbon ring in a cup. Later assemblies use a ballbearing. If the carbon ring has worn thin so that there is a danger of the cup contacting the release plate, renew the assembly. It is not possible to fit a new carbon ring into an old cup. **If the assembly uses a ballbearing do not try to degrease it or clean it in solvents because it is packed with grease and sealed.** If the bearing feels rough it must be renewed. To release the bearing, lever out the wire clips from each side. These have hooked ends which engage behind the operating fork arms as shown in **FIG 5:7**.

Check the fit of the operating shaft in the transmission casing bushes. The bushes can be renewed if necessary.

5:4 Dismantling the clutch

It must be understood that this is an operation which the inexperienced should not attempt. A press is needed to dismantle and reassemble the clutch and very careful setting of the release plate and levers is needed if there is to be no trouble with a fierce or juddering clutch.

If the owner feels competent to carry out the work, the following instructions will enable him to do so. He must, however be prepared to renew the three bolts and special nuts 7 in **FIG 5:1** as they are inevitably damaged during the unlocking process.

1 The first operation is to mark the relative positions of the cover and the pressure plate and the release levers with respect to the cover. In this way the original components can be reassembled so that the balance is correct. If major components need renewal it is recommended that a VW Service Station be consulted, as balance will certainly be affected.

2 Place the clutch in the flywheel and put the two assemblies under a press. Using three distance pieces, press down on the cover flange until it contacts the

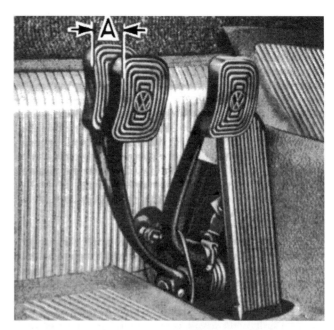

FIG 5:2 Clutch pedal free play is measured at **A**. It should be not less than $\frac{7}{16}$ inch or more than $\frac{13}{16}$ inch

flywheel. Proceed to unlock the three nuts from bolts 7 and unscrew them. Remove the springs from the release plate and levers, release the plate and finish dismantling.

3 Checking of all the parts then continues. A warped or grooved pressure plate 14 in **FIG 5:1** must be reground or renewed. Maximum permissible runout is .004 inch. Also check the fit of the pressure plate lugs where they pass through the coverplate as slackness here will cause faulty clutch operation. Check the tightness of the pins in the plate. Check the thrust springs 8 against the information given in Technical Data. Never renew one or two springs but always a complete set. Check the cover for cracks or warping. Renew it is cracked and straighten it if warped. Check the release levers 6 and release plate 4, renewing any parts which are cracked, worn or distorted. Renew the release lever springs 5 if they have weakened. It will be understood that the contact face of the flywheel is also part of the clutch and its condition must also be checked.

5:5 Reassembling and refitting the clutch

There are a few points to be noted before reassembling and refitting the clutch. **An important one is that a new driven plate must be used in order to adjust the release mechanism correctly.** Note also that Transporters from Engine No. 3478036 have been fitted with a driven plate having a shock-absorbing hub with six springs. This type of plate can be fitted in earlier vehicles. Before April 1958 the driven plate rim was not divided into springy segments to provide a flexible mounting for the linings and the old type of solid plate should be replaced by the new. The bolt and nut 7 which carries the outer end of each release lever has been superseded by an eyebolt carried on a split tubular pin and provided with locking flats for the nut. It is extremely difficult to unlock the nuts without ruining them and replacements are always necessary.

Reassemble the clutch as follows:

1 Insert the release lever bolts into the pressure plate. On the latest type using the tubular pivot pins and eyebolts, fit the pins so that the slots face away from the pressure plate. Always fit new parts.

2 Place the flywheel on the bed of the press and refit the new driven plate and the pressure plate. Fit the spring caps into the cover 9 in **FIG 5:1**, then assemble the springs 8 with spring seats. Fit the cover over the pressure plate so that the three lugs line up and the marks made before dismantling line up too. Check that the spring seats are correctly located in the plate. Take a 2 incn bolt and screw it into one of the cover fixing holes in the flywheel. This will ensure that the cover lines up with the flywheel holes.

3 Compress the cover on to the flywheel, taking care that the pressure plate lugs enter the square holes in the cover correctly. Bolt the cover in place and remove the guide bolt. Release the press.

4 Put a touch of lithium grease on the release lever pivot points and fit them, taking care to check the marks made before dismantling so that balance will not be affected. Install the nuts, or the washers and nuts on later models, always using new parts. Adjust the levers

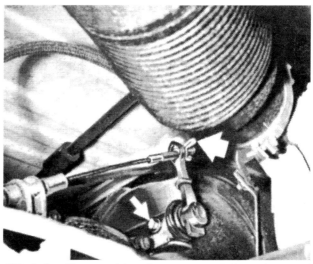

FIG 5:3 Clutch cable adjustment on lefthand side of transmission casing. Top arrow shows adjusting wingnut (or hexagon nut and locknut on early models). Lower arrow shows bolt which locates shaft bush

FIG 5:4 Checking the squareness of the clutch release plate using a steel straightedge. Measure at several points on the clutch periphery

to the same height provisionally. Use a little lithium grease on the contact points of the release plate 4. Install the plate and the sets of springs.

5 Refer to **FIG 5:4** which shows the method of checking the alignment of the release plate when the clutch is fitted to the vehicle. This method is also used when the clutch has reached the point of assembly in Operation 4. Adjust the release lever nuts until the release plate working face is $1.023 \pm .008$ inch away from the flywheel. Check the runout of the plate at several points. It must not exceed .012 inch. Now press down on the release plate several times to operate the clutch and recheck the adjustment. When satisfied, lock the adjusting nuts by peening.

6 Remove the clutch from the flywheel by undoing the nuts a little at a time, working diagonally to prevent tilting and distortion. At the same time block the release levers or press down on the release lever plate.

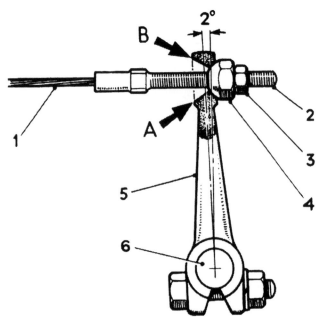

FIG 5:5 Correct setting of clutch withdrawal lever. With release bearing contacting release plate, lever 5 must incline forward not more than 2 deg. See text for setting at A and B

Key to Fig 5:5   1 Clutch cable   2 Adjusting thread
3 Locknut   4 Adjusting nut   5 Withdrawal lever
6 Operating shaft

5:6 The release mechanism

While the transmission casing and the engine are apart it will be a good opportunity to check the condition of the release mechanism. The removal and examination of the release bearing has been covered in **Section 5:3**. To remove the clutch operating shaft 1 in **FIG 5:1**, first remove the outside lever to which the cable is connected. Early models had a lever fitted with a clamping bolt. Later models have a lever located on the shaft by a circlip. Remove the bolt or the circlip and pull off the lever, followed by the return spring and the spring seat.

The shaft runs in bushes in the transmission casing. Remove bolt indicated by lower arrow in **FIG 5:3**. This secures the lefthand bush. Slide the shaft to the left and remove the bush, the washer and the spacer sleeve. Note that on recent models the bush is a plastic one with a rubber seal on each side. The removal of the bush gives the clearance required to slide the shaft to the right inside the casing so that it can be removed. Check both shaft and bushes for wear. Renew the return spring if it is weak.

Reassemble in the reverse sequence, lubricating the shaft with lithium grease. Refit the operating lever and check it against **FIG 5:5** after the engine and clutch have been refitted. This operation is covered in **Section 5:8**.

5:7 Refitting the clutch

Before bolting the clutch into place, clean the transmission shaft splines and then coat them with some molybdenum-disulphide powder applied with a piece of clean cloth or a brush and the surplus blown away. Pack needle bearing 10 (see **FIG 5:1**) with 10 grams (.35 oz) of universal grease.

The next step is to provide a mandrel to centre the driven plate while the clutch cover is bolted to the flywheel. As shown in **FIG 5:1**, it is essential for the driven plate hub 11 to be in-line with needle bearing 10 before the transmission drive shaft can be pushed into place while the engine is being fitted. If available, a spare drive shaft can be used or a stepped mandrel fashioned on the lines of the one shown in **FIG 5:6**. For one application only, it would be enough to turn up a wooden mandrel from a piece of dowel rod. One diameter must enter the needle bearing and the other would be a neat fit in the driven plate hub splines.

Having centralized the driven plate, fit the clutch cover and tighten the securing bolts evenly and diagonally a little at a time to avoid tilting the cover. While the mandrel is still in place, operate the release mechanism a few times and check the alignment of the release plate. This operation can also be performed if the engine has just be removed and the owner wishes to check the condition of the driven plate. The mandrel must be in place and the release plate pressed a few times. Measurements are then taken as in **FIG 5:4**, working in three or four positions round the periphery. If the dimension is down to 1.45 inch then the linings are worn and the plate must be renewed. Remove the mandrel.

Refit the engine, taking the greatest care to ensure that the weight of the engine does not hang on the main drive shaft. If everything is kept square there should be no chance of damage to the release bearing.

5:8 The operating cable

When the cable is reconnected to the operating lever it will be possible to check the angles according to **FIG 5:5**. On the early type illustrated, it will be seen that the adjusting nut has a spherical face in contact with the lever. On this type the lever will be correctly positioned if the cable thread just lightly touches the edge of the hole in the lever at **A**, with the clutch engaged. When the release bearing can just be felt to be in contact with the release plate the lever must incline not more than 2 deg. When the pedal is depressed and the clutch withdrawn, the upper edge of the hole at **B** must not touch the cable

FIG 5:6 Using a mandrel to centre the clutch driven plate

FIG 5:7 The clutch release bearing. Inset shows one of the two clips securing the bearing to the operating fork

thread. Any trouble at these points will lead to buckling and failure of the cable. Often the fault lies with a worn release bearing. Apply a little grease to the face of the adjusting nut.

Renewing a clutch cable:

Raise the vehicle on trestles and disconnect the cable from the operating lever. Remove the rubber boot from the guide tube and pull the cable through the boot. At the front, remove the coverplate below the pedal linkage. Remove the lockwasher from the clutch cable operating lever and detach the cable. Slide the rubber boot off the guide tube and pull the cable through from the front.

The cable is re-installed in the reverse order of dismantling. From Chassis No. 539286 the threaded rear end of the cable was increased to a diameter of 7 mm, and a larger bore of sleeve was fitted. The new cable can be used as a replacement but a new adjusting nut and locknut will be required. A new cable sleeve will not be needed. Always renew the rubber boots if they are defective, as water and road grit will make the cable stiff to operate, with consequent clutch trouble. Adjust pedal free play as instructed in **Section 5:2.**

The clutch cable linkage at the pedal can be serviced as follows:

1 Jack-up the vehicle and support it on stands or trestles. Detach the clutch cable from the lever at the rear end.
2 Remove the coverplate below the clutch pedal linkage. Detach the pedal arm from the rod and withdraw the pedal upwards. Detach the accelerator pedal shaft from the pedal rod.
3 Disconnect the accelerator cable from the operating lever and turn the pedal shaft downwards. Remove the circlip and washer from the clutch pedal arm pivot pin.
4 Pull the pedal off the pivot pin, remove the fixing nut, take off the lockwasher and withdraw the pivot pin and cap washer.

Replacement is the reverse of removal but note the following:

1 Check the pedal arm bushing and pivot pin for wear and renew if necessary. The bushing can be driven out with a shouldered drift. As the bushing is self-lubricating it is only necessary to apply some universal grease when reassembling.
2 Make sure that the felt seal of the clutch pedal rod seats properly against the floorboard. Lubricate the adjusting nut at the rear end with universal grease and adjust the clutch pedal free play as instructed in **Section 5:2.**

Setting the clutch cable guide tube:

This adjustment is carried out if the cable proves to be stiff in operation. Refer to **FIG 5:8** which shows the rear end of the guide tube and cable. If the guide tube is bent down too much the cable will be stiff to operate and may also be liable to break. A small bow is deliberate and gives a slight degree of friction to the cable to prevent clutch chatter and also makes the cable smooth in operation.

If the bow is too much the guide tube can be shortened slightly by removing the tube and cable. To increase the amount of bow, insert washers at the point indicated. These must go between the guide tube and the bracket which is part of the transmission cover. On early vehicles a bow of $\frac{3}{4}$ to $1\frac{1}{4}$ inch will be found suitable, while on more recent vehicles the bow should be between 1 and $1\frac{3}{4}$ inch.

5:9 Fault diagnosis

(a) Noisy clutch

1 Drive shaft bearing in gland nut worn
2 Driven plate fouling pressure plate
3 Weak or unequal release lever springs
4 Defective release bearing

(b) Chatter or grabbing

1 Transmission case mountings loose
2 Bow in cable guide tube incorrect
3 Uneven pressure plate
4 Release plate running out of true
5 Unequal strength of pressure springs
6 Distorted cushioning segments in driven plate centre
7 Grease or oil on friction surfaces

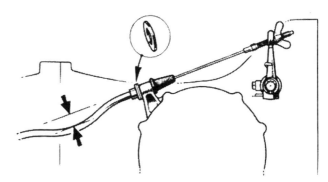

FIG 5:8 Amount of bow in clutch cable guide tube indicated by lefthand arrows. Correct figures are given in Section 5:8. Adjustment is made by fitting or removing washers as shown

(c) Dragging or incomplete release

1 Excessive clutch pedal free play
2 Bow in cable guide tube too great
3 Driven plate or main drive shaft running out of true
4 Uneven setting of driven plate cushioning segments
5 Driven plate friction linings broken
6 Needle bearing in gland nut defective or not greased
7 Tightness of drive shaft and driven plate splines
8 Sticky friction linings
9 Felt sealing ring in gland nut tight on main drive shaft
10 Stiffness in operation of clutch pedal, cable and release mechanism

(d) Slipping

1 Lack of free play of clutch pedal
2 Grease or oil on clutch linings

CHAPTER 6

THE TRANSMISSION

6:1 Description

The three basic forms of transmission are illustrated in **FIGS 6:1** and **6:2**. Prior to May 1959 on Transporters, the transmission casing was split vertically and housed either a 'crash' type set of four-speed gears or a set with synchromesh engagement on the second, third and fourth gears. With the change-over to synchromesh engagement on all four forward speeds the casing was also changed to a tunnel type with the gears and shafts fed in from the front and the assembly completed by fitting a cover as shown in **FIG 6:2**.

On 3-synchromesh assemblies it will be seen that second, third and fourth gears are helical and are in constant mesh to ensure silent operation. This also applies to first gear on 4-synchromesh assemblies.

On 'crash' gearboxes, third and fourth gears are helical and in constant mesh.

The reverse gears on early systems were housed in the gearbox and meshed with the first-speed gears. In the later system shown in **FIG 6:2** a gear 15 meshes with reverse gear to drive shaft in the opposite direction to the main drive shaft.

Gear selection on the 3-synchromesh transmission can be followed by referring to the top view in **FIG 6:1**.

The clutch driven plate is splined to the righthand end of drive shaft 11 so that when the clutch is engaged all the gears on that shaft are revolving. Second-, third- and fourth-speed gears on the shaft of pinion 8 are in constant mesh with the three on the clutch drive shaft but are free-running on the pinion shaft. Any one of these gears can be engaged, through the agency of typical synchromesh cones and sliding dogs, to hubs which are splined to the pinion shaft to complete the drive. First gear is selected by sliding the lower gear of the pair 7 to the right to engage the small gear on the main drive shaft. The reverse gears, which are not shown, engage gears 7 to provide a contra-rotating motion.

The all-synchromesh gearbox operates as follows. The front main drive shaft 9 in **FIG 6:2** carries fixed first and second gears and also drives the hub of synchromesh selector 5. The third and fourth gears run freely on needle roller bearings. The shaft of drive pinion 24 carries a similar arrangement, but the lower gears of pairs 4 and 7 are keyed to the shaft together with the hub of synchromesh selector 10. Forks slide the outer members of the synchromesh assemblies 5 and 10 to right or left to select each of the four forward gears, the driving dogs meshing when the synchromesh cone clutches have matched the

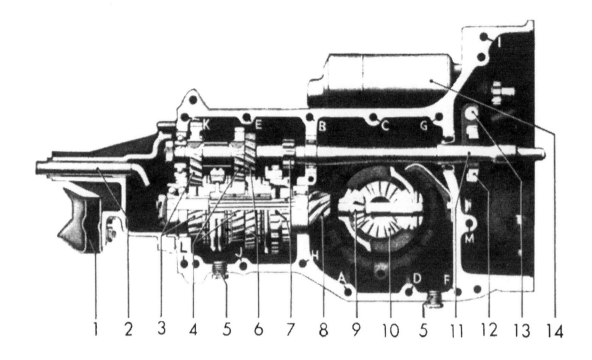

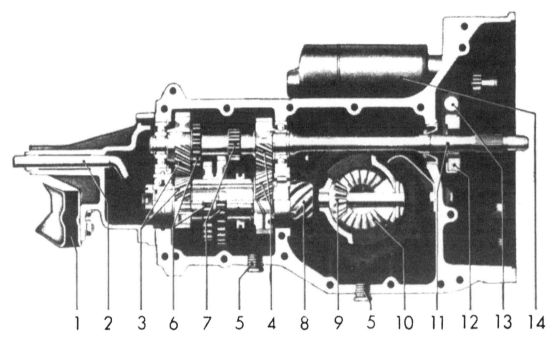

FIG 6:1 Earlier transmissions with casing split vertically. Top view shows 3-synchromesh transmission and lower view shows the 'crash' or non-synchromesh system

Key to Fig 6:1   1 Front rubber mounting   2 Gearshift rod and lever   3 Fourth-speed gear train   4 Third-speed gear train   5 Drain plug   6 Second-speed gear train   7 First-speed gear train   8 Drive pinion and shaft   9 Differential pinion   10 Differential side gear   11 Main drive shaft   12 Clutch release bearing   13 Clutch operating shaft   14 Starter

speeds of both members. The gear teeth on the outer ring of synchromesh assembly 10 are meshed with a sliding gear (not shown) to provide reverse gear.

The final drive pinion and the crownwheel are made in matched pairs and their correct relative positions are most important if silent running is to be ensured. Sideways adjustment of the crownwheel and differential assembly is made by shims. Fore and aft adjustment of the drive pinion is made by shims 13 in **FIG 6:2**. In the gearboxes illustrated in **FIG 6:1** the adjustment is made by shimming

between the fourth-speed gear on the pinion shaft and the front double-row ballbearing. Also in these two boxes, the two front bearings are located in the casing by spring rings in or abutting their outer races and by the end cover. As the rear bearings are not positively located endwise in the casing it can be appreciated that the shims behind the front bearing of the pinion shaft will adjust the fore and aft position of the pinion, positive location being assured by the clamping of the front bearing under the front cover.

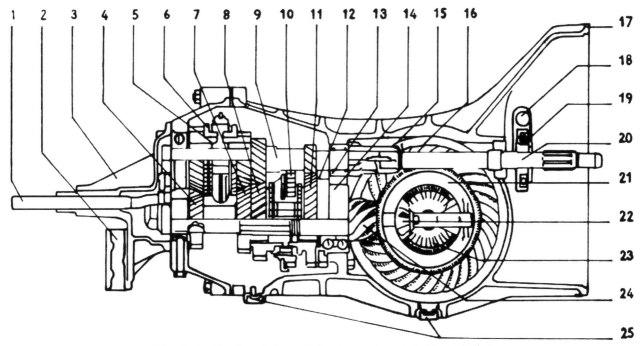

FIG 6:2 Sectional view of the 4-synchromesh transmission

Key to Fig 6:2 1 Gearshift lever 2 Front rubber mounting 3 Gearshift housing 4 Fourth gear train
5 Synchronizer sleeve and hub for third and fourth gear 6 Synchronizer stop ring for fourth gear 7 Third gear train
8 Second gear train 9 Main drive shaft (front) 10 Synchronizer sleeve and hub for first and second gear 11 First gear train
12 Bearing retainer 13 Shims for drive pinion meshing 14 Bearing (ball or taper roller) 15 Reverse drive gear
16 Crownwheel 17 Transmission casing 18 Clutch operating shaft 19 Clutch release bearing
20 Main drive shaft (rear) 21 Differential housing 22 Differential pinion 23 Differential side gear
24 Drive pinion 25 Magnetic drain plug

Before proceeding with instructions for servicing the transmission we must stress that official VW Service Stations use many precision devices to set the pinion and crownwheel positions correctly. It will also be understood that when the gears and shafts are assembled in the tunnel type of casing shown in **FIG 6:2** it is not possible to check the assembly, nor the correct functioning of the selector forks. Official VW methods employ a fixture in which the shafts and selectors are assembled and checked before they are fitted into the casing. As these fixtures and devices are not available to the normal owner we advise him to entrust the assembling of a transmission which incorporates new parts to a VW Service Station. The alternative is to use the Exchange system. There is no reason why the transmission should not be dismantled providing every care is taken to record the position and thickness of shimming for correct reassembly. Those parts which do not affect the position of the selector forks or the drive pinion can be renewed. Renewal of the casing halves, the pinion and crownwheel, the differential cage and bearings and the pinion shaft bearings will all require the special techniques for accurate location just mentioned.

6:2 Transmission maintenance

This is confined to topping up or changing the lubricating oil, but there is an associated adjustment which has a great effect upon the satisfactory working of the gearchange mechanism inside the transmission casing. This adjustment is to the clutch operation. Refer to **Chapter 5** and make sure that the clutch pedal clearance is maintained at the correct figure. Any tendency for the clutch to drag will have a bad effect on the synchromesh cones, causing them to wear rapidly.

Every 6000 miles check the oil level in the transmission by removing the level plug in the lefthand side of the casing just forward of the axle tubes, as shown in **FIG 6:3**. Top up with SAE.90 hypoid oil until it starts to overflow. Too hurried a filling may give a false impression, so wait a few minutes and add more lubricant if the level inside has fallen. There is only one filler plug, as the gearbox and rear axle are lubricated from a common source.

Every 30,000 miles drain the oil completely while it is still warm. Remove both drain plugs as indicated in **FIG 6:4**. On all synchromesh gearboxes the drain plugs are magnetic, so clean them of adhering particles of steel. Refill with hypoid oil, using slightly less than 4 pints. Sudden overflowing from the filler hole may be due to rapid filling, so pause now and then to allow the oil to settle inside the casing. The oil level should be up to the bottom edge of the filler hole. A newly-assembled transmission will take almost $4\frac{1}{2}$ pints.

If the drained oil is contaminated with many metallic particles and these also adhere in quantity to the magnetic drain plugs it is advisable to remove and dismantle the transmission to find the cause of excessive wear.

6:3 Removing transmission assembly

Any dismantling of the transmission system entails the removal of the gearbox and rear axle as a unit. This operation is fully covered in **Chapter 7, Section 7:4** on the rear axle.

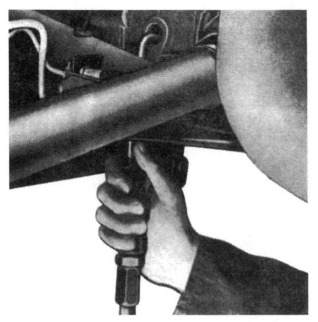

FIG 6:3 Location of filling and level plug for lubricant

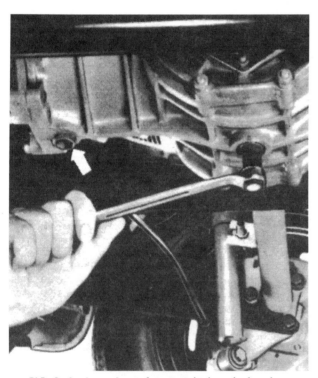

FIG 6:4 Location of transmission drain plugs

6:4 Servicing non-synchromesh transmission

This is the 'crash' type gearbox illustrated in the lower view of **FIG 6:1**. It is important to appreciate that the two halves of the transmission casing are machined in pairs. **Never try to renew one half alone.** Remember too that renewal of the casing calls for adjustment of the preload on the differential ballbearings and possibly of the pinion and crownwheel meshing, operations best entrusted to a VW Service Station. Renewal of the casing does not necessarily imply renewal of the gearchange housing too.

To dismantle the transmission, proceed as follows:

1 Remove the gearchange housing from the front end. Remove the clutch release bearing 12 and disconnect the clutch lever return spring. Remove all the casing bolts and lift off the righthand half.

2 Lift out both shafts complete. With a soft-faced mallet drive out the differential and axle shaft assembly from the lefthand casing. **Take particular care to note the number and position of the shims on the differential cage.** Remove the reverse gear and shaft.

3 Cut the locking wire and remove the selector fork screws. Pull out the selector rods from the front end, covering each detent hole with a finger to prevent the spring from jumping out. The principle is shown in **FIG 6:9**. Remove detent balls and springs, and the two interlock plungers shown in **FIG 6:16**.

Check all parts for wear and damage. Clean the casing joint faces and remove any burrs. Check the starter shaft and clutch shaft bushes for wear. Renew the detent springs if they are less than .9 inch in length. The correct length is 1 inch. When balls and springs are installed it should take a load of 45 lb to move the selector rods.

The main drive shaft:

To dismantle:

1 Remove circlips from each end of shaft 11. Press the bearings and gears off the shaft. The two straight-toothed gears are part of the shaft. Clean the parts and check for wear.

2 Try the fit of the rear end pilot in the bush in the fly-wheel gland nut. Check all splines for wear and the oil seal seating for scores and pitting. The removable gears and the ballbearings must be a press fit on the shaft. **Gears 3 and 4 must be renewed in pairs.**

3 Check the shaft between centres. Maximum runout must not exceed .002 inch at the centre bearing seat. The shaft may be straightened cold. When assembled, the runout of the rear end pilot must not exceed .008 inch.

To reassemble:

Fit the two keys, heat the gears and bearings to 180°F in an oil bath and press them onto the shaft. Do not forget the bearing retaining ring before fitting the front bearing. Refit the circlips.

The drive shaft:

To dismantle:

1 Unlock and remove the nut then pull off the spacer and shims. Remove lower gear 3 and lower gears 6 and 7.

2 Remove the guide sleeve, engaging pins and selector ring. Remove the retaining ring and pull off the lower gear of the pair 4.

3 Remove the roller bearing retaining ring and pull off the roller bearing, noting how the inner race is made up of two parts. Clean all parts, paying attention to the oil passages in the shaft.

Check all parts for wear and if the pinion is worn, have the replacement pinion and crownwheel fitted and correctly meshed by a VW Service Station. Wear of the engaging pins and grooves in the sleeve may be the cause of gears slipping out. The gears can be renewed without affecting the assembled position of the pinion with respect to the crownwheel.

To reassemble:

The roller bearing must be a press fit. Heat the inner race to 194°F in an oil bath and press into place. The friction washer must face the third-speed gear. Install the retaining ring. This can be expanded with pliers but do not overstrain it. Renew if loose.

Fit the third-speed gear followed by the retaining ring. End float of the gear can be corrected by fitting a replacement retaining ring with flat sides. This is .09 inch thick compared with .08 inch for the standard round-sectioned ring. Oil all parts liberally.

Stand the guide sleeve on end with the internal splines downwards. Fit three engaging pins equally spaced and hold them while engaging the selector ring in the grooves in the pins. The internal shoulder of the ring must face downwards. Fit the remaining six pins. If fourth-speed gear tends to disengage, special pins are available to cure the trouble. Slide the sleeve onto the shaft, making sure the splines engage correctly with the shaft. Refit the double gear, large gear first. Install the fourth-speed gear and bush. End float of the gear should not exceed .0098 inch.

Replace the shims. These must not be altered if no parts affecting the meshing of the pinion and crownwheel have been renewed.

Press the bearing into place with the ball-assembling groove in the outer race facing to the front. Tighten the nut to 108 lb ft torque and loosen it. Retighten to 45 to 50 lb ft, **tightening still more** if necessary to align the splitpin holes.

Reassembling transmission:

Fit the shafts to the lefthand casing. Install the clutch operating shaft. **Do not forget to do this as the shaft cannot be fitted after the casing halves are bolted together.**

Install the selector rods, fitting the third and fourth gear rod and fork first, followed by the first and second rod, and finally the reverse rod. Do not forget the interlock plungers. Check for correct interlocking by selecting a gear. The shaft next to the one selected should be immovably locked. When the centre shaft is engaged, both outer shafts should be locked. The selector fork screws must fit in their recesses and be locked with iron wire after tightening.

If a new bush has been fitted to the reverse gear and peened over to secure it, ream it out to a diameter of .6336 to .6319 inch.

Having checked the meshing of the gears and the correct bedding of the ballbearing retaining ring, the next step is to determine the amount of preload required on the outer races of the two front ballbearings. Use **FIG 6:5** for reference purposes. This must be done before assembling the casing halves.

A depth micrometer should be used for measuring, but it is also possible to use 'Plastigage'. The first step is to move the two shafts fully to the rear with light taps of a soft-faced hammer. Measure distances **D** and **E**. These are the projections of pinion shaft bearing 2 and main shaft bearing 1 beyond the face of transmission case 4. Also measure the depth of recess **C** in the gearchange housing 3.

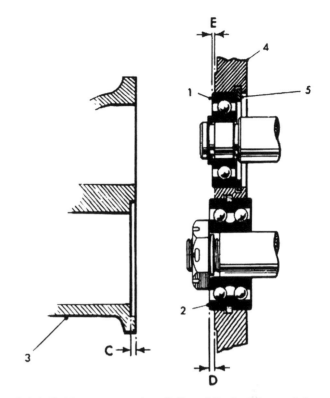

FIG 6:5 Measure at points C, D and E when determining the preloading of the outer races of the front bearings (non-synchromesh or 'crash' transmission)

Key to Fig 6:5   1 Main drive shaft front bearing
2 Pinion shaft front bearing   3 Gearshift housing
4 Transmission casing   5 Retainer ring

Bearing 2 must be preloaded by .0008 to .0043 inch. This is done by selecting an appropriate thickness for the housing gasket. Subtract dimension **C** from dimension **D**. Say that the difference is .012 inch. In order to preload the bearing by .004 inch, the gasket must be .008 inch thick.

If dimension **E** is .008 inch and the gasket is .008 inch thick as just determined, it means that there will be no preload on bearing 1 when the housing is bolted on. To obtain the required preload of .004 inch use a thicker retaining ring 5. The three thicknesses which are available are .079, .083 and .087 inch.

Use extra care to obtain the correct degree of preloading as excessive pressure may cause noise and lead to premature wear of the bearings.

Before assembling the case halves and the gearchange housing, check the shift rod bushes in the housing. New bushes should be reamed to .5925 to .5918 inch.

Press the differential ballbearings into the casings, making sure they are squarely seated and right home. Fit the differential cage and axle shafts to the lefthand casing. It is most important to ensure that the shims which position the cage in the bearings are fitted exactly as they were removed or the mesh of the pinion and crownwheel will be wrong and serious trouble could result.

Coat the clean burr-free faces of the casing halves with jointing compound and drop the righthand half into place. Tap the casing carefully into place in the vicinity of the differential bearing so that it is firmly seated and the joint faces have met. Fit and tighten the bolts to a torque of

FIG 6:6 The shaft assemblies in position in one half of the transmission casing (3-synchromesh transmission)

FIG 6:7 The reverse gear shaft locking pin on 3-synchromesh transmissions. Make sure this does not fall out when turning the casing over

15 lb ft, using the alphabetical sequence indicated in the top view of **FIG 6:1**. Put the three selector rods in the neutral position and fit the gearchange housing, using the correct gasket to give the desired preload on the two front bearings. Fit the earth strap to the stud from which it came.

6:5 Servicing 3-synchromesh transmission

The top view in **FIG 6:1** shows this transmission in section. All the gears on the main drive shaft 11 revolve with it. On the pinion shaft below, there are constant-mesh gears 3, 4 and 6 which can turn freely on bushes. Between clusters 3 and 4 is a synchromesh assembly the hub of which is splined to the pinion shaft. Moving the outer sleeve to left or right brings the synchromesh cone clutches into action. When the two parts of a clutch are turning at the same speed, dogs are meshed which provide a drive from either of the lower gears, through the hub to

the pinion shaft. Moving the lower first-speed gear and sleeve 7 to the left brings a similar synchromesh clutch into action to complete the drive from lower gear 6, giving second-speed. When lower gear 7 is moved to the right it meshes with the small gear on the main drive shaft to give bottom gear. In the position illustrated it is possible to slide two gears (not shown) into mesh with gears 7 to provide reverse gear. These can be seen in **FIG 6:7**.

The casing is split vertically and has a gearchange housing bolted to the front face. The web across the centre of the casing carries the housings for the main drive and pinion shaft bearings. Early transmissions have a ballbearing for the rear end of the main drive shaft and a roller bearing for the pinion shaft as in the lower view. Later transmissions have needle roller bearings on both shafts as shown.

The following points must be made so that the operator can decide whether to proceed with a comprehensive overhaul of the transmission. The first point is that the relative positions of the pinion and crownwheel are determined by shims and very accurate measurements. The equipment to carry out perfect meshing is available only at Official VW Service Stations, and is necessary if such parts as a new pinion and crownwheel, a new differential cage or new casing halves are fitted. Any part which affects the axial position of either gear cannot be renewed without the meshing having to be checked with precision equipment. Dismantling and the renewal of parts which do not affect the positions of the pinion and crownwheel is simply a matter of using the following instructions. Otherwise, the owner is advised to have his transmission serviced by a VW Service Station or to use the Exchange system.

The second point is that the casing halves are machined in pairs. It is not possible to renew one half alone and new casings can be obtained only as a pair. This does not imply that a new gearchange housing must also be fitted at the same time. The match pinion and crownwheel must be fitted as a pair.

To dismantle the transmission:

1 Remove the gearchange housing from the front of the casing. Remove the clutch release bearing 12 in **FIG 6:1** (upper view). Remove the flange bolts from the casing and also the single nut on the lefthand side low down in front of the axle retainer plate.

2 Use a soft-faced hammer to separate the casing halves. Lift the righthand half up and over the axle shaft. Lift out the main drive shaft 11 and the pinion shaft 8 from the lefthand casing. The appearance of the casing with the shafts in place can be seen in **FIG 6:6**.

3 Use a copper hammer to drive the axle shaft and differential assembly out of the casing half. There are shims between the differential cage and the ballbearings in the transmission casing halves. These position the crownwheel with respect to the drive pinion and it is most important to keep a note of the shims removed from each side. **If this is not done, the correct meshing of the drive gears will be upset and serious damage could result.**

4 Lift out the locking pin for the reverse gear shaft as shown in **FIG 6:7** and then remove the shaft and reverse gears. From the righthand case remove the two

screwed plugs shown in **FIG 6:8,** the holes giving access to two of the lockscrews for the shifting forks. Also remove the lockscrews in the reverse gear fork. Before pulling out the shifter rods, blank off each detent hole with a finger as shown in **FIG 6:9.** As the end of the rod clears the hole a ball and spring will pop up and could otherwise be lost.

5 Having removed all three rods and the selector forks, also retrieve the two interlocking plungers which lie in a drilling across the three selector rod holes in the front wall of the casing as shown in **FIG 6:16.** Remove the clutch release shaft. If necessary, remove the differential ballbearings from the casing halves.

Clean the casings and remove all jointing compound from the faces. Clean and check the internal parts, testing the ballbearings when dry. Check the length of the detent springs for the selector rod balls. The correct length is 1 inch and the low limit .9 inch.

The main drive shaft (see FIG 6:10):

To dismantle:

Remove the retaining ring from the rear of the central bearing and press the bearing off the shaft. At the front end, unlock and remove the hexagon nut. Remove the front ballbearing and the fourth-speed gear. Prise off the slotted spacer and press the third-speed gear off the shaft. Remove the two Woodruff keys.

Check the shaft between centres. Maximum runout at the centre bearing seat should not exceed .002 inch. If necessary, the shaft may be straightened **cold.** In connection with runout of this shaft it must also be checked when assembled in the casing. Maximum runout of the spigot bearing at the extreme rear end must not exceed .008 inch. This is the part of the shaft which runs in a bearing in the central nut for the flywheel. Having examined all parts for wear and made renewals where necessary, the shaft may be reassembled.

To reassemble:

Press on the rear ballbearing. Lubricate the shaft well and press on the bearing retaining ring. Fit the two keys.

The gears must be heated in an oil bath to 180°F before pressing on to the shaft. Third-speed gear must be fitted tightly against second-speed gear, followed by the slotted spacer. The slot can be expanded with a screwdriver to facilitate fitting. Fit the fourth-speed gear and large ballbearing. The locating ring in the outer race of the bearing must face to the front. Fit the retaining nut and lockwasher, locating the tongue in the washer in the slot in the shaft. Tighten the nut to a torque of 22 lb ft and secure it with a tab of the lockplate.

Before leaving the drive shaft we must repeat an earlier warning about renewing the gears. It is not permissible to renew any of the gears singly. Damage to a drive shaft gear calls for the renewal of its mating gear on the pinion shaft as well.

The drive pinion and shaft (see FIG 6:11):

The fore and aft location of the pinion with respect to the crownwheel is obtained by shims. Any alteration to the shimming, or the renewal of those parts which actually make contact with the shaft (except the nut and lockwasher) will affect this endwise location. Renewal of the

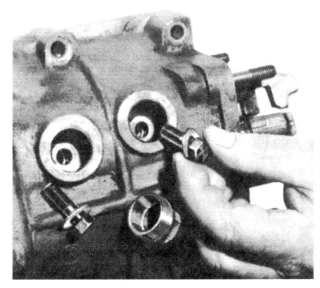

FIG 6:8 Remove the screwed plugs to reach the selector fork locking screws (3-synchromesh transmission)

FIG 6:9 Finger over detent hole when removing selector rod. This prevents loss of spring-loaded ball (3-synchromesh transmission)

gears and synchromesh clutches will not. It is therefore recommended that renewal of worn bushes, synchromesh hubs and bearings is entrusted to a VW Service Station so that correct meshing of the pinion and crownwheel can be ensured.

To dismantle:

1 Hold the pinion by soft jaws in a vice, unlock and remove the nut, which will be very tight. Take off the shims after removing the double-row ballbearing. **Keep these shims wired together for correct replacement.** Remove the thrust washer.

2 Remove the fourth-speed gear, the synchromesh cone and the stop ring. These parts can be seen in **FIG 6:11.** Remove the gear bush.

3 Remove the synchromesh selector ring and hub complete. Do not attempt to dismantle it until the later

FIG 6:10 Main drive shaft components for 3-synchromesh transmission. The two gears at the front end of the shaft are secured by Woodruff keys with a slotted spacer between

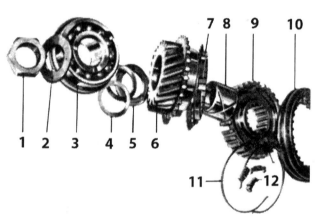

FIG 6:11 Pinion shaft components at front end of 3-synchromesh transmission

Key to Fig 6:11   1 Retainer nut   2 Lockwasher
3 Double-row ballbearing with spring ring   4 Shims
5 Washer   6 Fourth-speed gear and cone assembly
7 Synchronizing stop ring   8 Bush   9 Synchronizer hub
10 Synchronizer sleeve   11 Spring ring for shifting plates
12 Shifting or blocker plates

instructions have been read. Take off the next stop ring and cone, followed by the third speed gear. Pull the bush off the splines.

4 Remove the second-speed gear and stop ring. Wrap the first-speed gear assembly in a piece of cloth and press off the gear ring. This will release the small shifter plates, springs and snap ring. These can be seen in **FIG 6:12**. Pull off the synchromesh hub.

5 **Take great care of the shim which is the next part to be removed.** This must be correctly replaced or it will affect the position of the pinion. Pull off the ring and the roller bearing. If renewal is needed pull off the inner race of the bearing. If micrometer measurement of the width of the new inner race shows that it is identical with the old one there will be no change in the location of the pinion shaft when refitted.

Clean all the parts and use compressed air through the drillings in the shaft and bushes. Renew only those parts which were mentioned at the beginning of this operation. All other renewals, including the pinion shaft, must be entrusted to a VW Service Station. Replace the gears in pairs even though the one on the main drive shaft may be unworn.

Check the synchromesh components for wear. First clean the inside of each stop ring with a stiff wire brush. Press the stop ring 2 onto the correct synchronizer cone and measure the clearance indicated at **A** in **FIG 6:14**. The wear limit is .012 inch. Below this the stop ring must be renewed. Frequent need to renew worn stop rings is traceable to clutch trouble. If there has been difficulty in engaging a gear with the clutch fully withdrawn, the stop ring slots may be worn so that the teeth are not aligned with those in the operating sleeve. Renew the stop ring in this case.

Owners of older vehicles will be interested in the following changes in design. The early first gear synchronizer hub had no groove in it. Later models have a groove which prevent first gear from jumping out. The early third-speed gear on the pinion shaft had 28 teeth meshing with 23 on the gear on the main drive shaft, later models have 27 teeth meshing with 22. Be careful to get the correct replacement. Top gear on early models was obtained with 22 teeth on the pinion shaft gear, meshing with 28 teeth on the top shaft. The larger gear was later modified to have only 27 teeth. The new parts can be fitted to older boxes.

Reassembling the pinion shaft:

This is a reversal of the dismantling procedure but also use the following instructions:

1 Heat the roller bearing inner race to 194°F in an oil bath. It must be a press fit on the shaft. Follow up with the shim. .004 to .008 inch shims are available to control end float of parts assembled on the splined section of the shaft. Shim thickness is determined after the synchronizer hub for third and fourth gear is assembled on the shaft.

2 Fit the snap ring into the hub of the first speed assembly and slide the hub onto the shaft. Fit the three coil springs and the shifter plates with their stepped ends located under the snap ring. An assistant will be useful to press the shifter plates inwards while the first-speed gear is fitted with its selector fork groove facing forward. **It is most important to make sure that the chamfered splines slide over the shifter plates.**

3 Fit the second-speed stop ring with its slot engaging the shifter plates. Fit the second- and third-speed gears with the internal splines, lubricating well beforehand. Slide the assembly onto the shaft. Fit a synchronizer stop ring (the remaining two are interchangeable).

4 Take the outer sleeve which is slotted for the selector fork and fit it to the synchronizer hub. Fit the three shifter plates. Now the spring snap rings one on each side so that they engage the small lips on the shifter plates. The open ends of the rings should be positioned

halfway between two plates. Fit this assembly to the pinion shaft with the shifter plates entering the slots of the stop ring already fitted.

5 The synchronizer hub should be virtually flush with the face of the splines on the shaft within a tolerance of .002 inch, and if it is not, there is something wrong with the assembly. Check and reassemble. Adjust a small discrepancy by the shim mentioned in Operation 1, preferably so that the hub is just flush with the face of the splines. Too much standing proud of the splines may affect the meshing of the pinion in the crownwheel.

6 Fit the last stop ring with its slots engaging the shifter plates, followed by the fourth-speed gear and its bush. Fit the thrust washer, the shims removed during dismantling and then the bearing, with its filling slot for the balls facing forward. Fit a new lockplate, lubricating it with graphite grease, and tighten the retaining nut to a torque of 43 to 50 lb ft. Do not slacken the nut to obtain the correct torque. Lock the nut. **If any part has been renewed which will affect the axial position of the pinion with respect to the crownwheel, the assembly must be entrusted to a VW Service Station for correct meshing.**

Reassembling transmission:

Before reassembling, check the following points. First check the starter bush for wear and renew if necessary. Check the bushes for the clutch operating shaft. Renew the reverse gear shaft and bush if worn. Secure the bush by peening and then ream to .6319 to .6329 inch.

If there has been difficulty with gearchanging, check the selector rod detents before fitting the pinion shaft. Fit each rod, detent spring and ball and check that a force of 35 to 45 lb is required to move the rod. The free length of a detent spring should be 1 inch.

Renew the oil seal at the rear of the main drive shaft if leakage into the clutch housing has been troublesome. Oil the lip of the seal before fitting the shaft. Check the selector forks for excessive wear of the contact faces. If they were removed, fit the differential bearings, taking great care that they are squarely seated in their housings. Check the differential gears for wear, and renew as follows. This will not affect the meshing of the crownwheel and pinion providing the differential cage or housing is not changed nor the crownwheel and pinion renewed. The locking pin for the differential pinion shaft is shown in **FIG 6:1**. The hole will be peened over to prevent the pin working out so clean away the peening with a drill before trying to drive out the pin. Drive out the shaft and lift out the two small gears and the larger side gears which drive the axle shafts. Check gears for wear of the teeth and the spherical seatings of the small pinions where they contact the differential cage. Check the side gears and axle shaft trunnions as instructed in **Chapter 7**. Renew the pinion shaft if shouldered.

Reassemble the differential and fit the locking pin to the pinion shaft. Peen the holes to secure the pin.

There have been various changes in design of the differential parts so that it is important to verify that the correct spares are obtained. Remember that renewal of the differential cage or housing will entail reassembly by a VW Service Station to obtain the correct meshing of the drive gears.

FIG 6:12 Synchronizer hubs on 3-synchromesh transmission. On left, hub for third- and fourth-speed gears with shifting plate and retaining ring. On right, hub for second-speed gear with shifting plates, springs and retaining ring

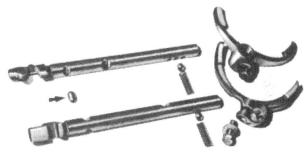

FIG 6:13 Forward speed selector rods and forks, showing the detent balls and springs. Interlocking plunger is arrowed (3-synchromesh transmission)

Assembly process:

Oil all parts liberally and then proceed as follows:

1 Install the selector rods and forks in the lefthand casing starting with the reverse rod. Do not forget the detent ball and spring, pressing them down and sliding the rod into place. Fit the reverse gear and shaft, locking the shaft with the pin shown in **FIG 6:7**. **When turning the casing about, make sure this locking pin does not fall out.** Later models have a modified reverse gear which can be fitted to early gearboxes but it necessitates rounding off the upper end of the selector fork.

2 Fit the first and second gear selector rod and fork and then the third and fourth rod and fork, taking care to replace the two interlocking plungers between the three rods as shown in **FIG 6:16**. Move one of the outside rods as if engaging a gear. The shaft next to it should then be locked and immovable. When the centre rod is moved to engage a gear, both of the other rods must be locked. Fit the fork locking screws but do not tighten until after gear shifting has been checked.

3 Drop the two shaft assemblies into the casing with the selector forks properly engaged in the operating grooves. The retaining rings in the outer races of the two front ballbearings must be correctly seated with their gaps slightly above the joint face of the casing. Tap both shafts lightly to the rear as far as the retaining rings will allow.

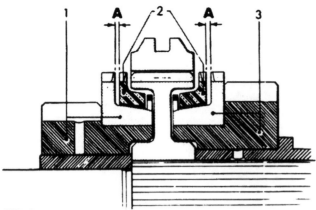

FIG 6:14 Synchromesh assembly for third and fourth gears on 3-synchromesh transmission. Stop ring clearance is measured at A

Key to Fig 6:14 1 Fourth-speed gear 2 Synchronizer stop rings 3 Third-speed gear
Clearance at **A** to be not less than .012 inch

4 Adjust the forward gear selector forks. Check that the centre rod and fork correctly engage first- and second-speed gears. If, for example, second gear only partially engages, move the fork nearer to that gear. Position the third and top selector fork so that both gears engage the same amount. Tighten the locking screws to a torque of 18 lb ft, and replace the two plugs in the casing. Refit the differential and axle shaft assembly into the lefthand casing, replacing the shims exactly as they were removed. This is vital to the relative positions of the crownwheel and pinion and any fault here can only be rectified by a VW Service Station.

5 Run through all the gearchanging movements once more to see that all is well. Remember to fit the clutch operating shaft assembly before joining the casing halves. Clean the joint faces of the casing thoroughly and make sure that there are no burrs. Coat the faces and oil seal seatings with sealing compound and tighten the screws to a torque of $14\frac{1}{2}$ lb ft in the alphabetical order shown in **FIG 6:1** (top).

The main drive shaft oil seal:

This seal, which is just in front of the clutch release bearing, can be renewed without removing or dismantling the transmission. First remove the engine and then the clutch release bearing. Prise out the old oil seal, taking care not to damage the housing. Lightly coat the outer surface of the new seal with sealing compound and oil the drive shaft and lip of seal. Very carefully slide the seal into place so that the spring ring round the sealing lip is not displaced. Keeping it quite square with the housing, drive it into place with a thick-walled tubular drift.

Fitting the front cover:

When the cover is bolted in position there should be a slight interference fit on the outer races of the two bearings so that they are securely located in the casing housings. This will ensure that the shafts cannot move endwise. The amount of interference or loading of the outer races is between .001 and .0045 inch and is adjusted by using different thicknesses of paper gaskets. These are shown in **FIG 6:15**. Note that the ring gasket 4 is to be stuck to the cover gasket 5.

The first step is to tap the shafts rearwards to the fullest extent. Then use an accurate depth gauge to measure depths **X, Y,** and **Z**. Measurements can also be made by assembling the cover without gaskets and using 'Plastigage' between the cover and the smaller outer race and between the cover and casing faces. Do not tighten the securing nuts excessively or the cover will be distorted.

As an example let us say that the difference between **X** and **Y** is .012 inch, giving excessive loading of the larger race if the cover is fitted without a gasket. If a gasket .010 inch thick is used it will reduce the loading to the satisfactory figure of .002 inch. Having settled the loading on the outer race of the large bearing 3 and found that dimension **Z** is .006 inch for the outer race of smaller bearing 2, we find that if gasket 4 is .008 inch thick it will load the bearing by .002 inch, which is the same as that determined for the large bearing. Gasket 4 must be glued into place so that it will bear on the outer race of bearing 2.

Before fitting the cover examine the gearshift bushes. Worn ones should be renewed and reamed out to .5925 to .5918 inch. Set the three selector shafts in the neutral position, engage the gearshift lever and fit the cover. Connect the earth lead to the correct stud.

6:6 Servicing 4-synchromesh transmission

Refer to the sectional view of this transmission system in **FIG 6:2**. It will be noted that the casing is of the tunnel type with a deep front gear housing and gearshift housing 3. The main drive shaft is in two parts 9 and 20, joined by a coupling 15 which incorporates a pinion used in the reverse gearing assembly. The large bearings for the differential housing make it possible to remove the axle shafts and side gears 23 without dismantling the complete unit. It can also be seen that the first- and second-speed synchromesh unit 10 is mounted on the pinion shaft, the synchromesh unit 5 for the third- and fourth-speeds being located on the front drive shaft 9. It must be appreciated that the renewal of any parts which call for readjustment of the selector fork positions must be entrusted to a VW Service Station because the adjustment cannot be made with the transmission assembled in the casing. The Service Station uses a special jig which holds the assembly in the relative position it will occupy in the casing and permits the adjustment to be carried out.

The differential side bearings are preloaded by .004 to .007 inch by selecting suitable shims. These shims together with those at the other end of the differential housing also control the sideways position of the ring gear or crownwheel 16 relative to the drive pinion 24. Endwise location of the pinion with respect to the crownwheel is determined by the thickness of shims 13. If either the pinion and crownwheel, the casing, the bearing 14 or the differential housing is renewed, the meshing of the drive gears must be checked and reset by a VW Service Station equipped with the necessary precision gauges and assembly jigs. Renewal of the side plates carrying the differential bearings, or the bearings themselves, may call for crownwheel readjustment only. **Note that the pinion and crownwheel are produced in matched pairs and must be renewed together.** Worn changespeed gears must also be renewed in pairs and never singly. Any adjustment of the pinion position will affect the selector forks and these will also need readjustment.

From the preceding remarks it will be realized that servicing this type of transmission should not be lightly undertaken, particularly if it is thought that the renewal of many worn parts might be needed. If the parts to be renewed do not affect the adjustment of the pinion and crownwheel or the selector forks then the following instructions can be used. **During dismantling it is most important to record the position and number of shims so that they can be replaced in their original positions on reassembly.**

Dismantling transmission:

This can proceed after the axle shafts and side gears have been removed as instructed in **Chapter 7**. Then do the following:

1 Remove the front mounting 2 and the housing 3 together with the gearshift lever 1. Move the reverse selector rod and the third and fourth selector rod so that the simultaneous engagement of reverse and one of the forward gears will lock the shafts. Flatten the lockwashers and remove the nuts from both shafts. These washers must be renewed upon reassembly.

2 Remove the nuts securing the gear housing, noting the positions of the earthing strap and throttle cable guide. Turn the transmission so that the righthand side plate is on top and unscrew eight nuts.

3 With great care, remove the side plate, keeping it square all the way. Use a soft-faced hammer if force is needed. Use a wooden block to drive out the differential assembly and housing from the opposite side. **Keep the bearing shims together in sets so that they can be replaced correctly upon reassembly.**

4 Remove the circlip to the rear of the reverse gear coupling 15, pull the gear back and unscrew the rear drive shaft 20. Withdraw the shaft to the rear, taking care that the splines do not damage the oil seal just in front of release bearing 19. Remove the remaining side plate.

5 Round pinion 24 will be seen four bolts which retain the pinion bearing 14. Prise up the locking tabs and unscrew these bolts. Using a lever and wooden blocks, press the pinion to the front so that the tranmission is pushed out of the casing. **Make a very careful note of the shims 13 under bearing retainer 12.**

6 Remove the circlip and reverse drive gear from shaft. Prise out the key and tap the shaft out from the rear. The shaft runs in needle roller bearings and these can be drifted out after removing a setscrew which locates the spacer between them. Remove the setscrew retaining the needle roller bearing for the main drive shaft 9 and drift out the bearing. Remove the clutch release bearing 19 and shaft 18.

7 Remove reverse shifter fork and gear. Use soft jaws to clamp housing in a vice. Loosen the clamp screws of the selector forks **after marking or taking measurements** to ensure that they can be replaced in their original positions. Remove first- and second-speed selector fork from gear 10. Withdraw the selector shaft for third- and fourth-speed gears out of the selector fork.

8 Fit a strong rubber band round the first-speed gears 11 to keep the shafts together and press out the shafts

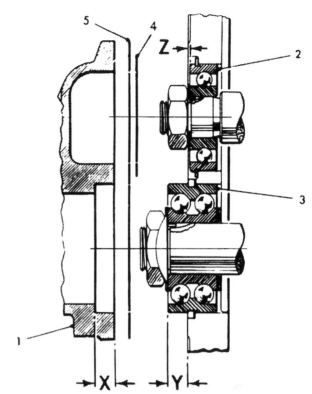

FIG 6:15 Measure at **X, Y** and **Z** to determine preload on outer races of front bearings (3-synchromesh transmission)

Key to Fig 6:15   1 Gearshift housing   2 Main drive shaft front bearing   3 Pinion shaft front bearing   4 Paper ring gasket   5 Housing gasket

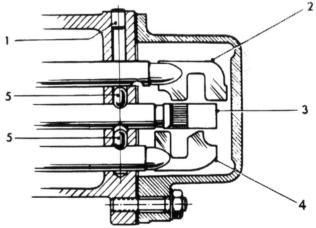

FIG 6:16   Selector rods and interlocking plungers

Key to Fig 6:16   1 Plug   2 Selector rod for reverse   3 Selector rod for first and second gears   4 Selector rod for third and fourth gears   5 Interlocking plungers

from the front end. This must be done simultaneously so that the drive pinion cannot tilt and damage the needle roller bearing at the front end of the pinion shaft. This bearing can be pressed out after removing the long setscrew. The main drive shaft ballbearing can be pressed out from the rear.

9 Remove the screw from the reverse lever guide, withdraw the reverse selector shaft and remove the

lever guide. Withdraw the selector shaft for first- and second-speed gears and remove the reverse lever from its support. Remove the selector shaft for third- and fourth-speed gears. Take out the interlock plungers and balls and remove the plugs from the outside of the housing adjacent to the selector rod holes. Lift out the springs with a thin screwdriver. See **FIG 6 : 16** for a similar assembly.

The free length of new detent springs is 1 inch with a wear limit length of .9 inch. In cases of difficulty with gear changing, check the force required to move the selector rod shafts with the pinion and main drive shafts removed. It should need 33 to 44 lb effort to overcome the detent balls and springs.

Dismantling main drive shaft:

This is the assembly on shaft 9 in **FIG 6 : 2**. Proceed as follows:

1 Remove the thrust washer and fourth-speed gear 4, the needle bearing and stop ring 6. Press the bearing race and assembly off the shaft and remove the needle bearing and third-speed gear 7.
2 The synchromesh assembly can be dismantled by prising out the spring rings and removing the three small blockers, making note of the shape of the latter for correct reassembly.

After cleaning the parts, check for wear. Put the shaft between centres and check the runout of the bearing surface for the third-speed gear. It should not exceed .0006 inch. Check the front section of the shaft for wear and check the reverse gear splines. Check the needle bearings and surfaces. If it is necessary to renew the needle rollers ensure that they are all the same length. Clean the internal cones of the stop rings with a wire brush. Renew the gears if worn, but only in pairs with the mating gear on the pinion shaft. As the first- and second-speed gears are solid with the shaft, worn teeth imply renewal of the shaft. In this case it is not necessary to renew the mating gears on the pinion shaft as well.

Check the clearance between the stop ring face and the small teeth on each gear with a feeler gauge as shown at **A** in **FIG 6 : 17**. Normally it should be .043 inch with a wear limit of .024 inch. If worn near to the wear limit renew the stop rings. Abnormal wear of the stop rings may be due to a worn clutch or incorrect operation of the clutch. Wear of the stop ring slots causes misalignment of the stop ring teeth with the splines of the operating sleeve. This condition makes it difficult to engage a gear even though the clutch is fully depressed.

While checking the front shaft it is a good plan to check the rear shaft 20 as well, first trying the pilot at the extreme rear end for fit in the gland nut bearing in the flywheel. Check the splines for wear and the working surface for the rear oil seal for pitting and scoring. Check the reverse gear and renew if worn.

Reassembling main drive shaft:

1 Assemble the synchromesh unit, noting that the sleeve which engages the selector fork is paired with its hub and these must be renewed together. The 1 mm groove in the sleeve must face towards the fourth-speed gear on assembly and the hub has a chamfer on the third-speed gear side to help when pressing it onto the shaft.

Note in **FIG 6 : 17** that there is an etched line to assist in the correct assembly of the sleeve and hub. The marks must be in-line.

2 Fit the three shifting or blocker plates in their slots and install the spring rings with ends offset to each other. Check that the rings engage properly behind the blocker plates.
3 Fit the Woodruff key in the shaft and put the stop ring for the third-speed gear into place. Press the synchronizing hub and sleeve into position on the shaft, lifting the third-speed gear slightly and turning it until the slots in the stop ring engage the three blocker plates. Some synchromesh assemblies are stamped with the numeral 4 which should face the fourth-speed gear. Press the inner race for the front needle bearing on to the shaft, then fit the bearing, the stop ring and the gear 4. Renew the thrust washer if it is worn or scored.

Dismantling pinion shaft:

Before starting work on the shaft, remember that renewal of the shaft or the double-row ballbearing (or taper roller bearing) will call for readjustment of the final drive gears by a VW Service Station. Proceed to dismantle as follows:

1 At the front end, press the shaft out of the inner race of the needle bearing and the fourth-speed gear 4 (lower). Prise out the Woodruff key. Take off the spacer sleeve, the concave washer shims and the concave washer which precedes the third-speed gear 7 (lower). Remove the gear and second-speed gear 8 (lower), the needle bearing cage and the synchronizer stop ring.
2 Remove the clutch gear assembly 10 complete with spring rings, shifting or blocker plates and sliding gear. Dismantle by prising out the spring rings, noting the correct way round for the shifting plates to ensure correct reassembly. Remove the stop ring, the first-speed gear 11 (lower) and the shims controlling first gear end float.
3 Hold the pinion by soft jaws in a vice and unscrew the round nut from the shaft, removing any burrs from the side faces of the nut afterwards. Remove the needle rollers, thrust washers and bearing inner race by pressing off the double-row ball or taper roller bearing. Note, in the case of the taper roller bearing that there are two types in use. One has a spacer ring between the two inner races. The other type has inner races which touch each other. See **FIG 6 : 18** for a typical assembly. Clean and inspect all the parts.

If the drive pinion is worn or damaged, a matched pair of pinion and crownwheel gears must be fitted and correctly meshed by a VW Service Station. This must also be done if the double-row bearing is renewed. Worn third- or fourth-speed gears must be renewed in pairs with the mating gear on the main drive shaft. First- and second-speed gears are renewed in pairs, but only if the teeth are damaged.

Refer to the preceding section on dismantling the main drive shaft for details of the manner of checking the clearance of the stop rings according to **FIG 6 : 17**. The same clearance is required and the same comments about premature wear also apply. Check all thrust washers and shims and renew if obviously worn.

72

Reassembling the pinion shaft:

If facilities do not exist for checking the torque required to turn the taper roller bearing type of pinion shaft when it is installed, the assembling must be entrusted to a VW Service Station. This torque must lie within a certain range and can only be corrected by renewal of the large bearing, the pinion or the housing.

1 Heat the inner races of the pinion bearing and the needle bearing in an oil bath to 100°C or 212°F. Fit the first inner race, install the bearing and press the second inner race into position. When dealing with earlier ballbearing types, fit the inner races so that the numbers stamped on one face of a ring are in-line with those on the second ring.

2 Fit the thrust washer and inner race of the needle bearing. Cool the pinion to room temperature in paraffin and press the parts fully home in a powerful press. Fit the needle bearing and thrust washer and tighten the round nut to a torque of 90 lb ft for ballbearing types and to 108 to 144 lb ft for taper roller bearing types.

3 If the pinion shaft is fitted with taper roller bearings, install the pinion in the housing and tighten the bolts of retainer 12 to a torque of 36 lb ft. Turn the pinion 15 to 20 revolutions in each direction and then use a gauge to record the torque while turning steadily. With new bearings the torque should be 5 to 18 lb in. After vehicles have covered at least 300 miles the torque should be 1.7 to 6.1 lb in. **Never run the pinion if the gauge shows no torque or if there is end float in the bearing.**

4 Refer to **FIG 6 : 18** and fit the shims for first-speed gear. Fit the bearing retainer and the first-speed gear and the hub of synchromesh assembly 10. Check the end float between the first-speed gear and the thrust washer at **A**. It should lie between .004 and .010 inch. Correct by using suitable shims which are available in five thicknesses. Fit the first-speed stop ring. This differs from the second-speed stop ring by having smaller recesses for the shifting or blocker plates and a larger number of oil scraper grooves.

5 Assemble the synchromesh assembly 10. Slide the outer sleeve and gear over the hub so that the slots for the shifting plates are in-line. The longer boss of the hub must face away from the pinion as shown in the illustration. Fit the shifting plates and spring rings. The rings should be offset to each other so that their ends do not coincide and they must be properly engaged behind the steps on the shifting plates or blockers. Slide the assembly onto the shaft and turn the first speed stop ring until the shifting plates engage in the slots.

6 Continue the assembling by fitting the second-speed gear, the needle roller bearing and the third-speed gear. The hubs of the synchromesh assembly and of the third-speed gear must not be tight on the shaft, so test by hand for backlash or free movement. This backlash of not less than .002 inch is controlled by a concave washer which is fitted in front of the third-speed gear and which exerts a pressure on the gear and hub to prevent vibration in the drive. It is fitted to newer pinion shafts and checking instructions are given in Operation 7. The pressure should be about 220 lb. If the hub and gear are tight on the shaft or the concave washer

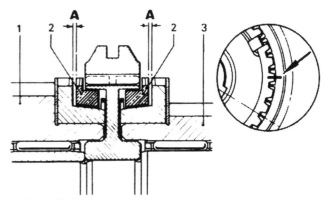

FIG 6 : 17 Stop ring clearance on synchronizing assembly is measured at A. Inset shows marks on sleeve and hub correctly aligned (4-synchromesh transmission, main drive shaft)

Key to Fig 6 : 17   1 Fourth-speed gear   2 Synchronizer stop rings   3 Third-speed gear
Clearance at **A** not less than .024 inch

presses too heavily on them the transmission may be noisy. Conversely, if the washer is not tight enough, second gear may tend to jump out. Special devices are needed to find the thickness of shims required to give the desired result and this is part of the VW Service Station equipment. The principle is readily understood if it is realised that the fourth-speed gear 4 (lower) is pressed on to the pinion shaft against a shoulder and it also presses on the tubular spacer to the rear, between the fourth and third-speed gears. The spacer does not fill the gap because it must also accommodate the concave washer and the shims. The concave washer is always .041 inch thick and its action as a spring must be restricted to .007 inch. The length of the spacer is measured accurately and subtracted from the distance between the shoulder on the pinion shaft and the front face of the third-speed gear. If this difference is .08 inch and the combined thickness of the concave washer and its prescribed spring travel is .048 inch, the space to be filled by shims is .08 —.048 inch=.032 inch. Nine thicknesses of shim are available and the nearest to the figure is selected.

7 The concave washer follows the third-speed gear, backed up by the shims and the spacer. Heat the fourth gear and the front needle roller bearing inner race to 90°C or 194°F, and after fitting the key in the shaft the parts are pressed home. The wider shoulder on the gear should abut the spacer. Older transmissions had a gear which was stamped or marked in black and the mark should face to the front. **Note that the concave washer can only be installed on newer pinion shafts** (from Chassis No. 602615). Check by measuring the distance from the second shoulder on the pinion shaft (the one which locates the rear face of the fourth-speed gear) to the front face of the pinion. This distance is 164.5 —1.0 mm for early shafts and 165.9 —.4 mm for later shafts (or 6.476 —.039 inch and 5.531 —.016 inch).

Servicing the differential assembly:

Before tackling this operation, note that renewal of the differential cage or housing, or of the crownwheel, means that the meshing of the drive gears must be readjusted

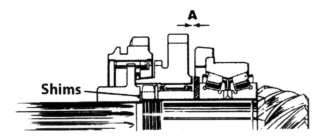

FIG 6:18 First gear end float is measured at A. Shims are used to obtain required end float of .004 to .010 inch (4-synchromesh transmission)

by a VW Service Station. The renewal of worn parts must therefore be confined to the differential gears and shaft. It can be seen in **FIG 6:2** that there is a locking pin through the shaft of pinions 22. Remove any peening round this pin and drive it out. The shaft can then be drifted out and the differential pinions removed. Check the teeth and the spherical bearing surfaces at the back of the pinions, and inside the housing, for wear and renew the shaft if it is shouldered. The crownwheel can be removed if necessary, bearing in mind that renewal will also mean renewal of a matched drive pinion and readjustment of the meshing. The wired bolts on later transmissions are also fitted with spring washers on some models. If spring washers are fitted to a housing without machined recesses to accommodate them, check that the bolt heads do not foul the casing. Before refitting the crownwheel remove all dirt and burrs from the mating surfaces. Tighten the bolts to a torque of 45 lb ft and wire the heads so that any tendency to unscrew will tighten the wire. Generally speaking it is preferable to replace the wired bolts with the later self-locking bolts with integral washer.

When reassembling the differential gears, peen round the hole after the locking pin for the shaft has been driven home.

Adjustment of drive pinion and crownwheel :

These are produced in matched pairs and cannot be renewed singly. To ensure silent running and correct tooth contact, the pinion must be adjusted endwise, and the crownwheel given a backlash of .0067 to .0098 inch. **FIG 6:19** shows the markings given on each pair of gears but note that markings have also been given on the face of the pinion instead of on the shaft. The gear sets are made either by Gleason or Klingelnberg and identified by **G** or **K**. The deviation from **R** is given as r and stamped on the pinion face as well as the crownwheel. The figure represents hundredths of a millimetre, and is added to **R** to give the correct endwise position of the pinion with respect to the centre line of the differential assembly.

Normally it is only necessary to readjust the meshing of the pinion and crownwheel if parts have been renewed which affect the position of the two gears. If the differential housing, side covers or differential bearings are renewed it is only necessary to rest the position of the crownwheel. Both gears must be reset if the transmission casing, the two gears or the rear bearing on the pinion shaft have been renewed.

Referring to **FIG 6:2** it can be seen that adjustment to the thickness of shims 13 will enable the dimension **R + r**

to be determined. Then the ring gear is adjusted to give the required backlash by altering the thickness of shims. It must be remembered however, that the side covers are fitted in such a way that they preload the differential bearings by .0028 inch on each side, so that shims to that thickness must be added to each end of the differential housing.

VW Service Stations use a number of specialized jigs and precision measuring devices when carrying out the measuring of the gears and it is not an operation which can be lightly undertaken by the normal owner. It is therefore recommended that the adjustment is entrusted to them.

Renewing the main drive shaft oil seal :

This is the seal at the rear end of the drive shaft 20, just in front of the clutch release bearing. This can be renewed with the transmission installed in the vehicle. To remove the old seal, remove the engine and the clutch release bearing 19. Prise out the seal, taking care not to damage the transmission casing. To fit the new seal, lightly coat the fitting surface with sealing compound and oil the shaft and the sealing lip. Slide the seal into place, being careful not to damage the lip on the splines nor to displace the spring surrounding the lip. Keep the seal square and drive it home with a tubular drift.

Reassembling the transmission :

Being satisfied that all worn parts have been renewed and that the clearance between the selector forks and the operating sleeves does not exceed .004 to .012 inch, oil the parts well and proceed as follows:

1 Refer to **FIG 6:2** and fit the selector rod detent springs into the three outside holes in gear housing. Fit new plugs to close the holes. Fit a detent ball and insert the reverse selector rod complete with reverse lever and guide. The ball can be pressed down as the rod is inserted.

2 Perform the same operation with the two remaining selector rods, remembering that there are two interlock plungers to be introduced into the drillings between the three selector rod holes. There will then be a plunger between each outside rod and the centre one. Engaging a gear by moving either of the outside rods should lock the centre one. Engaging a gear by moving the centre rod should lock both the outside rods. The principle can be understood by referring to **FIG 6:16**.

3 Fit the bearings for the two shafts, locking the needle bearing outer race with the long setscrew. Prepare to fit the two shafts by fitting a strong rubber band round the small gear 11 (upper) at the rear of the main drive shaft and the large gear 11 (lower). Press the gear carrier bearings on to the shafts after placing selector fork into the sleeve for assembly 5. When pressing, lift the drive pinion slightly, make sure the selector fork is fitted to the selector rod and see that the fork does not jam on the shaft.

4 Install the selector fork to engage in assembly 10. Fit the reverse sliding gear with fork and attach to reverse lever. If no parts have been renewed which will affect the position of the selector forks, restore them to the marks or recorded measurements made during dismantling and tighten the clamping screws to a torque of 18 lb ft. Tighten the reverse lever guide screw to

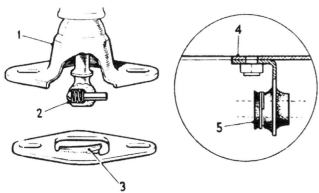

FIG 6:20 Details of gearlever mounting. Inset shows bush in tunnel for shift rod

Key to Fig 6:20   1 Gearlever cover   2 Peening to retain locating pin   3 Lever stop plate with turned-up edge
4 Tunnel   5 Shift rod bush

Gearshift housing:

From January 1966 the housing has a sealing ring pressed in to make a better seal for the gear shift rod. From August 1966 the housing is also tapped so that a reversing light switch can be fitted.

Starter outboard bush:

This has been reduced in bore from 12.5 mm to 11 mm on later models.

Higher ratios:

From Chassis No. 614456 the gears were altered so that third-speed gears had 28 and 23 teeth instead of 29 and 22, and fourth-speed gears had 23 and 28 teeth instead of 24 and 27. The newer gears can be identified by a groove in the teeth.

Synchromesh assemblies:

1966 models had improved synchromesh assemblies for first and second-speed gears. The cones on the gears were increased in diameter and the stop rings became almost the same size, so that care is needed not to interchange them. The first-speed ring has narrower slots and an increased number of oil slots in the inner cone.

The synchromesh hub for first and second-speed gears was modified to have six centring lugs for the outer sleeve. The shifting or blocker plates were flatter and had an inside groove to accept the spring ring. The modified hub needs thicker shims to adjust first gear end float. The parts can be fitted to older transmissions, but do not fit new-type stop rings to earlier hubs.

Selector rod:

The rod for first and second-speed gears was lengthened and supported by a bearing in the web between the transmission gears and the final drive. This rod cannot be installed in earlier transmissions.

First-speed gear:

The gear was widened on later models from 11.8 to 13.55 mm and the oil groove dropped. The teeth were widened 2 mm and the bearing retainer bolts modified to give clearance for the gear.

6:8 Gearlever and control rod

Removing and refitting lever:

Proceed as follows:

1 Remove the front floor mat and then the screws retaining the gearlever cover to the tunnel. Lift out the lever assembly.
2 Turn the spring to remove it clear of the pin. This spring-loaded pin is not fitted to very early models. It can be seen in **FIG 6:20**.
3 Remove the top plate from the tunnel and clean all components. Renew the rubber boot if deteriorated. Check the spring-loaded pin for free movement. The ball end of the lever is peened over to retain the pin.

To refit the gearlever, first grease all the working parts. Fit the diamond-shaped stop plate to the tunnel with the turned-up lip on the righthand side. Fit the lever assembly so that the pin at the lower end engages in the slot in the shifting rod socket inside the tunnel. The flanges of the ball housing must then fit over the stop plate. Fit the retaining screws and tighten when the lower part of the gearlever is vertical when in neutral. Difficulty in selecting gears may be cured by moving the ballhousing slightly and it may be necessary to enlarge the slotted holes slightly.

Removing and refitting shift rod:

1 Raise the vehicle on blocks and release the handbrake. Remove the gearlever as just instructed.
2 Remove the cover plate under the pedal linkage. Cut the locking wire and remove the front screw from the forward shift rod coupling. Detach the handbrake cables from the equalizer.
3 Withdraw the shift rod and guide towards the front and remove the guide.
4 To remove the rear shift rod, remove the rear screw of the coupling instead of the front one. Withdraw the rod rearwards and take the front rubber boot off the sleeve. Remove the rear shift rod coupling. Remove the rear rubber boot and bushes from the rod.
5 Check guides, bushes, rubber boots and rods for wear and check rods for misalignment. Coat the rods with grease and lubricate the guides and bushes.
6 Fit the rods and secure the coupling screws. Check the gear selecting and fit locking wire to the coupling screws when satisfied. See that the rubber boots are fitted to the protection sleeve for the rear rod. Finally, adjust the handbrake and check its operation.

In cases where the rear shift rod touches the bottom of the protection tube, make sure the correct rubber mounting has been fitted to the gearshift housing at the front end of the transmission. From Chassis No. 503026 the mounting holes were positioned lower down and harder rubber introduced. This was identified by a red paint spot. If it is found that the shift rod is lower than a central position in the tube (it is preferable for it to be about .040 inch above), then slacken the mounting nuts and lift the transmission until the rod is in the correct place. Some temporary packing can be introduced between the rod and tube to hold it in position while the work goes on. Prepare some eccentric washers of plates about .10 inch thick which will fit in place of the spring washers and bear against the upper ridge of the mounting when the nuts are tight. This will prevent the transmission from dropping. Sufficient hole clearance for moving the mounting plate can be obtained by filing the holes downwards.

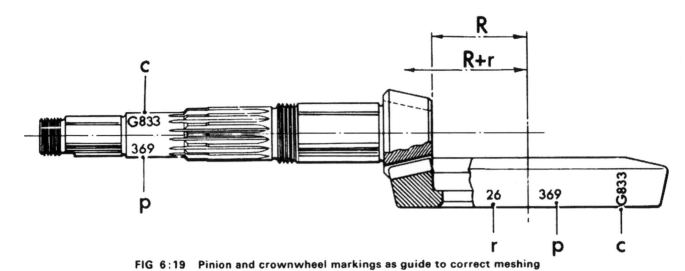

FIG 6:19 Pinion and crownwheel markings as guide to correct meshing

Key to Fig 6:19 **R** Standard dimension from crownwheel centre line to drive pinion face 58.70 mm **r** Deviation from **R** in hundredths of a millimetre **p** Matching number of gear set **c** Type of teeth (G = Gleason, K = Klingelnberg) and number of teeth 8 to 33

14 lb ft. **If the selector forks must be reset, the adjustment can only be done in a special jig which simulates the assembly in the transmission casing. This is used in VW Service Stations and is the only satisfactory way of positioning the selector forks correctly.** It is suggested that if an old transmission casing is available it is possible to cut holes to see what is happening when the gears are selected and to reach the fork clamping screws. It is important to adjust the forks only after the drive pinion has been correctly adjusted for mesh with the crownwheel and after tightening the shaft nuts at the front end to the correct torque values. Tighten first to 87 lb ft, slacken off and then retighten to 43 lb ft. Always fit new lockplates.

5 Before fitting the completed assembly into the main transmission casing, check the starter motor bush for wear. Also check the bushes and shaft for the clutch release mechanism. Note that reverse drive gear 15 must not be too loose on the splines or vibration of the main drive shaft may cause trouble with a worn oil seal, lost lubricant and a slipping clutch. If a new transmission casing is fitted it will be necessary to readjust the meshing of the crownwheel and pinion. A new side cover means the resetting of the crownwheel only.

6 Insert the needle bearings and spacer for reverse shaft, locking the spacer with the shouldered setscrew. Fit the main drive shaft needle bearing and secure. Fit the reverse gear shaft with the thrust washer. At the rear, fit the Woodruff key and reverse drive gear. Check that the circlip has not been strained and fit it.

7 Set the pinion shaft with the pinion uppermost and fit the shims 13. Fit two temporary studs about 4 inches long in opposite holes in the bearing retainer 12 to act as guides. Fit a new gasket to the gear carrier and insert the gear assembly into the transmission casing whilst engaging the reverse gear with its shaft. Use a rubber hammer to make sure that the drive pinion is fully home, remove the two temporary studs and tighten the bearing retainer setscrews on new lockplates to a torque of 36 lb ft. On later models there is

an extended selector rod which may not move freely because of an adjacent retainer setscrew. Turn the screw until there is clearance but do not exceed the stipulated torque figure and check the rod for freedom. Use only setscrews of 10K grade.

8 Oil the rear seal and fit the rear half of the main drive shaft. Screw the shafts together and then back off until the splines are in line. **The shafts must not be screwed tightly together.** Slide reverse gear into place and fit the circlip, making sure that it is not strained as it must fit securely in its groove.

9 Fit the differential assembly. Early models had covers which were sealed with jointing compound, but a paper gasket was fitted later. The thickness of this gasket will affect the preload on the differential bearings and the position of the crownwheel so use a genuine spare part. **When installing the differential assembly make certain that the correct shims are fitted to each side.** Fit the second cover and tighten the nuts to a torque of 22 lb ft. Check the tightness after a run of 300 miles in case of settling. Tighten the gear carrier nuts to 14 lb ft.

10 Engage both reverse and third or fourth gears to lock the transmission and tighten the shaft nuts if they have not already been done. Use new lockplates, tighten to 87 lb ft, slacken off and retighten to 43 lb ft. Turn up locking tabs.

11 Set the three selector rods in the neutral position and fit the gearshift housing 3.

6:7 Transmission modifications

Rear oil seal:

On later transmissions there is an extension to the main casing in front of the oil seal and this is machined with an oil return thread to relieve the seal of excess lubricant. To make the thread effective, the ground part of the rear main drive shaft is extended forwards. If a new type of transmission casing is installed the new rear drive shaft must also be fitted. This new type of shaft can be used in older transmissions.

6:9 Fault diagnosis

(a) Difficulty in changing gear

1 Bent or worn gear shift mechanism
2 Faulty synchronizing mechanism
3 Faulty clutch or release bearing
4 Clutch cable maladjusted

(b) Crashing of gears when changing down

1 Check 2, 3 and 4 in (a)
2 Wrongly placed or broken synchromesh spring rings
3 Transmission oil too thick

(c) Slipping out of first and second gears

1 Weak or broken selector rod detent springs
2 Worn gear on pinion shaft
3 Excessive end float of pinion shaft gears
4 Worn bearings
5 Selector fork wrongly positioned
6 Gear shift mechanism worn

(d) Slipping out of third or fourth gears

1 Check 1, 4, 5 and 6 in (c)
2 Worn teeth on synchromesh sleeve
3 Excessive end float of main shaft gears

(e) Gearbox noisy in neutral

1 Worn bearings and bushes
2 Excessive end float of main drive shaft
3 Incorrect or insufficient lubricant

(f) Gearbox noisy in forward gears

1 Worn drive and pinion shaft bearings
2 Worn reverse idler or constant mesh gears
3 Incorrect or insufficient lubricant

(g) Oil leaks

1 Damaged or worn rear oil seal, scored shaft
2 Damaged joint washers or joint faces
3 Worn gear shift bushes
4 Loose cover nuts

Inches	Decimals	Milli-metres	Inches to Millimetres — Inches	Inches to Millimetres — mm	Millimetres to Inches — mm	Millimetres to Inches — Inches
1/64	.015625	.3969	.001	.0254	.01	.00039
1/32	.03125	.7937	.002	.0508	.02	.00079
3/64	.046875	1.1906	.003	.0762	.03	.00118
1/16	.0625	1.5875	.004	.1016	.04	.00157
5/64	.078125	1.9844	.005	.1270	.05	.00197
3/32	.09375	2.3812	.006	.1524	.06	.00236
7/64	.109375	2.7781	.007	.1778	.07	.00276
1/8	.125	3.1750	.008	.2032	.08	.00315
9/64	.140625	3.5719	.009	.2286	.09	.00354
5/32	.15625	3.9687	.01	.254	.1	.00394
11/64	.171875	4.3656	.02	.508	.2	.00787
3/16	.1875	4.7625	.03	.762	.3	.01181
13/64	.203125	5.1594	.04	1.016	.4	.01575
7/32	.21875	5.5562	.05	1.270	.5	.01969
15/64	.234375	5.9531	.06	1.524	.6	.02362
1/4	.25	6.3500	.07	1.778	.7	.02756
17/64	.265625	6.7469	.08	2.032	.8	.03150
9/32	.28125	7.1437	.09	2.286	.9	.03543
19/64	.296875	7.5406	.1	2.54	1	.03937
5/16	.3125	7.9375	.2	5.08	2	.07874
21/64	.328125	8.3344	.3	7.62	3	.11811
11/32	.34375	8.7312	.4	10.16	4	.15748
23/64	.359375	9.1281	.5	12.70	5	.19685
3/8	.375	9.5250	.6	15.24	6	.23622
25/64	.390625	9.9219	.7	17.78	7	.27559
13/32	.40625	10.3187	.8	20.32	8	.31496
27/64	.421875	10.7156	.9	22.86	9	.35433
7/16	.4375	11.1125	1	25.4	10	.39370
29/64	.453125	11.5094	2	50.8	11	.43307
15/32	.46875	11.9062	3	76.2	12	.47244
31/64	.484375	12.3031	4	101.6	13	.51181
1/2	.5	12.7000	5	127.0	14	.55118
33/64	.515625	13.0969	6	152.4	15	.59055
17/32	.53125	13.4937	7	177.8	16	.62992
35/64	.546875	13.8906	8	203.2	17	.66929
9/16	.5625	14.2875	9	228.6	18	.70866
37/64	.578125	14.6844	10	254.0	19	.74803
19/32	.59375	15.0812	11	279.4	20	.78740
39/64	.609375	15.4781	12	304.8	21	.82677
5/8	.625	15.8750	13	330.2	22	.86614
41/64	.640625	16.2719	14	355.6	23	.90551
21/32	.65625	16.6687	15	381.0	24	.94488
43/64	.671875	17.0656	16	406.4	25	.98425
11/16	.6875	17.4625	17	431.8	26	1.02362
45/64	.703125	17.8594	18	457.2	27	1.06299
23/32	.71875	18.2562	19	482.6	28	1.10236
47/64	.734375	18.6531	20	508.0	29	1.14173
3/4	.75	19.0500	21	533.4	30	1.18110
49/64	.765625	19.4469	22	558.8	31	1.22047
25/32	.78125	19.8437	23	584.2	32	1.25984
51/64	.796875	20.2406	24	609.6	33	1.29921
13/16	.8125	20.6375	25	635.0	34	1.33858
53/64	.828125	21.0344	26	660.4	35	1.37795
27/32	.84375	21.4312	27	685.8	36	1.41732
55/64	.859375	21.8281	28	711.2	37	1.4567
7/8	.875	22.2250	29	736.6	38	1.4961
57/64	.890625	22.6219	30	762.0	39	1.5354
29/32	.90625	23.0187	31	787.4	40	1.5748
59/64	.921875	23.4156	32	812.8	41	1.6142
15/16	.9375	23.8125	33	838.2	42	1.6535
61/64	.953125	24.2094	34	863.6	43	1.6929
31/32	.96875	24.6062	35	889.0	44	1.7323
63/64	.984375	25.0031	36	914.4	45	1.7717

UNITS	Pints to Litres	Gallons to Litres	Litres to Pints	Litres to Gallons	Miles to Kilometres	Kilometres to Miles	Lbs. per sq. In. to Kg. per sq. Cm.	Kg. per sq. Cm. to Lbs. per sq. In.
1	.57	4.55	1.76	.22	1.61	.62	.07	14.22
2	1.14	9.09	3.52	.44	3.22	1.24	.14	28.50
3	1.70	13.64	5.28	.66	4.83	1.86	.21	42.67
4	2.27	18.18	7.04	.88	6.44	2.49	.28	56.89
5	2.84	22.73	8.80	1.10	8.05	3.11	.35	71.12
6	3.41	27.28	10.56	1.32	9.66	3.73	.42	85.34
7	3.98	31.82	12.32	1.54	11.27	4.35	.49	99.56
8	4.55	36.37	14.08	1.76	12.88	4.97	.56	113.79
9		40.91	15.84	1.98	14.48	5.59	.63	128.00
10		45.46	17.60	2.20	16.09	6.21	.70	142.23
20				4.40	32.19	12.43	1.41	284.47
30				6.60	48.28	18.64	2.11	426.70
40				8.80	64.37	24.85		
50					80.47	31.07		
60					96.56	37.28		
70					112.65	43.50		
80					128.75	49.71		
90					144.84	55.92		
100					160.93	62.14		

UNITS	Lb ft to kgm	Kgm to lb ft	UNITS	Lb ft to kgm	Kgm to lb ft
1	.138	7.233	7	.967	50.631
2	.276	14.466	8	1.106	57.864
3	.414	21.699	9	1.244	65.097
4	.553	28.932	10	1.382	72.330
5	.691	36.165	20	2.765	144.660
6	.829	43.398	30	4.147	216.990

CHAPTER 7

THE REAR AXLE AND SUSPENSION

7:1 Description

To divide the transmission and rear axle system into two reasonably logical sections it has been decided to treat the gearbox and final drive gears as a unit in **Chapter 6**, and to cover the rear axles, universal joints, rear hubs and the suspension layout in this chapter.

The plan view in **FIG 7:1** shows how the rear axles and suspension components are arranged. The two axle shafts run inside tubes or casings 1, the outer ends of the shafts being supported in ballbearings. The splined ends of the shafts carry one-piece hubs and brake drums. The inner ends of the shafts are flattened to slide in slots in the differential side gears as shown in **FIG 7:2** and **7:6**. Each slot is shaped to carry a pair of trunnion blocks or fulcrum plates, and these allow the shafts to swing, yet continue to drive, as the outer ends move up and down with road undulations. The outer ends of the shaft tubes are constrained to move in an arc by thin steel radius arms 2. These arms are splined to the outer ends of two torsion bars mounted inside casing 3. The inner ends of the torsion bars are splined to a fixed anchor block on the centre line inside the casing.

The bearing housings at the outer ends of the axle tubes also have brackets to which the lower ends of tubular dampers 7 are connected. The top ends of the dampers are connected to brackets bolted to the body. The inner ends of the tubes can move freely in large spherical housings which form ball joints centring on the axle shaft universal joints. Dirt is excluded by rubber boots or dust sleeves 4. These parts are clearly shown in **FIG 7:4**, and may also be identified in the cross-sectioned view of the rear axle in **FIG 7:2**. The outer ends of the axle tubes carry cast iron housings 15 and 16 (see **FIG 7:2**). Inside each housing is a pair of reduction gears 13 and 14, giving the lower ratio needed for industrial use. The lower gear is splined to a shaft carrying the rear hub and brake drum 11.

7:2 Routine maintenance

The differential assembly and the transmission gears are contained in one housing and are lubricated with the same oil. For routine maintenance instructions refer to **Chapter 6, Section 6:2**.

The reduction gears at the outer ends of the halfshafts have a separate oil supply, the level of which should be checked at 3000 mile intervals. Every 30,000 miles the oil should be changed. Remove the drain plug shown in **FIG 7:3** while the oil is hot. Refill with .44 pints of SAE.90 Hypoid oil through the filler plug on top of the housing.

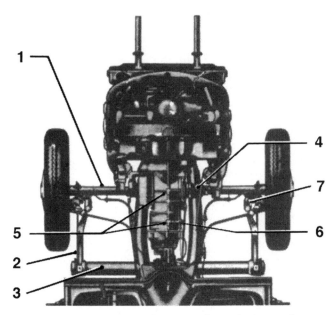

FIG 7:1 Plan view of the rear axle and suspension layout

Key to Fig 7:1   1 Axle tube   2 Radius arm (spring plate)
3 Torsion bar housing 4 Dust sleeve 5 Transmission drain plugs
6 Level plug   7 Telescopic damper

7:3 Removing and servicing axle shafts

On Transporters produced after May 1959:

Axle shafts can be removed with the transmission in the vehicle providing there is clearance to remove the retainer plate shown detached in **FIG 7:4**. Check this point before going too far, as the alternative is to remove the axles and transmission complete. The wheel bearing needs a special puller which fits between the races, but if the assembly is out of the vehicle, the axle can be pulled off with the bearing in place.

If there is clearance for the retainer plate, proceed as follows:

1 Loosen the axle nuts while the vehicle is still on the ground. **These are so tight that it is dangerous to try to slacken them initially while the vehicle is on jacks or stands.** Raise the vehicle and support firmly on stands. Remove axle nuts and rear wheels.

2 Pull off the brake drum after releasing the handbrake and slackening off the brake shoes. Remove rear brake drums and wheel cylinders as described in **Chapter 10, Sections 10:4** and **10:5**.

3 Remove brake cable retainer together with adjusting screws and nuts. Extract the leaf spring clicker. Unscrew four bolts from central bearing housing and pull off backplate. Remove adjuster screws and brake shoe anchor.

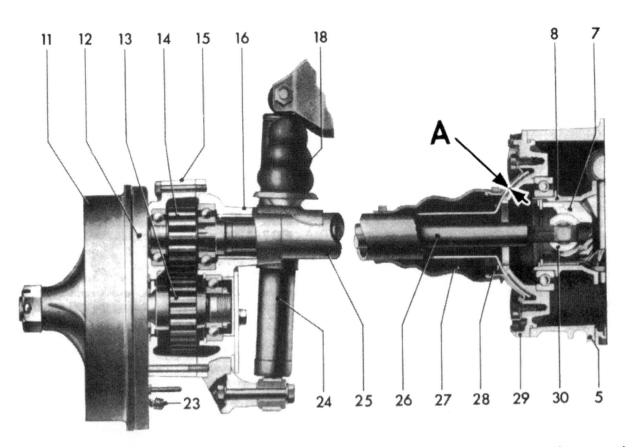

FIG 7:2 Sectioned view of Transporter rear axle, showing reduction gears. A indicates clearance between axle tube and retainer

Key to Fig 7:2   5 Transmission casing   7 Differential side gear   8 Differential housing   11 Brake drum
12 Brake backplate   13 Reduction driven gear   14 Reduction drive gear   15 Reduction gear cover   16 Reduction gear case
18 Bump rubber   23 Bleed screw   24 Telescopic damper   25 Axle tube   26 Axle shaft   27 Dust sleeve
28 Axle tube retainer   29 Final drive cover   30 Fulcrum plate

4 Extract the outer hub bearing and remove the reduction gear as described under 'Servicing the reduction gear'. Unscrew the rear damper lower mounting bolt. Refer to **Section 7:4** before releasing the spring radius arm from the housing flange.

5 Unscrew the six nuts securing the axle tube retainer 28 and pull off the axle tube 25 together with dust sleeve 27 and axle tube retainer 28 as shown in **FIG 7:4**. Remove gasket and plastic insert.

6 Remove the circlip and thrust washer from deep inside the transmission case as shown in **FIG 7:7**. Pull out the axle and, if necessary, remove differential side gear (7 in **FIG 7:2**).

On Transporters produced before May 1959:

On Transporters made before May 1969 the shafts cannot be removed until the transmission is removed from the vehicle. Refer to **Chapter 6** for this operation.

Servicing the dust sleeve:

One item which may need replacing is the rubber boot or dust sleeve (27 in **FIG 7:2**). The one-piece sleeve cannot be renewed without removing the bearing housing at the outer end of the axle tube. **This is pinned, and is also a press-fit. It may be damaged if suitable equipment is not available.** To avoid the need to carry out such an operation it is possible to cut away the old sleeve and fit a replacement part which is split for easy fitting. This is done as follows:

Remove the clips and cut the defective sleeve to remove it. Clean the axle tube and the retainer. Note that all this may be done without removing the axle tube from the transmission, if necessary.

Use a little jointing compound on the mating faces of the new split sleeve after checking that the large end is the correct size for the retaining plate. The split in the sleeve should be horizontal and face to the rear. Do not tighten the screws or the clips until the axle is in a loaded condition with the vehicle on the ground. See that the sleeve is not twisted or strained and then tighten the screws and clips moderately.

The axle tubes, shafts and side gears:

Inspect all parts for wear. The spherical surfaces of the transmission casing and the axle tubes must be smooth. Note that the spherical plastic inserts which are sandwiched between the metal faces were introduced in September 1958. Assemble the tube and retainer plate and check the end float or clearance as indicated at **A** in **FIG 7:2**. Early figures given are much in excess of those for more recent models, the original working clearance being given as .016 to .024 inch with a wear limit of .027 inch. Too great a clearance will result in wear and noise. The latest figures for clearance are a maximum limit of .008 inch with the retainer plate nuts tightened to 14 lb ft. Select gaskets which will give the required clearance. A small hole near one of the stud holes signifies that the gasket is .010 inch thick. A thicker gasket has two holes. If it is necessary to fit the retainer plate without a gasket, jointing compound must be used. The reduction of axle tube end play can be done with the axle in the vehicle.

FIG 7:3 Removing reduction gear drain plug on Transporter. Note four bolts securing radius arm to gear case

FIG 7:4 Removing axle tube from final drive casing. Gasket and split plastic insert are clearly shown

FIG 7:5 Removing circlip and thrust washer from side gear

FIG 7:6 Measuring clearance between axle shaft and fulcrum plates

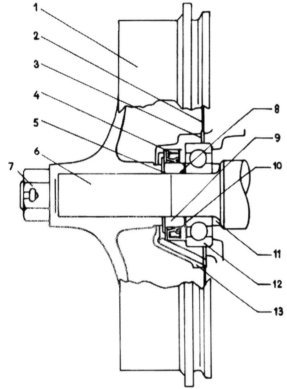

FIG 7:7 Section through rear hub and brake drum

Key to Fig 7:7   1 Brake drum   2 Brake backplate
3 Gaskets   4 Oil seal   5 Oil flinger   6 Axle shaft
7 Axle nut   8 Washer (1200 Transporter only)   9 Outer
spacer   10 Gasket   11 Inner spacer   12 Ballbearing
13 Bearing cover

Check the axle shafts, differential side gears and their thrust washers. The maximum permissible runout of the shaft at the point where the wheel bearing fits, is .002 inch. Small errors may be corrected by straightening the shaft **cold**. At the transmission end, assemble the shaft in a side gear with the fulcrum plates, as shown in **FIG 7:6**. Check the clearance between the flats and the plates with feeler gauges. It should lie between .001 and .010 inch. If the clearance is excessive renew the parts or fit oversize fulcrum plates, which are marked with a groove on the face.

The widest rounded part of the flattened end of each shaft must not have a clearance in the side gear which exceeds .004 inch, with a minimum of .001 inch. On some later shafts, one of these spherical surfaces is fitted with a spring-loaded ball which eliminates side clearance.

Shafts and side gears are mated in pairs and colour-coded in three groups, yellow, blue and pink, although there is also a pair coloured green for early models. The gears are marked with a spot in the recess, and the shafts by a painted ring six inches from the flattened end. The colour groups are graded as follows:

Paint mark	Inner diameter of side gear	Outer diameter of shaft
Yellow	2.3600 to 2.3610 inch	2.3570 to 2.3582 inch
Blue	2.3610 to 2.3622 inch	2.3582 to 2.3598 inch
Pink	2.3625 to 2.3638 inch	2.3602 to 2.3610 inch
Green	2.3641 to 2.3649 inch	2.3614 to 2.3622 inch

Note that excessive clearance at the transmission end of axle shafts may lead to noisy operation.

The following modifications are listed for Transporters.

The spring-loaded ball fitted in one edge of the flattened end of the axle shaft started at Chassis No. 589709. The modified shafts can be fitted up to Chassis No. 469447.

From Chassis No. 543946 the side gears have a wider face for the thrust washers. Modified gears can be installed only from Chassis No. 469447 (May 1959).

To keep the side gear to differential pinion backlash to .004 to .008 inch, a thrust washer 3.2 mm thick was installed from Chassis No. 522240 instead of one 3 mm thick as originally fitted. Then from Chassis No. 584155 a 4 mm thrust washer was fitted and the circlip groove moved out to suit. The modified housings are marked '4'.

The wheel bearing and oil seals:

If a suitable bearing puller is available, the wheel bearing can be removed after the brake backplate is taken off, and the axle shaft and tube need not be detached from the transmission. **FIG 7:7** shows the paper gaskets 3 which will be found when the bearing cover 13 is removed. After removing the cover and backplate, take off the outer spacer 9, the small sealing ring 10 round the shaft 6, and the washer 8 (1200 Transporter only). Note that later models do not have an oil deflector and tube fitted inside the brake drum, but have an oil flinger 5 like a large washer on the outside of the outer spacer. Extract the bearing 12 and the inner spacer 11 which is rounded on the inner face to fit the radius on the shaft. When an oil flinger is fitted, the cover has a lug and drilling on the lowest edge, and the gasket has a hole in it. This allows oil which passes the seal 4 to drain away behind the backplate.

Clean and examine the ballbearing when dry, renewing it if worn, or rough when spun. Renew the rubber sealing rings and the gasket. Renew the oil seal if oil leakage has been persistent or the lip is damaged but do not forget to insert the oil flinger washer into the cover first, on vehicles without a drain tube in the drum. Check the surface of the outer spacer where it contacts the lip of the seal. Remove scores and rust and polish with very fine emerycloth. Clean out the drain hole in the cover.

Check the splines on the shaft and in the brake drum and renew the parts if the splines are worn and slack. When renewing an oil seal, press it in with the sealing lip facing the bearing. On early models with the oil deflector

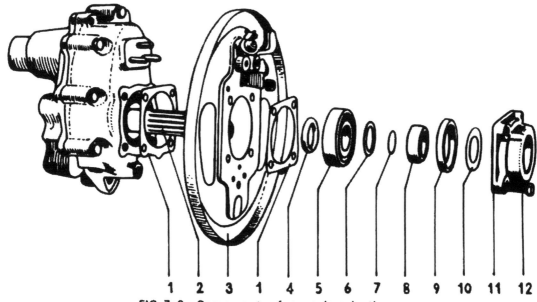

FIG 7:8 Components of rear axle reduction gear

Key to Fig 7:8 1 Gasket 2 Axle shaft 3 Brake backplate 4 Inner spacer 5 Ballbearing
6 Washer (1200 Transporter only) 7 Gasket 8 Outer spacer 9 Oil seal 10 Oil deflector
11 Bearing cover 12 Cover retaining screw

and tube fitted inside the brake drum, press the seal into the cover until its inner face is $\frac{3}{16}$ inch from the edge of the inner recess in the cover. It will then be almost flush on the outside.

To reassemble, fit the radiused spacer on the shaft and press in the bearing. Fit the washer and small sealing ring, followed by the outer spacer with its chamfered bore contacting the ring. The bevel on the outer surface then acts as a lead when fitting the cover and oil seal. Oil this surface lightly and carefully fit the backplate and cover on new gaskets. Make sure the drain hole is at the bottom, and tighten the screws to a torque of 40 to 43 lb ft. On models with deflector and drain tube in the drum, check that the tube is as close to the drum as possible so that it cannot foul the brake shoes. Fit the drum and tighten the nut moderately. When the vehicle is back on the ground, tighten the nut to 217 lb ft and fit a new splitpin. Do not slacken the nut in an attempt to align the splitpin holes. Check the transmission oil. Bleed and adjust the brakes.

Servicing the reduction gear :

Use **FIG 7:2** for reference. To remove the assembly, remove the brake drum and backplate as described in **Section 7:3**, remembering to slacken the axle nut before lifting the vehicle on jacks or stands. Remove the outer spacer, the shaft seal and washer and then the outer ballbearing. Remove the inner spacer which fits against the radiused shoulder of the shaft. Remove all the screws holding the gearcase halves together. Tap the casing cover with a rubber hammer to part it from the rear housing and lift off the gasket.

Remove the circlip from the axle shaft and pull off the outer bearing, the axle gear shaft gear and the inner ballbearing. The reduction gear shaft may be a press-fit into the inner bearing, in which case it can be withdrawn and the inner bearing removed. If the reduction gear shaft and inner bearing are of the type illustrated, it will be seen that

the bearing is located by a circlip, and a locking ring secures the inner race of the bearing to the shaft. In this assembly it is necessary to gain access through a plug in the rear housing, and if the bearing is unworn it would be inadvisable to tackle this operation. If the gear and bearing need renewal it would be best to consult a VW agent. Use the previous instructions when renewing the oil seal.

Clean the joint faces of the two housings. Clean and check the bearings for roughness and the gears for wear or cracking of the teeth. To reassemble, drive in the two inner bearings if the earlier type has been dismantled. Fit the drive gear and its outer bearing, renewing the circlip if it has weakened. Use a new gasket and fit the two housings together, tightening the screws evenly and securely. Replace all the driven shaft parts, fitting new gaskets when assembling the backplate and the bearing cover. If the cover has a lug which is drilled for drainage, this must be fitted at the bottom. After the drum is fitted, tighten the shaft nut moderately, and then to a torque of 217 lb ft after the vehicle is standing on the ground. **Lock with a new splitpin and do not slacken the nut in an attempt to align the holes.**

Put .44 pints of SAE.90 Hypoid oil in the reduction gear casing, check the transmission oil and bleed the brakes after adjustment.

Note that it is not advisable to try pressing the inner housing 16 off the outer end of the axle tube 25 as it is easily damaged beyond repair. This operation should be left to a VW agent.

7:4 Removing transmission and rear axle

For convenience when working it is often preferable to remove the complete transmission and rear axle from the vehicle. Before tackling this operation it is essential to point out that a clamp is needed when detaching or attaching the radius plate or arm to the reduction gear casing.

FIG 7:9 Releasing transmission front mounting (left). Arrows indicate transmission carrier bolts (right)

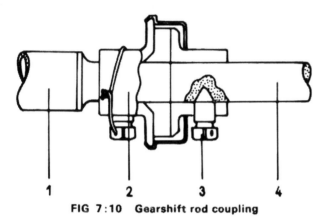

FIG 7:10 Gearshift rod coupling

Key to Fig 7:10   1 Gearshift rod   2 Coupling   3 Screw
4 Transmission shift rod

The fixing bolts can be seen above the spanner in **FIG 7:3**. Because the plate is heavily preloaded, the ends of the bolt threads will be stripped unless the load is taken by a clamp over the axle tube and under the edge of the plate. This clamp must be long enough to draw the spring plate into place when refitting the securing bolts. Proceed as follows:

1 Disconnect battery earthing strap. Remove the rear wheels as detailed in **Section 7:3**.
2 Remove the engine as instructed in **Chapter 1**.
3 Remove the rear brake components as detailed in **Section 7:3**. Disconnect rear brake hoses. Withdraw handbrake cables from backplate. If the rear axle is to be exchanged leave the brake drums on the axle and disconnect brake cables at the handbrake lever and pull them through the guide tubes. The cables remain on the axle, but the brake pipelines and fittings on the axle tubes should be removed.
4 Loosen dust sleeves (27 in **FIG 7:2**). Unscrew the rear damper lower mounting bolts. Disconnect clutch cable from operating lever, withdraw the rubber boot and remove cable and sleeve from the bracket on lefthand final drive cover.
5 Disconnect electrical cables from starter motor terminals 30 and 50. Refer to **FIG 7:10** and remove

locking wire and unscrew rear screw 3. Move the gear-lever in order to disengage coupling 2 from gear selector rod 4.
6 Place the clamp over axle tube and under the spring plate and take the load. Bend down the locking tabs and unscrew four spring plate mounting bolts. Repeat for the other side.
7 Unhook the accelerator cable from the retainer on the gear carrier.
8 Unscrew the nuts at the transmission housing front mounting as shown in **FIG 7:9**. Take the weight of the rear axle on a trolley jack. Unscrew two bolts on transmission carrier indicated by arrows in righthand view of **FIG 7:9**.
9 Withdraw the trolley jack complete with rear axle assembly. Take care not to bend or damage the main drive shaft. A good plan is to drill a hole in a block of wood to take the end of the drive shaft then bolt the wood to the transmission housing flange.

7:5 Installing transmission and axle

1 Lift the assembly into place and fit the two mounting bolts arrowed in the righthand view of **FIG 7:9**, after greasing them well. Now loosen the nuts attaching the rear carrier to the rubber mountings. This sequence must always be followed before the front mounting is secured.
2 Tighten the nuts of the front mounting plate as shown in the lefthand view of **FIG 7:9**. Then tighten the rear mountings. This will avoid distortion and premature failure of the rubber mountings.
3 Reconnect the gear shift rod coupling ensuring that the pointed end of rear screw 3 (see **FIG 7:10**) engages fully in the recess in the gear selector rod 4. Lock the screw with a piece of soft iron wire. The correct assembly of the coupling is important because it is possible that a defect at this point could lead to reverse gear being selected at the same time as second gear, with disastrous results. It might also make it difficult to drop down to first or second gear.
4 Refit the spring plate mounting bolts, using the clamp to draw the plate into position. Align the holes in the spring plate and the reduction gear housing using two tapered pins. Tighten the mounting bolts to a torque of 72 to 87 lb ft in the order shown in **FIG 7:11**. Securely tighten the damper lower mounting bolts.
5 Refit the engine as described in **Chapter 1**. Adjust the clutch pedal free play as described in **Chapter 5**. Bleed and adjust the brakes as explained in **Chapter 10**. Inspect the brake drum splines for signs of wear or damage. Renew the brake drum if necessary. Lightly coat the splines with graphite grease. Refit the rear wheels and lower the vehicle to the ground, tighten rear axle shaft nuts to a torque of 217 lb ft. Tighten the dust sleeve clips, ensuring that the sleeves are not strained or distorted.

7:6 Removing rear torsion bars

Before starting this operation the owner must realise that renewal of any of the parts of the suspension system or of the frame and transmission mountings means that the rear wheels will need realignment. If, however, it is only a matter of renewing a defective torsion bar, it is possible to reset the camber of the wheels by checking the angles of the two spring plates or radius arms which connect the axle tubes to the torsion bars. This check can only be carried out by setting the vehicle so that the body sill is level and by using a spirit-level type of protractor for measuring accurate angles.

To remove a torsion bar proceed as follows:

1 Stand the vehicle on level ground and adjust until the door sill is horizontal on both sides. As the rear wheel(s) must be removed, this implies that the vehicle must be supported on blocks or stands.

2 Disconnect the handbrake cables from the lever and withdraw them slightly to the rear.

3 Remove the lower damper mounting bolt. Remove the bolts securing the spring plate or arm to the bearing housing and pull the axle rearwards until it is clear of the slot in the arm. Remove the torsion bar cover as shown in **FIG 7:12**. Withdraw outer rubber bush. Early models had a longer outward extension of the arm at this point, a longer bush and a cover with a large central hole in it. The later bush has four irregularly spaced ribs on the outside rim and is stamped 'Oben' for top.

4 Pull the spring plate and inner rubber bush off the torsion bar, levering it away from the stop rib on the mounting bracket. Withdraw torsion bar from frame cross-tube. If the bar is broken, the inner part cannot be removed until the opposite torsion bar has been withdrawn and a long bar used to push out the piece.

5 Mark the bar(s) on the end so that it can be replaced on the same side as that from which it was removed. Although it was stated on early models before 1960, that the bars could be interchanged, this is definitely not so with bars which are stamped **R** for right and **L** for left on the outer end. These bars are prestressed in manufacture and must be fitted as marked. **It is most important to take the greatest care of torsion bars once they are removed. Do not mark or scratch them in any way or they may fail prematurely.** Make sure the protective paint remains intact as corrosion may also lead to failure. Replace a bar which is rusty or one which has splines with evident signs of wear.

7:7 Installing and setting torsion bars

It will be evident that the unloaded angle of the spring plate or radius arm will affect the camber of the rear wheel. This angle can be measured with an accurate protractor and adjustments made by rotating the torsion bar. The Transporter torsion bars have 44 splines on the inner end and 48 splines on the outer end. Turning the inner end by one spline alters the angle by 8 deg. 10'. Turning the radius arm by one spline alters the angle by 7 deg. 30'. Thus, the inclination of the arm can be adjusted to positions within 40' of the required figure.

Install a torsion bar as follows:

1 Grease the splines and install the bar and radius arm (spring plate). Check that the door sill is still exactly horizontal.

2 Place a spirit-level type of protractor on the upper edge of the arm. Lift the arm very lightly to take up any play. Check the angle against the required figure. The arm

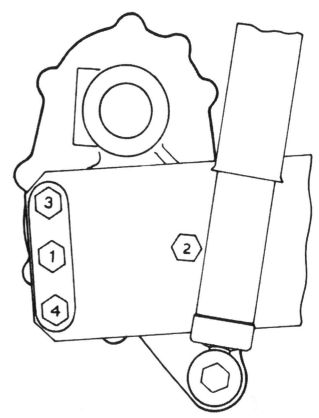

FIG 7:11 Tighten the spring plate mounting bolts in the order shown

FIG 7:12 Removing torsion bar end cover

must, of course, be otherwise free and not attached to the axle, nor against the stop on the bracket.

3 The radius arm setting varies according to model. The inclination of the unloaded radius arm or spring plate is given as 20 deg. ± 30', except on ambulances and fire appliances. These should be set at 18 deg. 40' ± 20', and 20 deg. 30' ± 20' respectively. In cases of difficulty with suspension settings it would be advisable to consult a VW agent.

The procedure for reassembling the radius arm is as follows:

Completing the installation of torsion bar and radius arm :

Having adjusted the setting of the radius arm to the correct position, proceed to complete the assembly as follows:

1 The cover or retaining plate over the outer end of the bar cannot be bolted down until the radius arm is over the stop rib along the bottom edge of the mounting bracket. It might be possible to use a jack to lift the arm until it can be tapped into place. The best way to tackle this operation is to make up a clamp from a length of screwed rod, one end of which hooks over the body mounting bracket above the middle of the arm. A loose hook fits under the lower edge of the arm, backed up by a nut on the screwed rod which forms the backbone of the clamp. Tightening the nut will slide the hook up the rod and raise the arm.

2 With the arm above the stop, press it home on the torsion bar. Coat the rubber bush with flake graphite, fitting the later type which has four ribs so that the word 'Oben' is at the top.

3 Fit the cover or retaining plate. Use two longer screws diagonally to pull the cover down until the other two can be inserted. On very early models, fit the torsion bar hub cap and secure it with a splitpin.

4 Clean the mating surfaces of the rear end of the arm and the axle bearing housing, swing the axle forward into the slot and align the nicks made before dismantling. Fit the bolts and new lockplates. Use a torque of 72 to 87 lb ft on the bolts.

5 Connect the handbrake cables to the lever and adjust according to the notes in **Chapter 10**.

At the beginning of this Section it was pointed out that renewal of any parts of the suspension and transmission system might affect the alignment of the rear wheels. After the radius arm setting is known to be correct it is essential to have the system checked by an optical alignment gauge if such renewal has taken place. This will ensure that details like the toe-in or toe-out of the rear wheels are correct according to the maker's specification for the model concerned.

7:8 Rear dampers

Standard dampers are not adjustable and it is difficult to test dampers without proper equipment. Clamping one end in a vice and moving the other by hand will show whether there is resistance, but it will not determine efficiency in operation. Trouble with poor road-holding and pitching over bad roads might be attributed to defective dampers. As they are not capable of being adjusted or topped up, the only cure is to renew them. If the dampers are used in conditions of tropical heat, continuous heavy loads or the likelihood of damage by stones, fit the special heavy duty dampers which are available. In this case, always fit a complete set of four. Where conditions are particularly bad it is recommended to fit the Koni adjustment type.

Removal :

Loosen the wheel nuts, lift the vehicle and take off the wheel. Remove the damper fixings at top and bottom and lift the damper away. Check the condition of the rubber bushes in the ends and renew them if the damper is fit for further service. If new dampers are to be fitted, make quite sure that they are the correct replacement type. The front and rear dampers are the same size but must not be interchanged. The rear dampers are painted grey for identification purposes.

Installation :

Inspect bushes and rubber grommets for signs of damage or wear, renew them if necessary.

Fit the dampers in the reverse order of removal. Fit the spring washers and tighten the nuts to a torque of 43 lb ft.

7:9 Fault diagnosis

(a) Noisy axle

1 Worn wheel bearings
2 Excessive clearance of transmission universal joint
3 Excessive clearance of axle tube spherical joint
4 Worn shaft and hub splines, loose nut

(b) Excessive backlash

1 Worn axle shaft, trunnion pads or side gear
2 Worn shaft and hub splines, loose nut

(c) Oil leakage

1 Defective seals or gaskets
2 Overfilling transmission oil

(d) Poor handling, bad road-holding

1 Torsion bars 'settled' or broken
2 Worn torsion bar splines
3 Radius arm (spring plate) setting incorrect
4 Wheel alignment incorrect
5 Dampers ineffective
6 Bump rubbers defective or missing
7 Equalizer spring defective
8 Faulty transmission mountings
9 Loose radius arm to housing fixings

CHAPTER 8

THE FRONT SUSPENSION

8:1 Description

The principles underlying the VW suspension system have remainded unchanged since its inception, but there have been many detailed improvements over the years. The cutaway views in **FIG 8:1** show the components of the assembly for a LHD installation, but it is only the alterations in the steering layout which need to be considered when dealing with RHD Transporters.

The assembly consists of two tubular beams 15, rigidly joined together and bolted across the front of the chassis frame. Shaped sideplates form the top anchorages of the telescopic dampers 12. Independent suspension is provided by a pair of trailing torsion arms 14 which pivot on bearings 6 and 8 inside the axle beam tubes. At these ends the torsion arms are coupled to the multi-leaf torsion bars 7 which are housed in the tubes. As each torsion bar assembly is held against twisting by an anchor block in the middle of each tube, this gives the effect of two torsion bars from one assembly, making four bars in all. The outer ends of the torsion arms are joined to the steering knuckle and stub axle 13, on early vehicles by adjustable linkpins and bushes, and on 1966 models onwards by ball joints 2, the top one being mounted in an eccentric bush which permits adjustment for camber angle.

A stabilizer bar 11 is attached to the lower torsion arms by rubber bushes and clips to prevent roll. Telescopic hydraulic dampers 12 are fitted with bump rubbers on the latest models, while earlier vehicles had rubbers mounted between the torsion arms.

The one-piece hubs and brake drums run on ball-bearings on the earlier vehicles and on taper roller bearings on later models.

8:2 Routine maintenance

The vehicle must be lifted until the front wheels are off the ground for the lubrication service to be effective.

On vehicles which have linkpins instead of ball joints in the torsion arms as shown in **FIG 8:1**, it is advisable to apply the grease gun every 1500 miles, or every 750 miles if road conditions are bad. **FIG 8:2** shows the four nipples on the axle tubes and **FIG 8:3** shows the kingpin and linkpin lubrication points.

From 1966 onwards, the introduction of ball joints reduced the number of grease nipples to the four shown in **FIG 8:3**, and these must be lubricated every 6000 miles or once a year if that mileage is not reached.

87

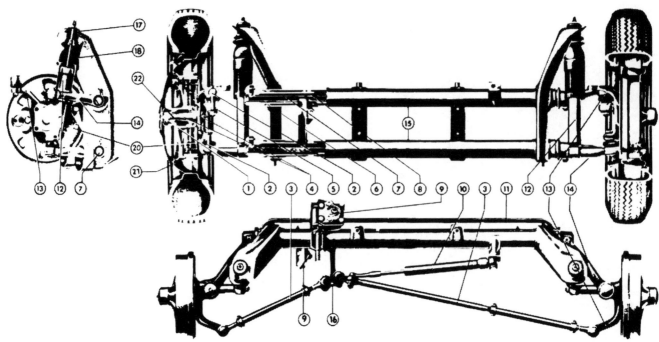

FIG 8:1   Layout of recent front suspension system using ball joint links (LHD illustrated)

Key to Fig 8:1   1 Clamp nut   2 Steering knuckle ball joint   3 Tie rods   4 Taper roller bearings
5 Eccentric bush for camber adjustment   6 Needle bearing for torsion arm   7 Torsion bar   8 Plastic and metal bush for torsion arm
9 Steering gearbo   10 Steering damper   11 Stabilizer bar   12 Damper   13 Steering knuckle   14 Torsion arm
15 Front axle beam   16 Steering drop arm   17 Damper ring   18 Rubber bump stop   19 Wheel lockstop
20 Brake backplate   21 Brake drum   22 Stub axle

Wipe the nipples free from dirt before applying the gun and continue pumping until fresh grease can be seen exuding from the seals. If grease gets on the tyres or brake hoses, wipe it off immediately as it will cause deterioration. While the grease gun is available it is also advisable to attend to the nipples on the steering gear as indicated in **Chapter 9.**

Every 30,000 miles the front hubs should be dismantled and the old grease cleaned out. The bearings must then be packed with fresh grease and each hub reassembled and adjusted as instructed in **Section 8:3.** Do not put grease in the caps.

For all front lubrication use a multi-purpose, lithium based grease.

Other maintenance jobs which will ensure trouble-free motoring will be attention to tyres and tyre pressures, the checking and adjustment of toe-in and a check of all the dust seals round the joints.

8:3 Attention to front hubs and drums

These instructions will cover the two types of hub bearings, the original ball type and the recent taper roller type.

Removing ballbearing hubs:

1 Prise off the hub caps 7 in **FIG 8:4** after removing the wheels. Before the lefthand cap can be removed it will be necessary to take out the cotterpin which passes through the squared end of the speedometer cable.

2 Lift the tabs on the locking plate and remove the two nuts 12 from each axle. The lefthand stub has a left-hand thread. Pull off the brake drums after backing off the brake shoes.

Clean inside the drums and examine the braking surfaces. If they are scored or out-of-true the drums can be refaced. Do both drums and then fit oversize brake linings. Clean the backplate free from abrasive dust.

Hub ballbearings:

It will be necessary to remove the bearings from the hub for cleaning and packing with fresh grease, or for renewal in the case of defects. The section in **FIG 8:4** shows the arrangement of the components of a hub, in this case it is the lefthand one, which carries the speedometer cable.

Dismantle it as follows:

1 Pulling off the drum will bring the outer ballbearing 8 with it. At the inner end of the hub will be found the outer race of the inner bearing 9 and the oil seal 10.

2 Draw the inner race off the stub axle, followed by the spacer 11. Note that the oil seal lip runs on the outer surface of the spacer.

3 Do not disturb the outer races of the ballbearings unless they are defective. Clean all the parts and examine for cracks and pitting. If required, press out the outer races and oil seal, working from the opposite end in each case.

Reassemble as follows:

1 If new outer races are to be pressed into the hub, they must be a tight fit. Slackness here will allow the races to move in the hub, causing wear which will lead to the scrapping of the hub and drum.

2 Fit the spacer first, after checking the sealing surface, which must be highly polished and free from cracks

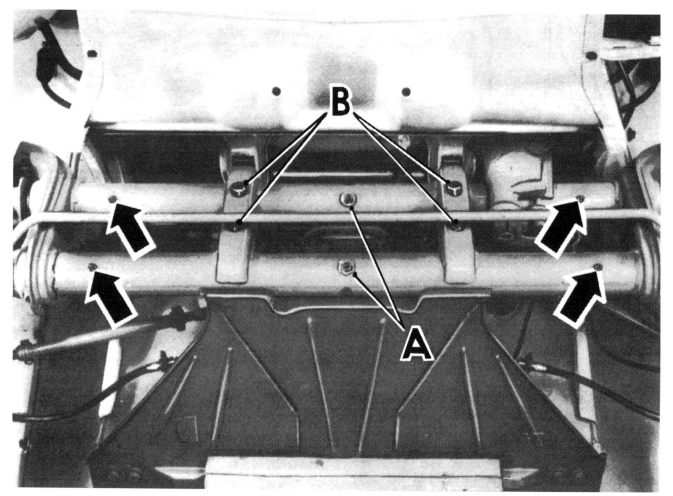

FIG 8:2 Arrows show torsion arm grease nipples. Central torsion bar fixings at **A**, axle beam to frame fixings at **B**

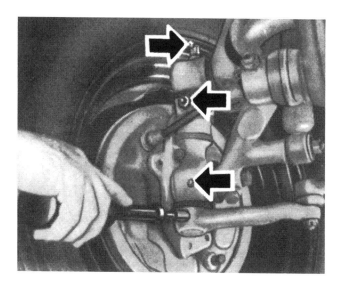

FIG 8:3 Kingpin and linkpin lubrication points indicated by arrows

or pitting. Drive the inner race onto the axle with a tubular drift.

3 Renew the oil seal if lubricant has been leaking into the brake. The lip and spring face into the hub. Pack the hub space between the outer races with multi-purpose lithium grease.

4 Grease and fit the inner cage and balls, then the oil seal. Fit the drum. Grease and fit the outer cage and balls and then drive home the inner ring of the outer race, being careful not to damage the balls and races with excessive force.

5 Fit the thrust washer and inner nut. Tighten this to take up all play. Fit the lockwasher and outer nut. It is now necessary to lock the two nuts together in such a position that the thrust washer can just be moved with a screwdriver, yet without perceptible play in the hub and drum. **The bearings must not be pre-loaded.** If the assembly tightens up when the outer nut is tightened, slacken off the inner nut a little at a time until satisfied. Then lock both nuts by bending up the tabs of the lockwasher. **Replace the hub cap but do not fill with grease.**

Note that all old grease must be removed, particularly if the grade is not known. Test the bearings after cleaning and drying them. Do not try to renew individual parts such as balls or cages alone.

Servicing hubs with taper roller bearings:

Prior to pulling off the drum and hub in the manner just described for the ballbearing type, slacken the pinch bolt which clamps the spindle nut and then unscrew the nut. The lefthand nut has a lefthand thread. The bearing parts can be seen in **FIG 8:1**.

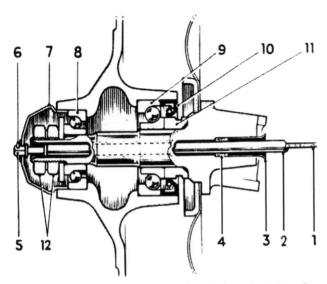

FIG 8:4 Section through earlier hub and stub axle, showing bearings and speedometer drive

Key to Fig 8:4   1 Speedometer cable   2 Plastic sleeve
3 Guide tube   4 Rubber seal   5 Squared end of
speedometer cable   6 Splitpin   7 Cap with square hole
to drive cable   8 Outer ballbearing   9 Inner ballbearing
10 Oil seal   11 Spacer   12 Axle nuts

Attend to all the components as instructed in the preceding section on ballbearing hubs. Assemble and lubricate them in the same way.

The bearings are adjusted so that there is a very small amount of free play. **There must not be any preloading or the bearings will be damaged.** First tighten the spindle nut to a torque of 11 lb ft, which will take up all slack. Then turn the nut back so that there is end play of the hub. This can be checked by dial gauge and should lie between the limits of .001 and .005 inch. At the higher figure there will be perceptible play in the hub but this is permissible and need only be reduced if there has been noise from the front wheels.

When the adjustment is correct, tighten the clamping bolt to a torque of 7 lb ft.

8:4 Adjusting early suspension

Jack up the front of the vehicle. Check end float of linkpins by rocking the front wheels. If play is perceptible, adjust the linkpins as follows:

The method of adjustment is shown in **FIG 8:5**. The spanner is shown fitted to the flats on a linkpin and the pinch bolts are indicated by arrows. The linkpins have helical grooves on their shanks and these engage the pinch bolts, so that turning a pin screws it in or out. Before trying to adjust the clearance, clean all parts free from dirt and hard lubricant, then apply the grease gun until fresh grease oozes out. Slacken the pinch bolts and tighten the linkpins fully. Slacken back about ⅛ of a turn and then retighten gently until the first resistance is felt, or until the torsion arms are free yet without sideplay. Tighten the pinch bolts and secure lower bolts with cotterpins. If adjustment is impossible, the shims may be worn and these must be renewed as instructed in **Section 8:5**. Worn pins and bushes can also be renewed.

After adjusting the linkpins, the toe-in of the front wheels must be checked as instructed in **Chapter 9**.

8:5 Servicing early suspension

To dismantle the suspension without removing the axle beam assembly from the vehicle, proceed as follows:

1 Raise the front end and support it firmly on blocks. Remove the front wheels. Detach the speedometer cable at the squared end (see **FIG 8:4**) by removing splitpin 6.
2 Disconnect brake hose from bracket and withdraw the hose from the clip. Remove the brake drum and brake assembly and then take off the brake backplate.
3 Detach the outer ball joints of the steering tie rods from the steering arms, checking in **Chapter 9** for the best method to use. Do not hammer on the threaded end of the pin.
4 Extract cotterpin from eye of lower torsion arm then remove the upper and lower pinch bolts. Tap out the linkpins 10 (see **FIG 8:6**) an equal amount each time until the stub axle 7 is free. Remove the dust covers 3.
5 Check that each linkpin has a total of eight shims 2, a retainer 9 and rubber seal 4. Note the arrangement of the shims.

Linkpin bearings:

When the dust covers 3 are removed, the linkpins and needle rollers can be pushed out. Remove the stop screw and press out the needle bearing bushes 12. Clean the parts and examine for wear. Always renew bushes and rollers in sets.

Press new bearing bushes into the kingpins 14 and 15 so that the ends do not protrude into the recesses which accommodate the shims. If the bushes are not a tight press-fit the kingpins are also in need of renewal.

Torsion arms:

Check the working faces of the torsion arm eyes for wear and reface them if necessary. Also check the arms to ensure that they are not bent. Do not try to straighten a bent arm, it must be renewed. Removal of the torsion arms and torsion bars is covered in **Sections 8:7** and **8:8**.

Kingpins and bushes:

To service the kingpins, bushes and stub axle, proceed as follows:

1 With the linkpins and bushes removed and the stop screw out of the way, unscrew the grease nipple 1.

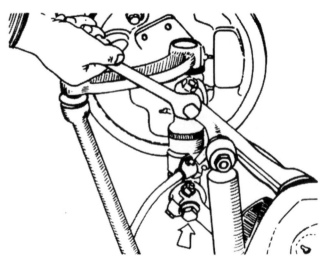

FIG 8:5 Adjusting end float of torsion arm linkpins on earlier suspension

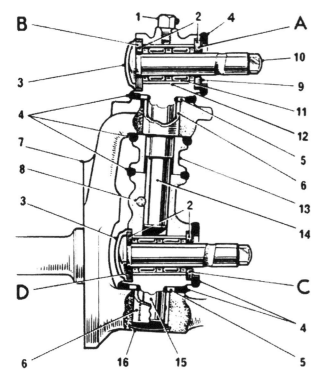

FIG 8:6 Linkpin and steering knuckle assembly. Note needle roller bearings for linkpins. **A, B, C** and **D** are the four positions for shim adjustment

Key to Fig 8:6 1 Grease nipple 2 Shims 3 Dust covers 4 Rubber seals 5 Thrust washer 6 Kingpin bush 7 Steering knuckle and stub axle 8 Knuckle stop screw 9 Seal retainer 10 Linkpin 11 Needle rollers 12 Roller bearing bush 13 Spacer 14 Upper kingpin 15 Lower kingpin 16 Blanking cap

2 Arrange a puller so that it lines up with the axis of the upper kingpin 14 and withdraw the pin. This will also release the spacer 13 to permit the removal of the lower kingpin 15.

Clean and inspect for wear. Apart from the kingpins and their bushes it may also be necessary to renew the thrust washers 5, and seals 4.

To renew the lower bush, press out cap 16. Both bushes can be pressed out without difficulty.

Press in new bushes so that their faces are flush with the stub axle eyes. Use a piloted reamer to size the bushes to a bore of .8677 to .8699 inch, turning the reamer in the cutting direction only. The kingpins should be a hand push fit without perceptible play. Insert the end cap at the bottom and peen it securely to make an oiltight fit.

Reassembling

Reverse the dismantling procedure, being satisfied that the stub axle is in good condition. If the wheel bearing inner races are not a tight press-fit on the stub shaft, due probably to repeated removals, the axle must be renewed. Then proceed as follows:

1 Fit the lower kingpin with thrust washer but no seal. Insert spacer 13 without rubber seals and check the end play. If it exceeds .006 fit an oversize spacer.

2 Grease and fit the lower kingpin with thrust washer and seal, lightly greasing both washer and seal. Clamp the axle in a vice and use a lever to compress the bottom seal 4 until it is possible to insert the spacer.

3 Having checked that the lower kingpin can be moved by hand, fit the upper thrust washer and seal, then press the upper kingpin into place, making sure that the working surfaces are greased.

4 Settle the rubber seals into position and fit the stop screw with its head to the rear and tighten the nut. Because of tolerances in the steering lock, three different head sizes are used. If it is necessary to renew the stop screw ensure that the replacement has the same size head.

5 Check both pins for freedom of movement, it should be possible to turn them by hand. Screw the grease nipple 1 into the top kingpin.

Fitting the linkpins:

Check the end faces of the torsion arm eyes for signs of wear or scoring. If necessary, the faces should be reconditioned by a VW agent. Place a straightedge across the top eye and measure the displacement of the lower eye. This should be .28 ± .08 inch. Correct if necessary by inserting .02 inch shims. The four positions of the shims are shown at A, B, C and D in **FIG 8:6**. The total number of shims is eight, arranged in accordance with the following table:

Displacement in inches	Number of Shims			
	A	B	C	D
.20	1	7	5	3
.22	2	6	5	3
.24	2	6	4	4
.26	3	5	4	4
.28	**3**	**5**	**3**	**5**
.30	4	4	3	5
.32	4	4	2	6
.34	5	3	2	6
.36	5	3	1	7

If the displacement is greater than .28 inch add shims to 'A' from 'B' and to 'D' from 'C'. If the displacement is less, add shims to 'B' from 'A' and to 'C' from 'D'. Work to the nearest dimension in the lefthand column. If the deviation exceeds the tolerance of ±.08 inch do not fit extra shims, but remove the torsion arm and check for excessive wear or bending. Renew the torsion arm if necessary. **Do not attempt to straighten a bent torsion arm.**

Lubricate the link bushes, shims and linkpins with universal grease and refit them to the torsion arms. If the alignment is correct and the shims arranged in accordance with the table, the linkpins should push in quite easily and the contact faces of the upper and lower torsion arms and shims should meet simultaneously. Insert both torsion arm pinch bolts from below on the lefthand side of the vehicle and the lower pinch bolt from below and the upper bolt from above, on the righthand side. Adjust and lock the linkpins as detailed in **Section 8:4**. Fit the brake backplate, brake assembly and brake drum as described in **Chapter 10**. Reconnect the brake hose, bleed and adjust the brakes as described in **Chapter 10**. Check the front wheel camber and toe-in as described in **Chapter 9**.

8:6 Servicing later suspension

In August 1965 a redesigned front axle assembly was introduced. This is the type shown in **FIG 8:1** where the following features can be seen. The main axle tubes 15 were spaced farther apart, the parallel linkpins were

FIG 8:7 Features of the latest suspension system. Arrow indicates notch in eccentric bushing

Key to Fig 8:7 1 Steering ball joint nut 2 Hexagon of eccentric bushing 3 Steering knuckle ball joint nuts 4 Stabilizer bar clips 5 Arm to torsion bar locking screws and locknuts

replaced by ball joints 2, taper roller bearings 4 were fitted to the front hubs and the top eye fixing of the dampers was changed to a mounting with rubber rings 17 and a progressive bump stop 18.

Dismantling without removing axle beams from vehicle:

1 Lift the vehicle and remove the wheel(s). Detach the brake hose at the bracket and seal the brake pipeline with a bleed screw dust cap.

2 Remove the outer steering ball joint from the steering arm, referring to **Chapter 9** for details of the best method to use. Never hammer on the end of the ball pin thread (1 in **FIG 8:7**).

3 Remove the nut at the top of the damper above item 17. A thin 42 mm spanner will hold the hexagon just above the rubber stop 18 to prevent the damper from turning.

4 Remove the brake drum and backplate, referring to **Section 8:3** and **Chapter 10**.

5 Remove the nut 3 from the ball pin of the upper joint in **FIG 8:7**. Loosen the large nut 2. This is part of a tapered eccentric bush used to adjust camber.

6 Remove the lower ball joint nut 3. Both ball joint nuts are self-locking and can be used again. With the upper ball joint out of the way, press out the lower ball pin using a long threaded bolt with a nut and large washer fitted as an abutment against the underside of the upper eye in the steering knuckle. In case of difficulty refer to the instructions on removing steering ball joints in **Chapter 9**.

Clean and inspect the parts. **Bent steering knuckles and steering arms must not be straightened.** If the fit of the inner bearing races on the stub axle is impaired, renew the steering knuckle.

Upper and lower ball joints:

These can be serviced after removing the torsion arms as in **Section 8:7**. Before attempting to remove the rubber dust seals it is important to remove all external dirt

If the seal has been damaged and road grit has entered the joint, fit a grease nipple in place of the plastic plug and force grease through until clean grease emerges. Use narrow feeler gauges to check the clearance of the ball in the joint. Clearance new is .020 inch with a wear limit of .080 inch. If the upper joint needs renewal the eccentric bushing 2 can be pressed off the ball pin. To reassemble, fit and secure the dust seal using 1 mm wire or a spring ring according to the method used. Fit the plastic clip and make sure the ring does not twist. Force in grease until the seal is full, remove the grease nipple and fit a new plastic plug.

The ball joints are pressed into the torsion arms, being knurled to ensure a tight press-fit. Never try to refit a joint once it has been removed but fit a new one. If the torsion arm eye is oversize, an oversize joint is available which is marked with two notches instead of one.

To press out the upper joint, fit a nut to the ball pin to prevent it from coming out of the eccentric bush. Press in a new joint after lining up the joint notch with the notch in the torsion arm. Press out the lower joint. If the ball pin comes out first, follow up by pressing out the socket. Line up the notches when fitting new joints.

Reassembling:

This is carried out in the reverse order of dismantling. Fit the steering knuckle and ball joints to the torsion arms. Notice the notch in the eccentric bush which is arrowed in **FIG 8:7**. This must be fitted so that it faces forward. The bush can be turned by the large hexagon so that the camber angle of the wheel can be adjusted as discussed in **Chapter 9**.

Use self-locking nuts on the ball pins, tightening the 10 mm nuts to a torque of 29 to 36 lb ft and the 12 mm nuts to 36 to 50 lb ft. Install the dampers as instructed in **Section 8:9**. Tighten the tie rod ball joint nuts and lock with new splitpins. Fit the brake backplate and brake drum and install the hoses free from twist. Adjust and bleed the brakes. Adjust the wheel bearings as instructed in **Section 8:3**. Adjust the toe-in and camber as instructed in **Chapter 9**.

8:7 Removing torsion arms

The bearings for early torsion arms were plastic bushes pressed into the axle tubes. After March 1960 these were changed to an outer needle roller bearing 4 and an inner plastic and metal bush 8 as shown in **FIG 8:1**. Removing and pressing in these bearings to the correct depth requires the use of special equipment. It is recommended that the axle beam assembly is removed as in **Section 8:10** and the work entrusted to a VW agent.

Whatever the type, torsion arms are removed as follows:

1 Remove the link and steering knuckle on early models as instructed in **Section 8:5**. Disconnect the damper from the lower arm. On models with ball jointed steering knuckles, remove the knuckle complete with brake drum, and if the lower arm is to be removed, disconnect the stabilizer bar and damper as instructed in **Section 8:9**.

2 Loosen the locknuts and unscrew the setscrews 5 in **FIG 8:7**. These lock the arms to the torsion bars. The arms can now be drawn out of the axle tubes and the dust seals removed if necessary.

Clean and check the bearing surfaces for wear. Wear limit in the bushes is .009 inch. Excessive wear in the needle bearings can be cured by fitting oversize bearings. Early torsion arms which run in plain bearings may be changed with those on the opposite side if wear at the bearing points is only slight, but note that upper and lower arms are not interchangeable.

On early models, check the eyes for wear and reface if necessary. On both types, check the arms for cracks and distortion. **Do not try to straighten bent arms.** Renew the dust seals if they are defective and reassemble the arms to the axle tubes using lithium grease.

8:8 Removing torsion bars

The torsion bars consist of leaves of flat strip steel stretching from end to end of the axle beams. The outer ends are clamped in the torsion arms and the centre of each bar assembly is locked against turning. Remove torsion bars as follows:

1 Remove the torsion arms from one side as instructed in the preceding Section. Disconnect the front gear shift rod from the coupling and push it out of the way.
2 Unscrew the locknuts and setscrews indicated at **A** in **FIG 8:2**. These secure the central parts of the torsion bars.
3 Move to the side where the torsion arms are still installed and pull both them and the bars out of the axle tubes. Note that it is not necessary to mark the bars for correct reassembly if they are completely detached. The direction in which they have been twisted has no effect on their life.

Clean the bars and examine them carefully for cracks or breaks. Fit new bars if necessary. Coat them well with grease before inserting and check that the correct assembly of leaves is being fitted. Transporters have nine leaves.

Line up the recesses in the bars before fitting the setscrews and locknuts. Replace all the parts in the reverse order of removal.

8:9 Servicing stabilizer bar and dampers

From August 1965 Transporters have a stabilizer bar which is secured to the lower torsion arms by rubber-lined clips 4 (see **FIG 8:7**). When both front wheels move in the same direction the bar is inoperative, but it reduces roll when one wheel moves up much more than the other, for example, when cornering.

Removing stabilizer bar:

Lift the vehicle and take off the front wheels. The clips round the rubber bushes are secured by clamps on the underside. Bend up the tabs on the inner ends of the clamps and drive them off in an outward direction by using a piece of flat steel bar and a hammer. Open up the clips and remove the plates, stabilizer bar and rubber bushes. Renew any defective parts.

Refitting stabilizer bar:

Fit the rubber bushes to the bar and lift into place. Fit the clips with the tapered slot narrowing towards the outer ends of the bar. Compress the clips with a powerful wrench so that the clamps can be fitted. Drive the clamps inwards, tab first until they are positioned and then turn up the tabs to lock them in place.

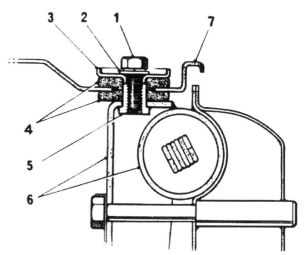

FIG 8:8 Body to axle beam mounting

Key to Fig 8:8   1 Body mounting bolt   2 Lockwasher
3 Spacer   4 Rubber packing pieces   5 Threaded bush
6 Axle beam   7 Body

Damper servicing:

The dampers are of the double-acting telescopic type and are not adjustable. If the front end of the vehicle pitches badly over bumpy roads or if, after bouncing the front end, the movement is not damped out almost immediately, then the dampers need checking. It is not enough to set the dampers vertically in a vice and test the resistance to movement up and down by hand. This will show that some damping is taking place but it is no check of efficiency.

Removal:

On early models remove the wheel, turn up the lockplates and remove the nut from the lower fixing and the bolt from the upper one. On later models, remove the wheel and the outer tie rod ball joint as instructed in **Chapter 9**. Removal of the ball joint will ensure that the tie rod is not bent. Also on later models, remove the lower eye from the torsion arm and unscrew the top nut while holding the large hexagon above the rubber buffer stop 18 (see **FIG 8:1**). Lift away the damper.

Testing:

Adequate testing can only be carried out on special equipment, but if there is no resistance to movement when the damper is compressed and extended, it is certainly due for renewal. Otherwise, if there has been any doubt about the damping effect, the only cure is proper testing or renewal. Slight leakage of fluid is not necessarily a serious matter if the damper is working. There is no provision for topping up, but there is an adequate reserve supply in the damper.

When renewing dampers, fit a pair and ensure that they are the correct type for the front axle. Rear dampers cannot be used. On recent models of the type shown in **FIG 8:1**, check the damper rings 17 and rubber buffer stop 18. It is possible to unscrew the top stud off the piston rod after pulling down the buffer. Check the rubber bush in the lower eye and have it renewed if necessary. A VW agent can fit a new oversize mounting pin to the lower torsion arm if the old one is worn or broken.

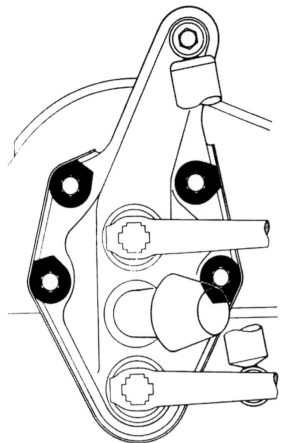

FIG 8:9 Refit the lockplates as shown

In conditions of tropical heat, high loading and possible stone damage there are heavy duty dampers available, but all four dampers must be renewed. For very arduous conditions the Koni adjustable damper is recommended.

Refitting dampers:

On early dampers with top and bottom eye fixing, this operation is simply a reversal of the removal procedure, but use new lockplates and tighten the nut and the bolt securely to prevent rattles. Lightly grease the lower pin.

On later dampers, lightly grease the lower pin, fit the damper and tighten the securing nut lightly. At the top end, fit the lower damper ring on the buffer stud with the spigot upwards. Feed the piston rod through the mounting bracket and fit the top damper ring with spigot downwards. Fit the top plate and nut. Tighten this nut fully, then tighten the lower nut to a torque of 22 to 25 lb ft.

8:10 Removing complete front axle

With some variations according to model, do the following:

1 Loosen the front wheel fixings, lift the vehicle and place on firm supports clear of the front axle and then remove the wheels.

2 Disconnect the hoses from the brake backplates or from the brackets, if hydraulic brakes are fitted. Plug the hoses with wooden plugs. With mechanical brakes, remove the front frame cover, disconnect the stoplight switch cable, remove the switch and unhook the cables from the brake push bar. Note that the brake cables must remain on the axle if it is being exchanged.

3 Remove cotterpin from speedometer drive in lefthand hub and pull cable out from behind stub axle.

4 Remove the coverplate under the pedal assembly. Remove the front gear shift rod and detach the clutch pedal cable. Disconnect handbrake cable at lever.

5 Detach the steering box drag link from the swing lever (see **Chapter 9**).

6 Remove the steering damper bolt and nut from the sidemember.

7 Take the weight of the axle, preferably on a trolley jack. The side brackets which carry the top mountings for the telescopic dampers are secured to the sidemembers by four bolts on each side as shown in **FIG 8:9**. Tap up the locking plates under the bolts and note how they are fitted. Lower the jack and wheel away the axle.

Dismantling of the axle has been covered in preceding Sections devoted to the individual assemblies. If the axle beam has been bent or damaged, remember that it is a welded assembly and must be renewed. **Do not try to straighten bent tubes.**

8:11 Installing complete front axle

This is the reverse of the dismantling procedure but check the clearance between the mounting plates and the sidemembers. If there is a gap when the axle assembly if offered up, fill it with compensating plates. These are available in thicknesses of .02 and .04 inch. Fit the lockplates in the positions shown in **FIG 8:9**, fit the eight bolts and tighten to 65 to 72 lb ft. It is advisable to check these bolts periodically.

Guide the draglink joint into the swing lever. Adjust the steering draglink. Refit the coupling on the front gear shift rod and lock the square-headed bolts. Adjust the clutch pedal free play. Connect the brake hoses without twist, then bleed and adjust the brakes as described in **Chapter 10**. Check front wheel alignment as described in **Chapter 9**.

8:12 Fault diagnosis

(a) Wheel wobble

1 Unbalanced wheels and tyres
2 Worn steering ball joints
3 Incorrect steering angles
4 Weak, broken or incorrectly angled torsion bars
5 Worn hub bearings

(b) Erratic steering

1 Check 1, 2, 3 and 4 in (a)
2 Bent torsion arms
3 Wear in linkpins or ball joints
4 Unequal torsion bar angles on opposite sides
5 Incorrect alignment of steering knuckles on linkpins, excessive end float
6 Uneven tyre wear or pressures
7 Defective dampers
8 Incorrect steering angles
9 Worn torsion arms and bearings, worn kingpins

(c) Rattles

1 Worn steering ball joints
2 Lack of lubrication
3 Excessive end float of steering knuckle on linkpins
4 Loose damper mountings, rubber bushes faulty

(d) Excessive pitching and 'bottoming'

1 Dampers inoperative
2 Bump or buffer rubbers missing or faulty
3 Broken torsion bar leaves

CHAPTER 9

THE STEERING

9:1 Description

Transporter are fitted with a ZF type steering gear which utilizes the worm and peg principle. This is illustrated in **FIG 9:1**. The inner steering column 9 has an integral worm machined at the lower end. A peg 11, which is mounted on a steering arm, engages with the worm and transmits rotary motion via a lever shaft 12 to drop arm 20. The steering linkage assembly is shown in **FIG 9:2**. The drop arm 6 is connected via a draglink 7 to a swing lever 8, which, in turn, is connected to the two steering knuckle arms 11 by a pair of tie rods 10. The steering box 4 is attached to the chassis by a bracket 5.

An adjusting screw 12 (see **FIG 9:1**) is provided to ensure correct engagement of the peg with the worm. End float of the worm can be eliminated by removing shims 15 from the lower end cover 16. The peg is free to rotate in a pair of tapered roller bearings 11 housed in the steering arm. The swing lever shaft is carried in a bracket which is welded to the lower suspension tube. Later vehicles are fitted with a steering damper, this is shown in **FIG 8:1** in **Chapter 8**.

Transporters with lefthand drive may be fitted with ATE type steering gear. This can be identified by the letters ATE stamped on the steering box. All the components of the two types are interchangeable except the following:
1 Steering box cover
2 Adjusting screw
3 Guide tube
4 Shim
5 Lockplate
6 Bearing flange for steering column tube

Replacement steering columns are supplied complete with upper and lower bearing rings, these must be changed before fitting to the ATE type steering gear.

9:2 Routine maintenance

Lubrication:

Check the level of oil in the steering gearbox every 3000 miles. The level and filler plug will be found as indicated by the righthand arrow in **FIG 9:3**.

The correct lubricant is SAE.90 Hypoid oil. An empty steering gear case will hold approximately $\frac{1}{2}$ pint. For topping up, add oil until it reaches the lower edge of the filler plug hole.

On vehicles fitted with grease nipples on the track rod ball joints, use a grease gun filled with universal grease

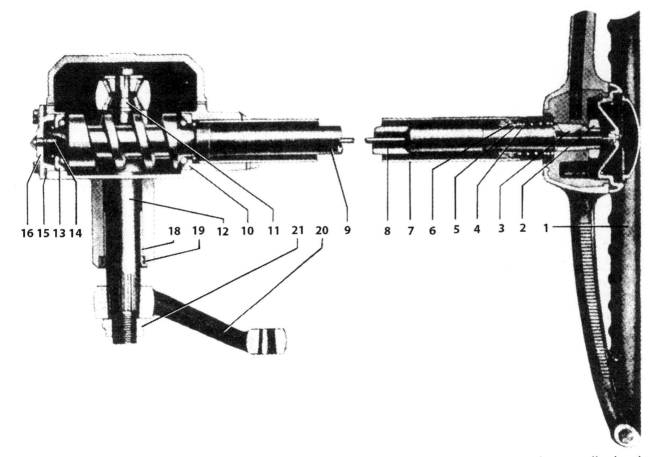

FIG 9:1 Components of steering gear. The peg which engages the worm is carried on opposed taper roller bearings

Key to Fig 9:1   1 Steering wheel   2 Steering wheel nut   3 Woodruff key   4 Spring   5 Expander ring
6 Ballbearing   7 Outer column   8 Horn cable   9 Inner steering column and worm   10 Upper ballbearing
11 Peg and taper roller bearings   12 Lever shaft   13 Lower ballbearing   14 Horn cable tube   15 Shims
16 Adjuster flange   18 Lever shaft bushes   19 Oil seal   20 Drop arm   21 Nut

at intervals from 750 miles upwards according to road conditions.

There are additional grease nipples for the drag link and for the swing lever bearings as shown by the arrows in **FIG 9:4**. After Chassis No. 829/681 the ball joints do not need lubrication.

The remaining lubrication points which affect the steering gear are for the kingpin bushes, as shown early in **Chapter 8.**

Adjustments:

Normally there is no need to adjust the steering gear. Wear at various points in the steering and suspension assembly may make adjustment or renewal necessary. Parts of the suspension system which will affect the steering are covered in **Chapter 8.** All other adjustments will be fully covered in the following instructions.

9:3 Removing steering wheel

1 Disconnect the battery earthing strap. Prise off the horn switch cover with a screwdriver and disconnect the cable from the switch. Remove the direction indicator switch.
2 Remove the steering wheel nut and spring washer and draw off the wheel

If it is necessary to use an extractor, leave the nut slightly above the top of the column to take the centre pad of the extractor.

Replace the steering wheel in the reverse sequence after putting some universal grease in the top bush. Make sure the Woodruff key is correctly seated, replace it if it is worn.

On recent models where the direction indicator switch is located just below the hub of the steering wheel, make sure the brass washer cut-out is exactly opposite and away from the lever with the front wheels in the straight-ahead position. The tongue of the cancelling ring must engage in the cut-out. Fit two spoke wheels so that the spokes are horizontal with the wheels set straight-ahead. Tighten the nut to a torque of 18 to 22 lb ft.

9:4 Removing and refitting steering gear

1 Disconnect battery earth cable. Remove horn button and direction indicator switch and steering wheel as described in **Section 9:3.**
2 Remove retaining plate rubber guard, lift off ignition switch cover and disconnect three cables. Loosen steering column tube rubber mounting retainer.
3 Remove ignition switch. Unscrew two bolts securing the retaining plate to underside of instrument panel.

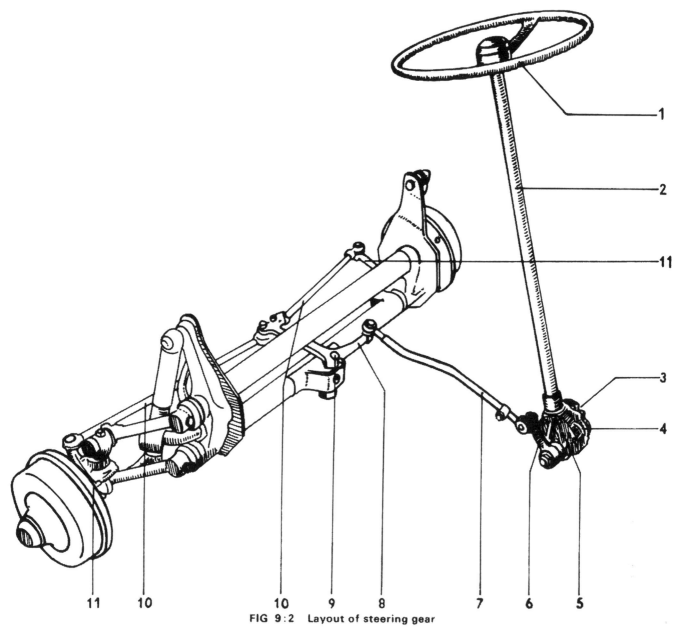

FIG 9:2   Layout of steering gear

Key to Fig 9:2   1 Steering wheel   2 Outer column   3 Oil filler plug   4 Steering box   5 Steering box bracket
6 Drop arm   7 Drag link   8 Swing lever   9 Swing lever shaft   10 Drag link   11 Steering knuckle

4 Lift front end of vehicle and support on blocks. Loosen clip on steering box bottom plate and withdraw horn cable. Remove coverplate under pedal cluster.

5 Pull off drop arm using extractor, after removing splitpin and nut 21 (see **FIG 9:1**) and drag link ball joint. Do not hammer on the end of threaded ball pin in order to loosen it.

6 Unscrew three bolts at the side of the steering box bracket and two bolts underneath bracket.

7 Withdraw the steering assembly downwards and forwards, sliding the rubber bush and retainer off the steering column.

Replacing steering gear:

Reverse the removal procedure but take the following precautions:

1 Check the oil level as suggested in **Section 9:2**.

2 Tighten the mounting bolts to a torque of 22 to 29 lb ft.

3 **Do not secure the top end of the column before the pinch bolts in the steering gear bracket are tightened or the column may be out of line and subject to bending stresses.** First slacken the pinch bolts in the mounting bracket so that the steering gear can be rotated in the bracket. Move the gear about in the bracket until the column is in the correct position, then tighten the pinch bolts. The bracket near the parcel shelf has slotted holes to ensure that alignment can be made without stressing the column.

4 If the drop arm has been removed, refit it and tighten the nut to a torque of 58 to 72 lb ft, locking it with a new splitpin. Set the front wheels in the straight-ahead position and find the mid-position of the steering wheel. The spokes should be horizontal and it should take about $1\frac{1}{4}$ turns to reach the limit of travel in each

FIG 9:3 Righthand arrow points to the filler plug on steering gearbox. Lefthand arrow points to the adjusting screw and locknut. LHD illustrated

direction. Adjust the length of the drag link so that the ball pins fit squarely into the holes in the drop arm and swing lever. Secure the nuts with new splitpins.

5 Push the horn cable up the column and tighten the clip. Secure the bolts by turning up the outer edges of the clip. Tighten the steering wheel nut.

If the mounting bracket has to be removed from the steering gearbox, do not dismantle it until the relative positions of the two parts have been carefully marked. To refit the bracket, drive it firmly against the gearbox casing, put new lockplates under the pinch bolts and tighten the bolts to a torque of 22 to 29 lb ft. **Do not overtighten the pinch bolts as the pressure on the lever shaft bushes may cause seizure.**

9:5 Dismantling steering gear

Refer to **FIG 9:1** and do the following:

1 Drain out the oil and then remove the splitpin from the top bolt of the adjuster flange at the lower end. Remove the flange 16 and shims 15 (four bolts).

2 Remove the gear case cover (four bolts). Push out the lever shaft 12 after removing the drop arm 20.

3 Take out the Woodruff key 3 at the top of the inner column 9 and remove the spring 4 and the expander ring 5. Refit the steering wheel nut until its face is slightly above the inner column and tap the column downwards. This will drive the column out of the gear casing. Remove the retainer rings to take off the ball-bearing cups. Clean the parts and check for wear. Renew the column and worm as an assembly.

4 Inspect the peg in the lever shaft when clean and dry. If the taper which engages the worm is worn and the bearing feels rough, renew the whole assembly. To dismantle it, hold the cylindrical part of the peg in a vice with the threaded end uppermost. Undo the nut after flattening the tabs on the lockwasher. Use a soft-faced hammer to drive the peg out from the threaded end. This will also release the rollers and the loose cone.

5 To reassemble the peg and bearing, take the clean dry parts and apply grease or petroleum jelly about $\frac{1}{16}$ inch thick to the tapered faces of the peg and loose cone. Stick the rollers in place with their large diameters resting on the shoulder of each cone. Carefully fit the loose cone and rollers into the upper race in the lever shaft. Insert the peg from below and tap upwards with a rubber hammer. Fit the lockplate and nut.

6 Adjust the bearing by gripping the cylindrical part of the peg in a vice. Tighten the nut until there is a slight drag when turning the peg. Check that the parts are fully seated by tapping on both ends of the peg, as this will often loosen one which is tight to turn. If this does not produce the desired result, slacken the nut and start again. It is a good plan to tighten a new assembly a little more than one which has seen service.

7 **Lock the nut with tabs which have not been used and break off those which were originally bent up.** Select two which are diametrically opposite and will bear on the flats of the nut at right angles. Check the feel of the peg again and then wash the bearing free from grease and dry it with compressed air.

8 If the lever shaft bushes 18 in the casing need renewal, first take out the oil seal 19. Lift up the rubber sealing lip with a wire hook and carefully pull out the spring with another hook. It will then be possible to push the seal out without damaging it. Fit new bushes by driving or pressing them into place with a suitable mandrel. Ream to a diameter of .999 to 1 inch. Preferably fit a new seal, but if the old one is to be refitted, install the spring first. When fitting the lever shaft, press the sealing lip outwards so that the splines on the shaft do not damage it.

9 The outer column tube 7 can be renewed if it is damaged or loose in the gear casing. It can be pressed out and a new one pressed in to a depth of 1.77 to 1.81 inch from the point of entry.

9:6 Reassembling and adjusting steering gear

Having renewed all worn parts, and this should include the lever shaft bushes in the casing, reassemble in the reverse order to dismantling as follows:

1 Using grease to hold the balls in place, install the top bearing and push the steering column upwards, tapping it home to ensure that it is properly seated. Do not forget to fit the bearing retainer rings.

2 If necessary fit a new bearing assembly at the top of the column before inserting the inner column. Follow up the fitting of the inner column and adjuster flange by dropping the expander ring and spring over the top end and then fit the Woodruff key for the steering wheel. Do not forget to fit the shims under the adjuster plate and tighten the bolts evenly. If new bearings and steering worm have been fitted, do not tighten these four bolts too much if the steering column becomes stiff to turn some time before they are fully tightened. The column should turn without stiffness or end float, and adjustment is made by shims under the flange. When correctly adjusted there should be no end float and no excessive pressure on the balls in the bearings. It should be possible to push the balls round the races without force.

3 Fit the lever shaft and then the casing cover, using a new gasket. Slacken off the adjusting screw before

fitting the cover and then tighten the cover bolts. Find the central position for the steering gear by halving the lock-to-lock turns of the steering column. Turn the adjusting screw inwards until there is a slight drag when moving the column through the mid-position. Hold the screw and tighten the locknut (see **FIG 9 : 3**). Lock the four bolts in the adjuster flange and put the correct grade of oil in the casing as instructed in **Section 9 : 2**. Do not overfill, but leave the final topping up until the assembly has been refitted in the vehicle.

4 Use the refitting instructions in **Section 9 : 4**. Before installing the drop arm make sure that the splines are in good condition. If the arm has been bent through accidental damage do not try to straighten it, but renew it. **Do not hammer the arm onto the lever shaft.** Tighten the nut to a torque of 58 to 72 lb ft and lock with a new splitpin.

Adjusting steering gear in vehicle :

Steering column end play is taken out by altering the shimming 15 under the flange at the lower end of the gear case. Follow the instructions in **Section 9 : 4** dealing with removal of the assembly but do not actually proceed beyond the point where the horn cable is pulled out. Then take off the adjuster flange and add or take away shims as required. With the steering wheel off it should be possible to move the column by hand from lock to lock. Insufficient play will make for stiffness and too much end play will give lost motion in the steering. The bolts in the adjuster flange must be evenly tightened.

Removal of backlash between the worm and stud should be undertaken after steering column end play has been tackled. Set the wheels in the straight-ahead position by turning the steering wheel from lock to lock and halving the number of turns. Slacken the locknut indicated in **FIG 9 : 3** and turn the screw clockwise until there is the slightest extra drag in the mid-position when the steering wheel is rocked to and fro. Hold the screw and lock the nut, then check by turning the wheel from lock to lock. The slight stiffness in the mid-position should disappear as the lock increases. This is a design feature in the shape of the worm and is not perceptible when under way. Check the adjustment on the road. When straightening up after a sharp bend, the steering wheel should try to return to the central position virtually unaided. Too much stiffness may lead to rapid wear of the worm and stud.

9 : 7 The swing lever

The location of the swing lever and its lubrication points is shown in **FIG 9 : 4**. A section is given in **FIG 9 : 5**.

Removing :

1 Remove the steering damper end from the swing lever.
2 Press out the drag link and track rod ball joint pins from the lever. Do not hammer on the threaded ends of the ball pins but use a proper extracting tool. If this is not available the tapers can be started by hammering on one side of the eye in the lever while holding a heavy steel block on the opposite side.
3 Remove the pinch bolt 3 through the lever and press the lever shaft 2 out of the lever and bracket.

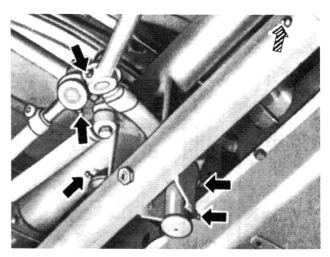

FIG 9 : 4 The two lowest arrows point to the swing lever grease nipples. The lefthand arrows point to ball joint grease nipples. LHD illustrated

Clean and check the parts. Renew the shaft and bushes 7 and 10 if worn. The bushes can be driven out after removing the top grease nipple. As the oil groove 10 is offcentre, fit the top bush with the groove nearer the bottom and the lower bush with the groove nearer the top as can be seen in the illustration. Also make sure that the top bush is correctly aligned with the grease nipple. Drive in the top bush so that .055 to .067 inch is left protruding. The lower bush should be flush. Ream to a diameter of .9449 to .9457 inch. Clean away all swarf, renew defective grease nipples and reassemble with adequate lubricant.

Reassembling :

1 Fit the swing lever and shaft, threading the seals into place in the order shown in the illustration. The spring washer 6 must provide enough end load to prevent rattling in service. Compression of the washer must be .024 to .031 inch and this is calculated by leaving off the spring washer but assembling the other parts. The end float should be the thickness of the spring washer (which is .189 ± .028 inch when free) minus the preload of .024 to .031 inch. If clearance is excessive, fit an extra thrust washer .020 inch thick between the dust seal 5 and the spring washer. If the spring washer is obviously weak, renew it.
2 Fit all the parts in the correct order and press the arm so that the spring washer is compressed in order to fit the pinch bolt. Use a new lockplate on the bolt and tighten it to a torque of 47 to 54 lb ft.

9 : 8 Track rods and steering damper
Servicing track rods :

The ball joints fitted to the ends of the track rods may be locked in place with clips and pinch bolts or by two nuts. Grease nipples will be used for lubrication service on early vehicles. Later vehicles will have sealed ball joints which are packed with grease and these do not need attention. The condition of the rubber seals is vitally important, particularly on the sealed joint. Renew the seals on early joints if no dirt has entered. Sealed joints

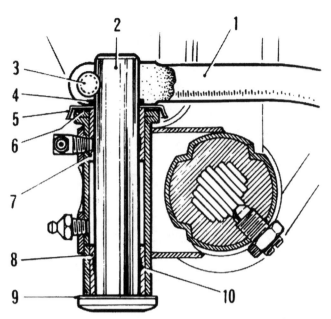

FIG 9:5 A section through the swing lever pivot

Key to Fig 9:5   1 Swing lever arm   2 Swing lever shaft
3 Pinch bolt   4 Plastic seal   5 Dust cover   6 Spring washer
7 Upper bush   8 Lower bush   9 Thrust washer
10 Oil groove in bush

must be renewed if the seal is damaged and every care must be taken not to squeeze grease out of them when they are being handled or taken off.

Removing:

1 Raise the front of the vehicle and remove the wheels. Detach the steering damper and unlock and remove the nuts securing the ball joint pins to the drop arm and steering arms.

2 Press the ball pins out with a special extractor made for the job. Do not hammer on the threaded end of the pin if the extractor is not available. It helps to jar the tapers loose by hammering on one side of the eye while a heavy steel block is held against the opposite side.

3 Before unscrewing the ball joints from the rods it is useful to record the position approximately, so that the joint can be refitted in much the same place. This will save time when checking the tracking.

Check the rods for damage. Bent rods must not be straightened but renewed. Check each ball joint by moving the pin about. It must do so without roughness and without shake. The thread on the pin must be undamaged. If old joints are considered satifactory, check that the grease nipples are clear and undamaged. Joints can be renewed individually, and the newer sealed type can be fitted as replacements of the early type with grease nipples, providing the joints are of the type requiring two locknuts.

Replacing track rods:

Install both rods so that the ball joints with lefthand threads are on the lefthand side. These are sometimes marked with a paint spot. On early vehicles fit the short track rod so that the bent end is attached to the drop arm. Tighten the ball pin nuts and lock them, then slacken the clips or nuts securing the joints to the track rods. Move

the joints until they are aligned with each other at both ends of a rod and tighten the nuts or clips. Refit the steering damper and check the tracking according to the instructions in **Section 9:9**.

Removing steering damper:

Remove the bolt from the bracket end and the nut from the track rod end and remove the damper. Check by pushing the plunger in slowly and steadily. The resistance should be uniform throughout the travel. Renew the damper if there are 'flat spots'.

The rubber bushes may need renewal. First press out the metal sleeve, followed by the rubber bush. Press in a new bush and then use a tapered and shouldered pilot to press in the metal sleeve. Put a smear of rubber grease on the pilot to assist penetration. Do not forget the bush and sleeve in the track rod and make sure the attachments are sound.

Refitting steering damper:

Insert a washer at the swing lever side between the bolt head and the damper eye. Tighten the inner nut at the track rod eye to 18 to 22 lb ft and secure with a locknut. Fit the bolt at the bracket end, using a new lockplate. Fit the plate with the open end pointing forward and the short angled end on the bracket. Tighten bolt to 18 to 21 lb ft and lock.

9:9 Steering geometry and tracking

If steering is to be smooth, accurate and without strain then several conditions must be met. These are, that lubrication is regular and adequate, that all parts are correctly adjusted, that the steering angles have not been thrown out by accident damage, that the tyres are not excessively out of balance and that they are running at the correct pressure. Tyre wear must be even, the dampers must be in working order and the tracking or toe-in must be correct.

Correct steering angles are specified by the manufacturers and they will be found in Technical Data. **FIG 9:6** shows the camber angle, the kingpin inclination and the castor angle in diagrammatic form. Wear and damage will affect these angles and may result in hard steering, excessive tyre wear, pulling to one side, front wheel 'shimmy', poor road holding and poor cornering.

Camber angle and kingpin inclination reduce the effect of road shocks on steering and keep down tyre wear, especially when cornering. Castor angle is noticeable because it induces the steering wheel to return unaided to the central position after passing through a sharp bend. Not enough castor angle makes the vehicle wander about over potholes and bad roads or under the influence of side winds. Too much increases the effort needed to deflect the wheels from the straight-ahead position.

Rough checks can be made to establish whether the angles are seriously out, but accurate measurements must be made by optical alignment gauges as used in Service Stations. The required conditions are that the vehicle is on a level, horizontal and smooth surface. The tyres must be at the correct pressure and the front wheel bearings correctly adjusted. The steering gear must be properly adjusted, the vehicle must be unladen except for the spare wheel and a full tank and the suspension must be well bounced before testing.

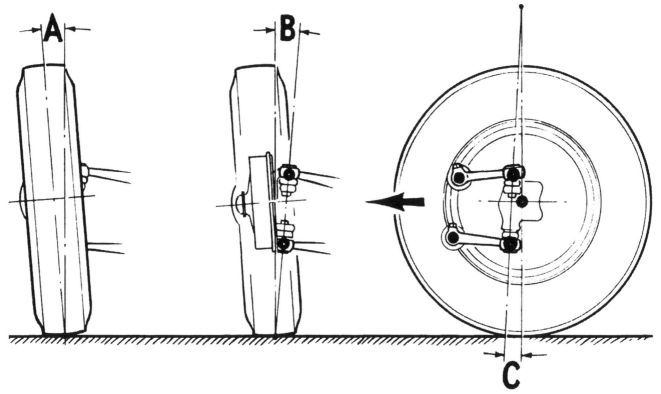

FIG 9:6 The angles which determine steering behaviour. A is the camber angle, B is the kingpin inclination, and C is the castor angle

Given these conditions, the camber angle can be roughly checked by dropping a plumb line from the top bulge of a front tyre and measuring the distance from the line to the bottom bulge. A simple drawing on a large sheet of paper will enable the dimensions to be set out and the angle measured with a protractor. It is advisable to check by rolling the vehicle forward for half a turn of the wheels, measuring again and taking the average. This method will enable a check to be made of the angles on each side.

Adjusting the tracking or amount of toe-in:

The front wheels are not parallel when at rest but 'toe-in'. This is done so that the wheels are parallel when under way because all the play which is present in the steering gear and suspension is taken out by the rolling resistance of the wheels. **FIG 9:7** shows that the amount of toe-in is the difference between measurements **A** and **A—**. Due to the geometry of the steering gear the wheels actually toe-out when they are turned for cornering at sharp angles as shown in the righthand view. This angle must also be checked in cases where there is trouble with the steering.

To carry out a rough check of the toe-in, satisfy the test conditions and then measure the distance between the rims at **A** and **A—** at wheel centre height above the ground. Roll the vehicle forward for half a wheel and measure again in order to compensate for uneven rims. The difference between measurements **A** and **A—** is the amount of toe-out or toe-in.

Adjustment is made by altering the lefthand track rod length. Set the wheels straight-ahead by halving the steering wheel turns from lock to lock. The ball joints at

each end of the track rod must be released by slackening the clips or unlocking and turning the nuts. Only one track rod is adjustable for length. Turn track rod in the required direction to rectify any error. Tighten the ball joint clips or nuts after setting the joints at each end of a rod in the same place. Recheck toe-in.

Adjusting the camber angle:

Assuming that accurate measuring facilities are available, it is possible to adjust the camber angle on vehicles made after August 1965 which are fitted with ball joints on the kingpins instead of the earlier type with plain linkpins. The adjustment is made by turning an eccentric bush which can be seen in **FIG 8:7** in **Chapter 8. Checking the camber angle is possible on earlier vehicles but errors can be rectified only by renewing faulty parts. The correction of camber angles by altering the position of shims on the linkpins might result in excessive wear and is definitely not recommended.** To adjust by means of the eccentric bush do the following:

1 Place the vehicle on a smooth level surface with the tyres correctly inflated and the front wheels exactly in the straight-ahead position.

2 Loosen the self-locking nut which secures the upper ball joint to the steering knuckle. Note the notch in one face of the hexagonal part of the eccentric bush. Initially, this notch is assembled in the straight-ahead position. For adjustment purposes it can be turned no more than 90 deg. in either direction. When satisfied with the setting, hold the hexagon and tighten the ball pin nut to a torque of 29 to 36 lb ft.

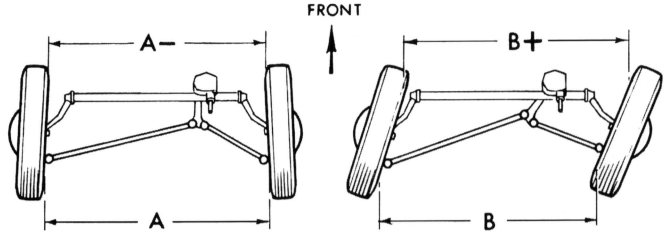

FRONT

FIG 9:7 Front wheel tracking. With front wheels straight-ahead, toe-in means that dimension **A—** is less than **A**. On large steering locks this becomes toe-out as indicated on the right. **B+** is then greater than **B**

Steering wheel spokes at an angle:

This condition **must not be cured by turning the wheel on the column splines.** The adjustment is made to the length of the drag link by releasing the front ball joint from the drop arm. With the wheels and steering wheel centralized, it is then a simple matter to make the drag link the correct length.

9:10 Modifications

Track rod joints:

The sealed type which needs no periodic lubrication, have no grease nipple. They can be fitted in place of the older type.

Track rod clamps:

Instead of the original two-nut locking of the ball joints to the track rods, clamps were fitted from August 1965. The new type cannot be fitted to earlier vehicles.

9:11 Fault diagnosis

(a) Wheel wobble

1 Unbalanced wheels and tyres, pressures uneven
2 Looseness in steering gear and connections
3 Front end damaged, incorrect steering angles
4 Incorrect toe-in adjustment
5 Worn or slack hub bearings
6 Faulty dampers

(b) Steering wander

1 Check 2, 3 and 5 in (a)
2 Smooth front tyres, pressures too high or too low

(c) Heavy steering

1 Check 3 in (a)
2 Low or uneven tyre pressures
3 Faulty steering gear adjustment
4 Lubrication neglected
5 Front suspension worn or out of alignment
6 Steering gearbox mounted out of line
7 Faulty steering damper
8 Weak or broken torsion bars
9 Steering column bent

(d) Lost motion

1 Loose steering wheel, worn splines
2 Worn ball joints and suspension pivots
3 Drop arm loose on shaft
4 Steering gearbox mounting loose
5 General wear and faulty adjustment of steering gearbox

(e) Steering pulls to one side

1 Check 3 in (a) and 2 in (c)
2 One front brake binding
3 Broken or sagging rear suspension
4 Bent front axle tubes

CHAPTER 10

THE BRAKING SYSTEM

10:1 Description

All versions of the VW Transporter are fitted with hydraulically operated drum brakes, the general layout of the braking system is shown in **FIG 10:1**. The brakes fitted to the 1500 Transporter are larger than those on the 1200, the sizes are given in Technical Data. The front brakes M are of the internally expanding type with two leading shoes and the rear brakes N have one leading and one trailing shoe.

The brake pedal A is connected by a pushrod B to the master cylinder C. When the pedal is operated, hydraulic pressure is generated in the master cylinder, the pressure is transmitted through the pipes E and hoses H to the wheel cylinders J. The hydraulic pressure operates a piston in each wheel cylinder, causing the brake shoes to expand onto the brake drum. A fluid reservoir D ensures that the hydraulic pipes and cylinders are always full of fluid.

The mechanically operated handbrake K is connected to the rear wheels brakes only by two cables which run in guide tubes L. The front brake is illustrated in **FIG 10:3**. Two single-ended cylinders 5 are coupled by a pipe 7 so that the leading ends of both shoes 2 are expanded. Each cylinder has a single serrated adjuster 6. The rear brakes are fitted with a single wheel cylinder as shown in **FIG 10:4**. The cylinder 4 houses two pistons, each provided with a sealing cup. Adjustment for wear is by means of two screws and nuts 6. The serrated nuts can be turned with a screwdriver inserted through a hole in the drum.

Later versions of the Transporter are fitted with dual circuit braking systems.

10:2 Routine maintenance

Adjusting the handbrake:

Remove the rubber boot at lower end of handbrake lever. Slacken the locknuts at top of cable (see **FIG 10:8**) then jack up the rear wheels. Tighten the adjusting screws so that the wheels can turn freely with the handbrake released. Pull the lever on two notches and check that there is equal resistance to turning the rear wheels. Tighten the locknuts and refit the boot. Check the operation of the brakes on a road test.

On Transporters before Chassis No. 614456, remove the coverplate under the pedal linkage and slacken the locknuts at the front ends of the two cables and adjust the two inner nuts as described in the preceding paragraph.

103

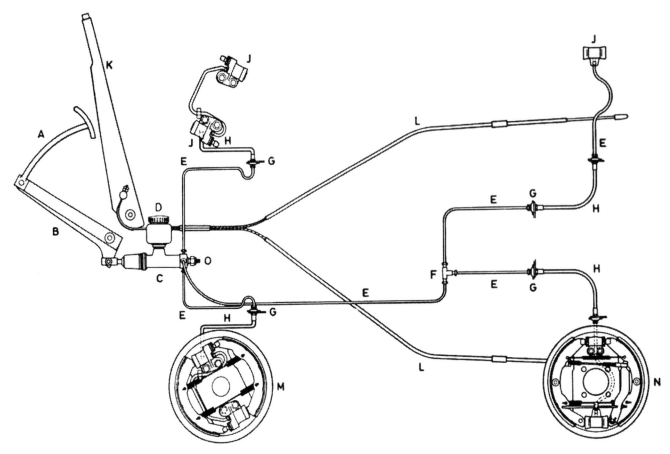

FIG 10:1   Layout of hydraulic braking system

Key to Fig 10:1   A Pushrod   B Brake pedal   C Master cylinder   D Fluid reservoir   E Steel pipeline
F Three-way union   G Hose bracket   H Flexible hose   J Wheel cylinder   K Handbrake lever   L Cable guide tube
M Front brake   N Rear brake   O Stoplight switch

Topping up hydraulic reservoir :

The reservoir is located under an inspection plate in the cab floor as shown in **FIG 10:5**. Clean all round the cap thoroughly so that dirt cannot enter when the cap is unscrewed. Check the fluid level. The reservoir must always be at least three-quarters full and when topping up the level must be to within $\frac{1}{2}$ to $\frac{3}{4}$ inch of the top. **Use only genuine VW or Lockheed brake fluid. Never put mineral oil in the system as this will ruin all the rubber seals. Be careful not to spill the fluid on paintwork.** Before restoring the cap, check the vent hole in it. This is sometimes blocked when a vehicle has been repainted.

If the reservoir needs frequent topping up there is a leak in the system. This must have immediate attention as further neglect might have dangerous consequences. The most likely places for leaks are at the pipe joints and past the sealing cups in the cylinders. Flexible hoses must also be checked.

Adjusting hydraulic drum brakes :

Before adjusting, check the front wheel bearing play. Apply the brake pedal several times to centralize the shoes. Raise the vehicle and release the handbrake. Remove the wheel caps.

Turn one of the wheels until the hole in the drum is in line with one of the adjusters. Consult **FIG 10:2** to determine the correct way to move the serrated adjusting nuts when taking up slack. Turn one nut, using the screwdriver as a lever, until a light drag on the drum can be felt. Repeat on the other nut, then back off both nuts by three to four teeth until the wheel will turn freely. Repeat on the other three wheels. **Never adjust one wheel alone.** Test by applying the brake pedal hard several times then check the adjustment.

10:3 Servicing the master cylinder

Removing master cylinder :

Jack up and securely support front end of vehicle. Remove coverplate under pedal linkage. Withdraw split-pin, remove washer and extract pushrod clevis pin. Disconnect cable from stoplight switch 6 (see **FIG 10:6**). Disconnect the three brake pipes from the end of the master cylinder and plug the ends. Bleed screw caps make useful plugs. Unscrew two bolts securing the master cylinder to the front crossmember and withdraw master cylinder, complete with pushrod, towards the rear of the vehicle.

104

FIG 10:2 Front brake (left), rear brake (right). Large arrow points to front of vehicle, small arrows show direction to turn adjusting nuts to take up lining clearance

Refitting master cylinder:

The master cylinder fitted to the 1500 Transporter has a shorter stroke than the master cylinder fitted to the 1200. The pushrod lengths are also different. The dimensions are as follows:

	Piston stroke	Pushrod length
1500 Transporter	1.181 inch	2.32 to 2.36 inch
1200 Transporter	1.417 inch	2.735 to 2.774 inch

Check the length of the piston pushrod, this dimension should be measured from the spherical end to the face of the nut as shown in **FIG 10:7**. Refit the master cylinder and tighten the bolts. Reconnect pushrod to the brake pedal and fit a new splitpin.

Check that there is .04 inch free play between the spherical end of the pushrod and the bottom of the recess in the master cylinder piston as shown in **FIG 10:7**. Adjustment is made by moving the pedal stop plate. Reconnect the stoplight cable. Refit the hydraulic pipes. Fill the reservoir with the correct grade of brake fluid and bleed the brakes as described in **Section 10:9**. Check that the stoplight operates. Test the brakes on the road then inspect all joints for signs of leaks.

Dismantling and reassembling master cylinder:

These instructions apply to all models, but those with dual braking systems will need to refer to **FIG 10:9** to identify the extra parts.

The essential point when dealing with all internal parts of the hydraulic system is to maintain absolute cleanliness of the components and the fluid. The efficiency of the rubber sealing cups is dependent on such cleanliness, as grit will destroy the sealing effect and may permanently score the cylinder bores. Any leaks in the hydraulic braking system can be dangerous. **When cleaning all parts use only clean brake fluid or methylated spirits; any other solvents may cause a breakdown of the rubber cups.**

Dismantle the master cylinder as follows:

1 Remove the rubber boot 19 (see **FIG 10:6**) and prise out the locking ring or circlip 17.
2 Remove the stop washer 16 and shake out the piston 14, followed by spring 9 and check valve 8. The check valve differs on some models and earlier types may have a flanged metal cup with an internal rubber valve and there will then be a rubber seating washer at the bottom of the bore. This can be removed.
3 **On vehicles with dual braking system,** remove stop screw 21 in **FIG 10:9** and then extract all the internal parts in the order shown.

Clean and examine all the parts for wear and deterioration. In **FIG 10:6** will be seen a small port 10 in front of the primary sealing cup 11. This must always be uncovered when the piston is fully retracted to enable fluid from the reservoir to recharge the system if necessary. Check that the port is clear and free from burrs. There are two ports in the master cylinder of a dual braking system. The piston(s) must be a suction fit in the master cylinder bore when clean and dry.

Always renew the rubber sealing cups on the piston(s) and the seating washer for the earlier check valve. Renew the check valve if there has been faulty operation. The parts are available in kits. Note that all the cups can be interchanged on the dual system with the exception of the cup for the rear circuit piston.

Reassemble the parts in the correct order, coating the piston(s) with genuine VW Brake Cylinder Paste. Be careful not to trap or turn back the lips on the cups. See that the circlip seats properly. On dual circuit master cylinders, place the cup washer, support washer, spring plate and spring on the front piston. Hold the cylinder with open end down and feed in the parts so that they do not fall off. To the rear piston fit the cup washer, primary

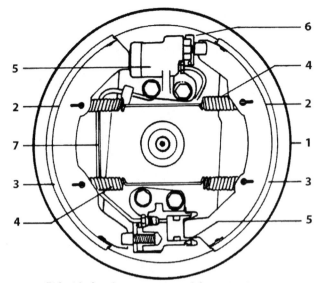

FIG 10:3 Components of front brake

Key to Fig 10:3   1 Backplate   2 Brake shoes
3 Brake linings   4 Shoe return springs   5 Wheel cylinder
6 Adjusting nut   7 Bridge pipe

cup, support washer, stop sleeve, spring and stroke-limiting screw and insert into cylinder. Fit stop washer and spring ring. Use the pushrod to press the front piston forward, well clear of the hole for the stop screw, which can then be fitted complete with sealing washer. Install stoplight switches and tighten to 11 to 14 lb ft. Fit the rubber boot with the breather hole underneath.

The residual pressure valves 19 which are shown in the illustration are used on systems which have drum brakes all round. They are fitted to maintain some pressure in the system.

Note that, on some models, master and wheel cylinders may be of two different makes. Look for marks **ATE** or **S** and obtain spare parts with the correct marking.

10:4 Removing drum brake shoes

Front shoe removal:

1 Jack up the front end and remove the wheels. Remove the hub caps, noting that it is necessary to remove the cotterpin which passes through the squared shaft of the speedometer drive before the front lefthand cap can be prised off.

2 On earlier models, unscrew the locknut, remove the lockplate and then the inner nut and thrust washer. Later models have a nut which is fitted with a clamping screw. Slacken the screw and remove the nut. The lefthand axle has a lefthand thread.

3 Back off the brake shoes before pulling off the drums. Brush dirt from inside the drums and examine for wear. Worn drums can be reground by VW agents and over-size brake linings must then be fitted. Attend to the hub bearings as instructed in **Chapter 8**.

4 **FIG 10:3** shows the front brake. Pull one shoe outwards until it is released from the slot in the adjusting screw. The shoe can then be released, which will make it possible to remove the second shoe. Take particular note of the way the return springs are fitted.

5 Brake linings are due for renewal if they are down to .1 inch thickness. It is not advisable to try riveting on

linings oneself, as replacement shoes have linings which are accurately bedded to the shoes and are concentric to the drums. **Never renew one set of linings alone and make sure the material of the linings is the same on all four brakes.**

6 While the shoes are off, make sure that the brake pedal cannot be depressed. If the wheel cylinders are not to be dismantled, put a clamp or a loop of wire over the pistons to ensure that they cannot be ejected by use of the brake pedal. Another method is to put a clamp on the flexible hose behind each brake backplate.

7 When replacing the shoes, be careful to fit the return springs correctly. Note in **FIG 10:2** how they are hooked in from the back. It is essential to see that the return springs do not contact the bridge pipe joining the two cylinders so that chafing cannot cause leaks. Fit one end of the lower spring only, at first. Shoes which are notched near the spring holes must be fitted with the notches at the cylinder end

8 Fit the shoes into the slots in the pistons and then into the slots of the adjusters. Check that the angled ends of the shoes and the adjusters coincide and line up.

9 Fit the retainer pins and locating springs and washers, and centralize the shoes. Check the oil seal and grease the hub and bearings according to **Chapter 8**. Fit the brake drum and adjust the wheel bearings. Adjust the brakes and then bleed the system as instructed in **Section 10:9**.

Rear shoe removal:

Before starting on this operation the owner must realise that the rear axle nuts are tightened to a torque of 217 lb ft. **It is dangerous to try to loosen these nuts with the vehicle on jacks or trestles. Always slacken and tighten the nuts when the vehicle is on the ground.**

1 After slackening the axle nuts, lift the rear of the vehicle and remove the wheels. Release the handbrake and back off the shoe adjusters. Remove the axle nuts and brake drums.

2 Remove the shoe locating springs and cups (if fitted) and then the retaining pins. Unhook the return spring. Unhook brake cable 9 (see **FIG 10:4**).

3 Pull the shoes outward to remove them from the adjuster slots and lift them away complete with lever

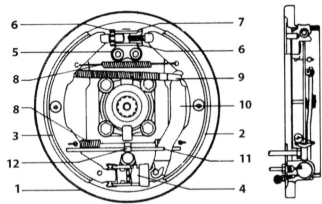

FIG 10:4   Components of rear brake

Key to Fig 10:4   1 Backplate   2 Leading brake shoe
3 Trailing brake shoe   4 Wheel cylinder   5 Wheel cylinder
anchor block   6 Adjusting nuts   7 Spring
8 Shoe return spring   9 Handbrake cable   10 Brake lever
11 Handbrake pushrod   12 Clip

10 and pushrod 11. The return springs on some Transporter models are in pairs hooked into holes in the backplate.

4 Put a clamp or wire loop over the pistons 10 so that they cannot be ejected by pressing the brake pedal. Alternatively, put a clamp on the flexible hose behind the backplate.

5 The handbrake lever can be detached if necessary by removing the anchor pin circlip.

6 Clean all parts and check linings and drums for wear. Have the drums reground by a VW agent if badly scored or out of true. Fit the same type of lining material to both brakes. Do not fit new linings to one side only. Refer to preceding instructions for front brakes.

8 Replace the shoes in the reverse order, fitting the return springs correctly and making sure they cannot contact other parts. Make certain that the shoes and angled slots in the adjusters line up.

9 Fit the drums and nuts but do not tighten fully until the vehicle is standing on the ground. Then tighten the axle nuts to a torque of 217 lb ft. If the cotterpin holes do not line up, tighten still further. **Do not slacken off.** Adjust the foot and handbrakes and bleed the system as described in **Section 10:9**. Carry out a brake test on the road.

10:5 Removing and servicing wheel cylinders

If wheel cylinders need renewal make sure that each replacement cylinder has the same bore as the original one.

To remove wheel cylinders proceed as in the previous section on removing brake shoes. When the shoes are off, disconnect the flexible hoses as outlined in **Section 10:7**. Remove cylinder mounting screws and take away the cylinders, after first removing the bridge pipe between cylinders in front brakes.

Service each cylinder by cleaning the exterior thoroughly. Using every care to maintain all internal parts in a state of absolute cleanliness, remove the dust-excluding boots and withdraw both pistons with pushrods. Take out the cups, the cup expanders and the spring. **Clean the parts in methylated spirit or clean brake fluid and no other.** When dry and clean, the pistons must be a suction fit in the cylinder. Always renew the rubber cups. Renew the cylinder and pistons if worn or scored.

Reassemble in the reverse order, coating the pistons with genuine VW Brake Cylinder Paste. When fitting the rubber cups be careful not to trap or turn back the lips. Connect up the hoses in the manner described in **Section 10:7**. Adjust and bleed the brakes and test on the road.

10:6 Dismantling drum brakes

Follow the instructions in preceding **Sections 10:4** and **10:5**. After the wheel cylinder is removed from a front brake, unscrew the adjusting screws and nuts and remove the leaf spring clicker and lift the backplate away.

To remove a backplate from the rear axle, remove the brake cable retainer. Remove the adjusting screws and nuts. Take off the leaf spring clicker. Remove the four bolts from the bearing housing cover round the axle shaft and pull off the backplate. Take out the adjuster screws and remove the brake shoe anchor.

FIG 10:5 Master cylinder fluid reservoir under cab floor

When replacing a front backplate, clean the contact surfaces of plate and stub axle. Tighten the mounting bolts to 36 to 43 lb ft. Tighten the wheel cylinder mounting bolts on recent models to a torque of 40 to 42 lb ft. Connect the cylinder bridge pipe under the lug.

To replace the backplate on the rear brakes, clean all the contact surfaces first. Before fitting the bearing housing cover check the oil seal and bed it correctly in its recess. Renew both gaskets for the cover and spacer. The oil drop lug on the housing cover must point downwards . Tighten the mounting bolts to 40 to 43 lb ft. The adjuster screw leaf spring can be set slightly if more tension is required. Apply some universal grease sparingly to the adjuster threads. When fitting the brake drum check the position of the oil deflector.

Finally, adjust all brakes, bleed the system and test on the road.

10:7 Brake hoses and pipelines

Brake hoses must not be painted or left in prolonged contact with oil, grease, paraffin or fuel.

To remove a hose, take off the wheel. Unscrew the union nut securing the metal pipeline at the inner end, release the retainer and pull the hose from the bracket. Unscrew the hose at the backplate. Transporters have an additional bracket secured to each steering knuckle by a grease nipple. On rear hoses release the union nuts at both ends.

Fit hoses with the axles free from load. **Most failures are due to twisting when installing or to chafing against nearby objects.** It is most important to ensure that neither of these defects can affect braking safety.

Install each hose without twisting so that it hangs down. Check that the hose cannot be strained at any steering angle or position of the suspension. It must not chafe against any part when the vehicle is under way with the

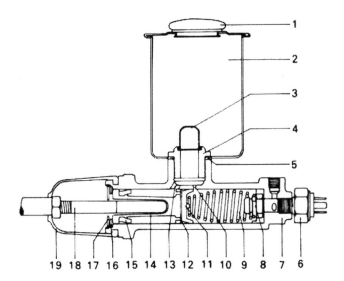

Key to Fig 10:6
1 Filler plug   2 Reservoir   3 Filter
4 Gland nut   5 Gasket   6 Stoplight switch
7 Master cylinder body   8 Check valve   9 Spring
10 Bypass port   11 Primary cup   12 Piston washer
13 Intake port   14 Piston   15 Secondary cup
16 Piston stop washer   17 Circlip   18 Pushrod
19 Boot

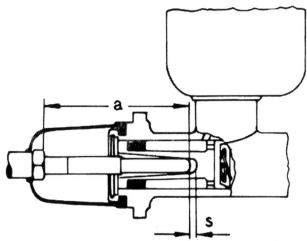

FIG 10:7 The pushrod length shown by dimension (a) must be 2.32 to 2.36 inch for master cylinder with stroke of 1.181 inch and 2.735 to 2.774 inch for master cylinder with stroke of 1.417 inch. The clearance shown by dimension (s) must be .04 inch

suspension moving up and down to the fullest extent. Tighten the hose and union hexagons to a torque of 10 to 14 lb ft.

Brake pipelines are of $\frac{3}{16}$ inch steel tubing and are subject to corrosion and to damage by stones after long periods of use. Check all sections and renew any which are faulty. The ends are double flared. Moisten these flares with a little brake fluid before tightening the union nuts. Check that the pipes are firmly clipped to the chassis.

10:8 Dual braking system

Servicing the dual braking system master cylinder has been covered in **Section 10:3** and **FIG 10:9** shows the parts exploded. The object is to provide the maximum safety in a hydraulic system of braking. This is done by separating the front and rear brake circuit and supplying

pressure to each by separate sections of the dual master cylinder.

FIG 10:11 shows the action diagrammatically. The first view shows the master cylinder supplying the needs of both circuits. The middle view shows what happens when the front brake circuit fails through leakage. The floating piston **A** is pushed fully to the left by the fluid between the pistons, so that it cannot force fluid into the faulty circuit. The rear circuit continues to function with an increase in pedal travel. The view on the right shows action when the rear brakes develop a leak. Piston **B** moves to the left until it contacts piston **A** which then provides fluid pressure to the front brake circuit. The brake pedal pushrod is on the extreme right. Note how the fluid reservoir is divided into two compartments so that loss of fluid in one circuit does not mean failure in the other one.

10:9 Bleeding the brakes

The following method will apply to all hydraulic systems. Use **FIG 10:10** for reference purposes.

The operation is necessary when there is air in the system because air is compressible and it will give a 'spongy' feeling to the brake pedal, which may also have excessive travel. Whenever any work is done on the braking system which calls for removal of the hoses, pipelines or cups from the wheel cylinders, then air will enter. This is bled out of the system in the following way:
1 Secure the services of a second operator. Have ready an extra supply of clean brake fluid of the correct grade. This must be either genuine VW or Lockheed Brake Fluid. Remember that fluid will be used from the reservoir shown in **FIG 10:5** and the level must be maintained throughout the operation. If the level falls so low that air can enter the master cylinder then the whole process must start from the beginning again.
2 Provide a clean glass container and a length of tubing which will fit over the bleed screw. On rear brakes it is

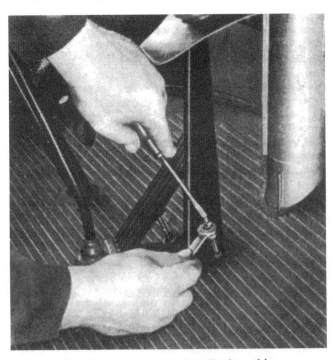

FIG 10:8   Adjusting handbrake cables

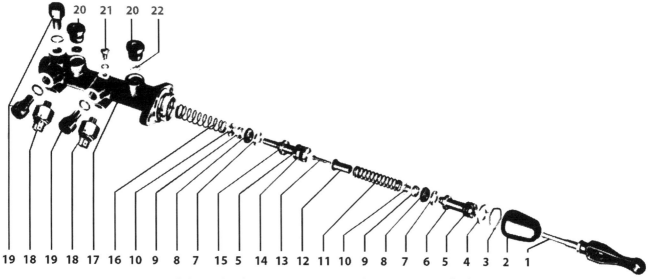

FIG 10:9   Components of dual-circuit master cylinder

close to the union where the hose or pipeline enters the wheel cylinder, behind the backplate. On front brakes it is opposite the hose. Remove the bleed screw caps.

3 Start with the brake which is farthest from the master cylinder. Fit the tubing to the bleed screw and immerse the free end in a small quantity of fluid in the jar. Open the bleed screw about one turn.

4 The second operator must now depress the brake pedal quickly for a full stroke and allow it to return slowly. Air bubbles will stream from the immersed end of the tubing.

5 When air bubbles no longer come out, ask the second operator to hold the pedal down at the end of a full stroke while the bleed screw is tightened. Repeat the process on all the other brakes in turn. Fit the caps to the bleed screws to exclude dirt. Check the fluid level in the reservoir.

It is not advisable to use the fluid in the jar for topping up. It will be aerated and may not be perfectly clean. If it is known to be clean it may be used again after it has been standing for twenty-four hours. Never leave brake fluid uncovered, as it will absorb moisture.

10:10 The handbrake

Removing lever:

Pull lever boot up and off the lever. Unscrew nuts from end of brake cable. Lift the vehicle and support firmly, release the handbrake. Remove the coverplate under the pedal linkage. Pull cables out from handbrake lever. Remove accelerator pedal spring and remove pedal push-rod. Remove circlip and push out lever pivot pin 3 (see **FIG 10:12**). Pull off handbrake lever. Press release button and remove ratchet.

Refitting lever:

Refer to **FIG 10:12**, clean and grease the pawl rod 1, button, pawl spring and ratchet 2. Insert the ratchet, ensuring that the recess fits over the lever bearing bush A and that the teeth engage with pawl 7. Refit lever with slot in ratchet engaged with mounting bracket C. Grease lever pin 3 and insert into handbrake lever and mounting bracket. Refit circlip. Connect pushrod to accelerator pedal and refit spring. Attach the cables to the handbrake lever, adjust handbrake as described in **Section 10:2** and lock the nuts. Refit the coverplate and the handbrake lever boot. Check the operation of the handbrake.

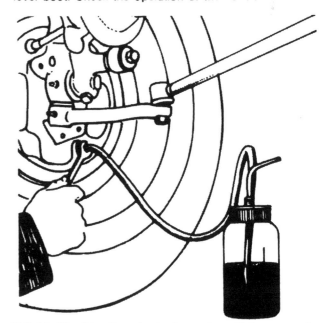

FIG 10:10   Bleeding the brake system. Tube connects bleed screw to liquid in container. Unscrew bleed screw with spanner as shown

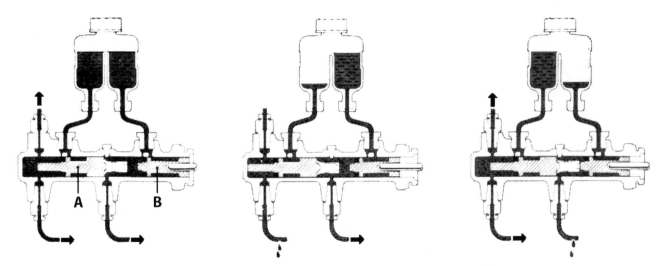

FIG 10:11 Diagrammatic principles of dual-circuit braking system. On left, movement of piston **B** by brake pedal is transmitted to piston **A** by fluid between. Fluid under pressure flows to three outlets, two on the left to front brakes, one on right to rear brakes. Central view shows failure in front brake circuit, piston **A** moves to stop on left, piston **B** provides pressure to rear circuit. On right, failure of rear brake circuit, piston **B** contacts piston **A** to provide pressure to front circuit only

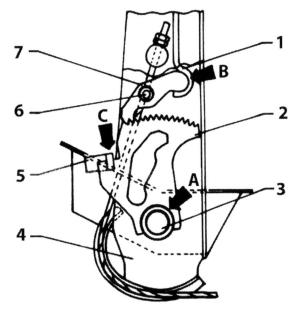

FIG 10:12 Handbrake lever assembly. When refitting ensure that ratchet seats properly on bearing bush at arrow **A** and that the pawl locates with rod as shown at arrow **B**. The slot in the ratchet must engage in the bracket as shown at arrow **C**

Key to Fig 10:12   1 Rod   2 Ratchet   3 Lever pivot pin
4 Handbrake lever   5 Bracket   6 Pawl pivot pin
7 Pawl

The handbrake cables:

These can be removed after the rear wheels and brake drums have been removed as instructed in **Section 10:4**. Remove the cable from the handbrake lever. Remove the rear brake shoes, detach the cable, remove the cable retainer from the backplate and pull the cable out of its guide tube from the front end. To install a new cable, check the length against the old one. Use universal grease on the cable before pushing it into the guide tube. When all operations are completed, check the action of the handbrake on the road.

10:11 Fault diagnosis

(a) 'Spongy' pedal

1 Leak in the system
2 Worn master cylinder
3 Leaking wheel cylinders
4 Air in fluid system
5 Linings not firmly bedded to shoes
6 Insufficient fluid in reservoir

(b) Excessive pedal movement

1 Check 1, 4 and 6 in (a)
2 Excessive lining wear
3 Too much free movement of pedal
4 Check valve in master cylinder defective
5 Linings excessively worn, clearance needs adjusting

(c) Brakes grab or pull to one side

1 Distorted drums
2 Wet or oily linings
3 Brake backplate loose
4 Worn suspension or steering connections
5 Mixed linings of different grades
6 Uneven tyre pressures
7 Broken shoe return springs
8 Seized cable
9 Seized wheel cylinder piston

(d) Pedal must be pumped to get braking

1 Air in system
2 Check valve in master cylinder faulty
3 Weak spring in master cylinder

(e) Brakes get hot when not used

1 Small drilling in master cylinder blocked by main cup
2 No free play of master cylinder pushrod
3 Weak or broken shoe return springs
4 Tight wheel cylinder pistons
5 Rubber cups swollen due to wrong brake fluid

CHAPTER 11

THE ELECTRICAL SYSTEM

11:1 Description

A 6-volt electrical system was used on all Transporter models until late 1966. During 1967 there was a change-over to a 12-volt system.

Although the basic function of all the components has been much the same throughout the years, there have been so many small changes in design that it would be impossible, in the space available, to cover every one. There is an added complication that generators and starters of Bosch or Volkswagen manufacture have been fitted alternatively. Fortunately, the general instructions we are able to give will cover both types reasonably well, and a little observation of the components when dismantling will enable any normal owner to service his equipment without serious difficulty.

The battery is charged by controlled output from the belt-driven generator, the controlling unit being a regulator. **This regulator is sealed and must be renewed or adjusted at an official Service Station if faulty.** It is mounted on the generator on all models until the advent of the 12-volt system.

The starter motor is mounted on the transmission casing and its shaft carries a sliding pinion. The pinion is moved into mesh with the ring gear on the flywheel by a solenoid and lever which comes into action as soon as current is supplied. When the pinion is fully engaged, the starter circuit is completed and the flywheel is turned. When the engine fires, an overrunning clutch prevents the pinion from being spun too fast and a spring returns it to rest.

Most headlamps have been of the renewable bulb type, but recent models are equipped with sealed beam units. Early direction indicators were of the swinging arm type but flashers are now standard. An electric windscreen wiper is fitted.

The instructions given in this Chapter are for the 6-volt system, but the maintenance and serving procedures apply also to the 12-volt system. The components shown in **FIGS 11:1** and **11:6** are basically similar for the 12-volt generator and starter respectively.

Instructions for electrical tests are given for the benefit of the owner who can use accurate test meters and there are some mechanical faults which can be rectified by a reasonably skilled person. Wiring diagrams are included in Technical Data at the end of this manual.

11:2 Battery maintenance

The negative terminal of the battery is earthed. The terminals and cables must be clean and dry. Brush away

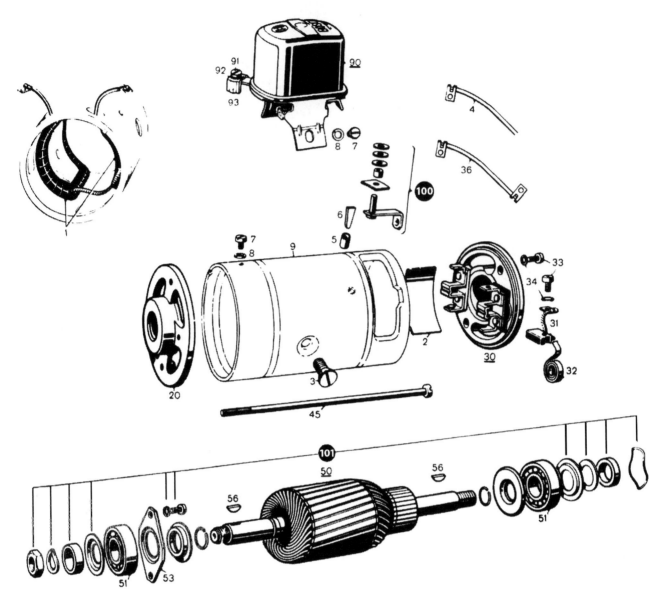

FIG 11:1   Components of a typical Bosch generator with regulator mounted on body

Key to Fig 11:1   1 Field coil   2 Insulating strip   3 Screw   4 Cable   5 Insulating bush   6 Key   7 Screw
8 Lockwasher   9 Body or frame   20 Drive end plate   30 Commutator end plate (with parts 31 to 36)   31 Carbon brush
32 Brush spring   33 Screw   34 Lockwasher   36 Cable   45 Screw   50 Armature (with parts 51 and 53)
51 Ballbearing   53 Bearing retainer   56 Woodruff key   90 Regulator (with parts 91 to 93)   91 Screw
92 Spring washer   93 Terminal bracket   100 Terminal assembly   101 Armature assembly

all corrosion, scrape the terminals and cable clamps to a bright metal surface and coat them with petroleum jelly before refitting. Make sure the battery is securely clamped.

Heavy demands are made upon a battery, particularly in the winter, and periodic attention is essential. On Transporters the battery is in the rear compartment on the righthand side.

With the cover removed, check the level of the electrolyte and top up if required, using distilled water. Some batteries have indicators. On those without, top up to a level slightly less than $\frac{1}{4}$ inch above the plates. Never add neat acid, and only top up with dilute sulphuric acid if some has been lost by spillage. To prepare the electrolyte, add sulphuric acid very slowly to distilled water. **Never add water to acid as this is highly dangerous.** Stir the liquid and test with an hydrometer until the specific

gravity is 1.285 when cool. Do not use rainwater or tap water.

The state of charge of the battery can be checked with the hydrometer. Remove the filler plugs and use the bulb to suck up enough electrolyte to lift the float. When fully charged the reading should be 1.285, when half-discharged 1.20 and when fully discharged 1.12. **A discharged battery must be recharged at once.** Never leave a battery in a discharged condition or it will become sulphated. If it is to be left unused for long periods, give it a freshening charge every six weeks.

Testing each cell with a hydrometer is not a real test of a battery. This method is only satisfactory if it is done while the battery is made to deliver a heavy discharge, and most garages have suitable equipment. The voltage of all cells should be 2. Any cell which is .2-volt less than the average is probably defective. If the voltage drops below 1.6 volts during a heavy discharge test, the battery is discharged. Charge again at a rate which is 10 per cent of the capacity. A 66 amp/hr battery will thus be charged at 6.6 amps. Remove all the filler plugs and keep naked lights away. Rapid charging of a sound battery is permissible in an emergency, but it is not recommended at frequent intervals.

Remove the negative cable from the battery when working on the cables of the electrical system. Short-circuits may cause serious damage, particularly if there is spilled fuel about.

11:3 Generator maintenance

There is no provision for regular lubrication. The ball-bearings are packed with high-melting point grease. Repack with fresh grease during a major overhaul, say at 20,000 miles. Never use ordinary grease.

Routine maintenance is confined to examination of the brushes and to the adjustment of the driving belt as instructed in **Chapter 4**.

Brushes:

To check the brushes remove the cover(s) from the rear end of the generator body. This will reveal the apertures at the righthand end of the body 9 (see **FIG 11 : 1**). Through these will be seen the brushes 31 and springs 32. Hook up the springs with a piece of bent wire and pull the brushes out of the holders. Try to keep them the right way round for correct replacement. It is possible that the latest models may not have a cover band.

The brushes must slide freely in their holders. If, after cleaning with a fuel-moistened rag, a brush still sticks, ease the sides by rubbing on a smooth flat file. If the brushes are soaked in oil or are so worn that they no longer bear on the commutator, they must be renewed. A very short brush also leads to low spring pressure. If the springs are weak they must be renewed. Check the condition of the commutator and recondition it as follows:

Commutator:

This is the segmented copper cylinder at the righthand end of part 50 in the illustration. The copper should be clean and smooth and the insulation between the segments must not stand proud or the brushes will not make electrical contact with the copper. If the commutator is only discoloured it can be polished by cleaning with a fuel-moistened cloth, pressing with a piece of wood. Then it should be rotated while holding a piece of very fine glasspaper in contact. Clean away all dust.

If the commutator is burnt and obviously worn, the generator must be dismantled and the armature run between centres in a lathe. A light cut with a very keen tool should be taken, removing as little metal as possible. Finally polish with very fine glasspaper. **Do not use emerycloth.** After this, the insulation between the segments must be undercut as shown in **FIG 11 : 2**. Grind the sides of a fine hacksaw blade until it is the width of the insulation then carefully cut between each pair of segments to a depth of approximately $\frac{1}{64}$ inch.

11:4 Generator and regulator testing

Visual indication of generator current is given by the red warning lamp on the instrument panel. A burnt-out bulb can be renewed.

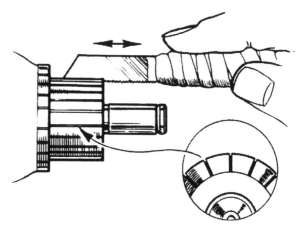

FIG 11:2 Undercutting commutator insulation with hacksaw blade ground to width between copper segments

Assuming that the bulb is working it should light up when the ignition is switched on and go out when the generator is charging the battery. If the bulb continues to glow even though the generator and regulator are known to be in order, there must be an excessive voltage drop between the regulator terminal B+ and the bulb. Check the connections as follows:

1 Run the engine at a fast-idle and switch on the head-lamps, screen wiper and indicators.
2 Connect a little over four yards of heavy insulated cable to terminal B+ on the regulator. Bare the insulation from the free end.
3 With the help of an assistant to watch the warning lamp, contact the following points in sequence: Lighting switch terminal 30. Fuse box terminal 30. Ignition/starter switch terminal 30. Fuse box terminal 15/54.
4 If the warning lamp stops glowing when one of the connections is made the poor connection causing the voltage drop lies between the last point of contact and the previous one. Look for loose connections, faulty cables and defective contacts in switches.

If the warning lamp continues to light up with the engine running fast, test the generator as follows:

Note that cables to the generator and regulator must not be connected or disconnected with the engine running. When the engine is stationary, disconnect cable B+ or 51, as a shortcircuit will damage the regulator. Be careful not to interchange the cables to D+ (or +) and F (or DF) as this will also damage the regulator.

Note that even if the warning lamp goes out when engine speed rises, it does not guarantee that the regulator is in order or that the battery is being charged properly.

Carry out the tests with two accurate moving coil meters, a 0—30 voltmeter and 50—0—50 ammeter.

Testing no-load voltage:

1 Disconnect the cable from terminal B+ (or 51) on the regulator. To the same terminal, connect the postive lead of the voltmeter and earth the negative lead of the meter.
2 Start the engine and increase the speed until the needle no longer rises. On 6-volt systems this no-load voltage

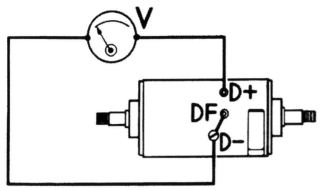

FIG 11:3 Checking generator output without regulator. Connect voltmeter between generator D+ and earth

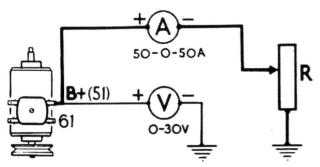

FIG 11:4 Checking regulator operation independently of the state of battery charge

should be 7.4 to 8.1 volts, or 6 to 7 volts on early generators. Shut off and watch the needle. Just before the engine and generator stop turning, the needle should drop suddenly to zero, indicating that the cut-out points in the regulator are opening correctly. If the cut-out points do not open the regulator will become very hot and the battery will become discharged through the generator.

3 On 12-volt systems using regulator VA.14V.30A, a tachometer is required as well as the meter. Use the greatest care not to shortcircuit the field coils when carrying out this test. Disconnect the two leads from the generator. Earth terminal DF. Connect the voltmeter across terminal D+ (or 61) and earth, start the engine and gradually increase speed. With a cold generator running at 1450 rev/min the output should be 14 volts. **Complete this test in a few seconds or the field coils may burn out. FIG 11:3** shows how the connections are made. Do not alter the length of the wiring from regulator to generator as cable resistance is matched with the 'Variode' device in the regulator.

Checking charging current:

1 Disconnect battery earthing strap. Disconnect cable from B+ on regulator. Insert an ammeter between the disconnected cable and the B+ terminal. Reconnect the battery strap.
2 Run the engine at a fast-idle. Switch on the lights and other current users. If the ammeter does not record on the positive side then the regulator is defective.
3 Reduce engine speed slowly to idling and watch the meter needle. It should cross the zero mark to the discharge side. Just before the speed drops to idling

the needle should flick back to zero which shows that the cut-out points in the regulator have opened. If, with the engine stopped, a heavy discharge is still indicated, remove the battery lead at once as the battery is discharging through the generator due to the cut-out points being welded together. The regulator must then be serviced or renewed. This test does not show whether the current control of the regulator is correctly set for battery charging at the required rate.

Checking regulator:

This should form part of the generator tests, before the generator is removed for servicing. The initial instructions refer to the 6-volt regulator.

Refer to **FIG 11:4** when making the connections. Equipment required will be a 30-volt meter, a 50—0—50 ammeter and an adjustable resistance capable of passing 50 amps. Carry out the test on 6-volt systems as follows, with the generator in the vehicle if desired:

1 Use heavy cables which are as short as possible. Disconnect cable from B+ (or 51) terminal on regulator. Connect the resistance in series with the ammeter and a good earth on the generator. Make the best connections possible, as extra resistance will give faulty readings.
2 Connect the positive terminal of the voltmeter to the same regulator and earth the other side.
3 Run the generator at approximately 4000 rev/min, remembering that this speed is not the same as engine rev/min. Set the resistance to show a reading of about 45 amps on the meter. The voltage indicated should be at least 6 to 7.5 volts on the 6-volt system. Renew the regulator if the reading is not within the limits. **Repair or adjustment is a job for an authorized Service Station.**

On 12-volt systems the regulator is sealed and no attempt should be made to adjust it. **Repair and adjustment must be left to an official Service Station.** It is possible to make a simple test to determine whether the regulator is working if the generator and battery are known to be in good order. Remove the rear seat to reach the regulator. Connect a moving coil 20-volt meter across regulator terminal B+ and a good earth. Battery voltage should be indicated. Run the engine and increase the speed. The meter reading should rise as the generator is cut-in by the regulator, but only by a small amount.

Repeating an earlier warning, connections to the generator and the regulator must be made with the engine stopped and cable B+ (or 51) disconnected. A shortcircuit will make the regulator unserviceable. Interchanging the cables to D+ (or +) and F (or DF), may affect the polarity of the generator.

11:5 Removing and installing generator

On 6-volt generators disconnect the battery earthing strap and the cables to the regulator terminals. Release the regulator from the generator body. Disconnect the two cables D+ (or +) and F (or DF) from under the regulator. On 12-volt generators simply remove the two cables.

On recent models remove the air cleaner and carburetter. Take off the fan belt and remove the generator retaining strap. Remove the cooling air thermostat by undoing the screws with a socket inserted through the holes in the lower air deflector plate under the engine. Detach the warm air hoses from the fan housing, remove the two fan housing screws at the sides and lift the housing, referring to **Chapter 4** if necessary. Remove the four screws from the fan housing cover and lift the generator and fan away.

On early models proceed as above, but instead of removing the thermostat, remove the two screws fixing the air regulating ring to the bracket in front of the fan housing (see **Chapter 4**). Remove the ignition cables and conduit tube. Lift the fan housing slightly, remove the four fan housing screws and remove the generator. The paper gasket under the generator must be sound.

Installing the generator:

Reverse the removal instructions. On early models the air regulating ring in front of the fan housing must be correctly centred (see **Chapter 4**). When the regulator is mounted on the generator the thick cable from one of the brushes is connected to D+ (or +) under the regulator. The thin field coil cable must be connected to the F (or DF) terminal under the regulator. If a new regulator has been fitted without curing any defects in the system, the generator is at fault. Bear in mind, however, that reversed generator leads may have reversed the generator polarity. Refer to the next section on generator servicing for instructions on restoring correct polarity.

11:6 Generator servicing

Use **FIG 11:1** for reference purposes. The illustration shows the Bosch generator but the VW generator will be found to resemble it fairly closely. The most likely differences will be in the bearing assemblies, so make a careful note of the sequence of circlips, washers, seals and spacers which will be found on the armature shaft or in the end covers.

Note that the generator and regulator must both be of the same make.

To dismantle a generator, do the following:
1 Remove the driving pulley and the fan. Disconnect the field coil terminal 100 from the holder of the positive brush.
2 Remove the two long through-bolts 45. Prise out the keys 56 and remove any burrs from the shaft of armature 50. Tap off the end cover 30.
3 At the other end, tap off cover 20 which will bring the armature with it. Check the position of the various washers, seals and spacers at the commutator end. Press the armature shaft out of the bearing in the end cover 20.
4 To remove the bearing in the end cover at the fan end, remove the two screws from retainer plate 53. Clean all parts except the windings with fuel and dry thoroughly, preferably with compressed air.

Check the condition of the brush gear and commutator as described in **Section 11:3**. Inspect the field coils and connections for breakdown of insulation. Check the dry bearings for cracks, pitting or roughness when spun. Check the armature laminations for the bright marks of actual contact with the field coil polepieces. **Never attempt to straighten a bent shaft or machine the armature laminations.** Test the armature and the field coils.

Armature testing:

Badly burned spots between the commutator segments indicate broken windings. Shortcircuits can be checked on a device called a growler which is part of Service Station equipment.

Field coil testing:

Test coils 1 with a battery and test lamp, trying each one for an open circuit. Test for earthing by putting a 230-volt test lamp across one end of each coil and the body of the generator.

Testing for a shortcircuit needs either an ohmmeter or an ammeter. Compare the readings of resistance. To use the ammeter, connect a 6-volt battery in series with the meter and check the current consumption of each coil. If the difference is more than half an amp there is a shortcircuit in one of the coils.

Reassembling generator:

Fill the bearings with high-melting point grease and no other. Reassemble in the reverse sequence to dismantling.

It is possible for a generator to have reversed polarity due to crossed leads or shortciruits. Before installing an overhauled generator, motor it for a short time, using a battery of the correct voltage. Connect terminal F (or DF) to earth, the positive terminal of the battery to D+ (or +) and the negative battery terminal to earth of D—.

Fit the fan and cover so that there is the correct clearance given in **Chapter 4**. Tighten the fan nut to a torque of 40 to 47 lb ft.

Starting with 1967 models the generator is cooled by air from the fan housing. The fan coverplate has a slot on the periphery for the cooling air intake, and it is most important to fit this cover to the fan housing with the slot at the bottom.

Finally, fit the pulley, adjust the belt tension and make the connections to the regulator. The red cable goes to terminal 51 and the blue cable to terminal 61.

11:7 Starter motor description and maintenance

The starter motor is flange-mounted on the righthand side of the transmission housing. In the transmission housing is an outrigger bush for supporting the extended armature shaft. Starting in August 1966, the starter pinion was modified to mesh with a new flywheel ring gear with 130 teeth instead of the original 109. The outrigger bush was also modified, having a bore which was reduced from 12.5 mm to 10.89 mm. On recent models there is a non-repeat lock in the ignition switch to prevent any attempt to actuate the starter while the engine is running. Before the starter can be operated again the ignition key must be turned right off. As mentioned earlier there are both Bosch and VW starters fitted to the various models. **FIGS 11:5** and **11:6** show Bosch starters in exploded form. The pinion and solenoid assembly on VW starters will be found to be different in design but similar in operating principles. If care is taken to note the sequence for removing the various shims, washers and locking rings from the armature shaft, there should be no difficulty in dismantling and reassembling either make.

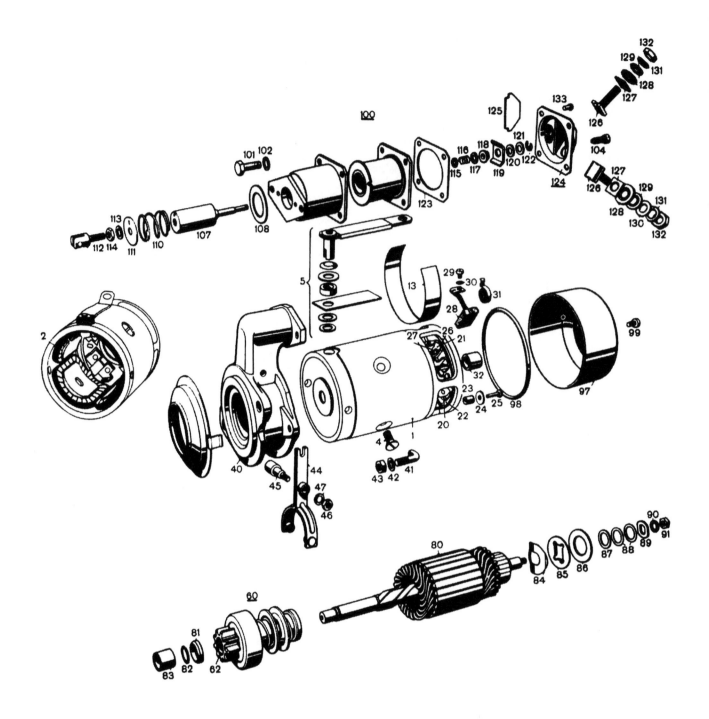

FIG 11:5 Components of earlier Bosch starter motor in the EED series

Key to Fig 11:5   1 Body or frame with commutator end bearing   2 Field coil   4 Screw for polepiece   5 Terminal assembly
13 Insulating strip   20 Commutator end plate   21 Brush-holder   22 to 25 Parts securing positive brush-holder
26 and 27 Parts securing negative brush-holder   28 Carbon brush   29 Screw   30 Lockwasher   31 Brush spring
32 Commutator end bearing   40 Intermediate bracket   41 Hook bolt   42 Lockwasher   43 Nut   44 Drive engaging lever
45 Bolt   46 Nut   47 Lockwasher   60 Driving pinion assembly   62 Bush for pinion   80 Armature   81 Stop ring
82 Circlip   83 Bush for transmission casing   84 Spring washer   85 Retaining washer   86 Insulating washer
87 Insulating washer   88 Shims (three thicknesses)   89 Dished washer   90 Lockwasher   91 Nut   97 End cover
98 Rubber gasket   99 Screw   100 Solenoid assembly (including parts 104 to 133)   101 Screw   102 Lockwasher
104 Screw   107 Solenoid plunger   108 Gasket   110 Plunger return spring   111 Retaining disc   112 Link fork
113 Lockwasher   114 Nut   115 Shim   116 Contact pressure spring   117 Washer   118 Insulating bush
119 Contact bar   120 Insulating washer   121 Cup washer   122 Retaining ring   123 Gasket
124 Switch cover (with parts 125 to 132)   125 Insulator   126 Contact bolt   127 Insulating plate   128 Insulating washer
129 Washer   130 Washer   131 Lockwasher   132 Nut   133 Cover rivet

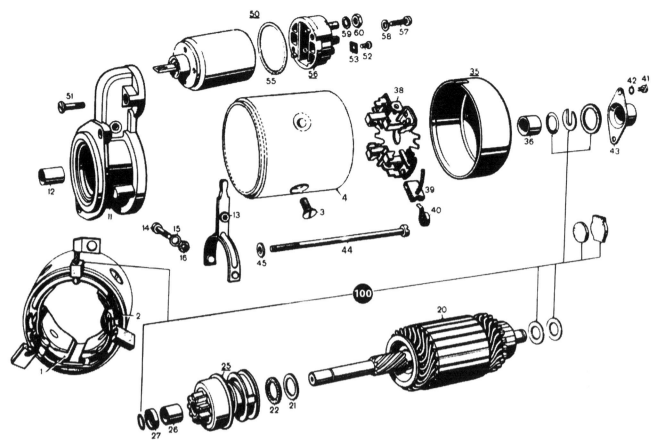

FIG 11:6   Components of Bosch starter motor in EEF series

Key to Fig 11:6   1 Field coil   2 Insulating strip   3 Screw for polepiece   11 Intermediate bracket
12 Bush for transmission casing   13 Pinion engaging lever   14 Screw   15 Lockwasher   16 Nut   20 Armature
21 Shim   22 Packing ring   25 Pinion assembly (with bush 26)   27 Stop ring   35 Commutator end bracket (with bush 36)
38 Brush plate assembly   39 Carbon brush   40 Brush spring   41 Screw   42 Spring washer   43 End cap
44 Screw   45 Washer   55 Solenoid assembly (with parts 55 to 58)   51 Screw   52 Screw   53 Lock plate
55 Packing ring   56 Switch cover   57 Screw   58 Lockwasher   59 Lockwasher   60 Nut   100 Kit of parts

Routine maintenance

The plain bushes which are used as bearings do not require regular lubrication. When the starter is due for overhaul, the bush at the commutator end can receive attention and when the starter is removed at any time, the outer bush in the transmission casing can be checked for wear and lubricated with grease.

The brushes should be checked every 6000 miles. Remove the brush inspection covers on the VW starter or the end cover 35 (see **FIG 11:6**) on the Bosch starter. Pull on the brush leads to check that the brushes 39 slide freely in their holders. Check the length of each brush. If the flexible lead is almost in contact with the metal brush holder it is time for renewal. While the brushes are out, examine the commutator. If badly burned or worn it will be necessary to remove the armature 20 to have the commutator skimmed. If the segments are just dirty or oily, clean them by rubbing a cloth dampened with fuel against them with a small piece of wood. Check that the springs 40 are not weak or broken. The renewal of brushes is covered under 'Starter motor servicing'. When refitting the brushes into their holders, make sure the flexible connectors are so placed that the brushes can move freely.

11:8 Starter motor servicing

Removal:

Dismantling (early type):

Refer to **FIG 11:5** and proceed as follows:

1 Detach the connector from the solenoid switch. Remove screws 101, slightly withdraw the pinion and remove the switch. Remove end cover 97 and lift up the brushes, trapping them clear of the commutator by letting the springs bear on their sides.

2 Using soft jaws in the vice, clamp the pinion end of the armature shaft and remove nut 91 from the other end. Release nuts 43 from the hook bolts 41 and lift off the intermediate bracket 40 and the armature 80. Keep a careful record of the arrangement of shims and washers 84 to 90.

3 Mount the armature in a vice, commutator end downwards and tap stop ring 81 further on to the shaft with a hollow drift. This will enable spring ring 82 to be prised out and the stop ring to be pulled off. Clean up any burrs round the spring ring groove. Withdraw the armature and remove the drive pinion assembly 60. Defective drive pinions can only be renewed as an assembly.

Dismantling (later type):

Refer to **FIG 11:6** and proceed as follows:

1 Release the connector strip from the solenoid 50 and remove screws 51 to release the solenoid from the intermediate bracket. Lift the solenoid until its slotted pullrod is clear of lever 13 and remove.

2 Remove end cap 43 and the sealing ring. Prise out the lock ring from the shaft and pull off the shims. Remove bolts 44 and end cover 35. This will also release the brush holder plate 38, but lift the brushes before pulling the holder off the armature shaft.

3 Separate the starter body from the intermediate bracket 11. Repeat preceding operation 3 to remove the pinion assembly. Remove the shift lever bolt 14 to release lever 13. A defective pinion assembly must be renewed complete.

These instructions will also be applicable to 12-volt starters.

Removing and dismantling VW starter:

1 Remove the connector strip from the solenoid, remove the two nuts and withdraw the housing with insulating disc. Remove the nut from the field coil lead and take off the specially shaped rubber seal.

2 Disconnect the connector strip at the end plate and remove the cap from the commutator end. From the end of the shaft, remove the circlip and the steel and bronze washers. Remove burrs from the shaft.

3 Lift off the two segmental brush covers, lift the brushes and wedge in position. Remove the two long through-bolts. This will enable the intermediate bracket at the drive end to be lifted together with the armature. Keep a careful note of the position of the various washers.

4 Disconnect the field coil lead from the brush holder and lift off the end plate. Remove the brake washer and thrust ring.

5 At the pinion end remove the spring clips and pivot pins from inside the bracket, pull out the insulating plate and turn the contact plate of the pointed solenoid core through 90 deg. Withdraw the armature, shifting linkage and solenoid core as a unit. Take off the circlip and retaining washers from the drive end of the shaft. Take the armature in one hand and the pinion in the other. Pull the shift collar about $\frac{3}{16}$ inch from the overrunning clutch and remove the drive assembly by turning clockwise and jerking slightly. Remove the shaft collar and the five steel balls from the overrunning clutch. The clutch cannot be dismantled.

Checking for defects:

Clean the parts in fuel but do not immerse the armature or field coils in it and keep it away from the porous bush at the commutator end. If the drive pinion is oily or has been reluctant to engage in cold weather it can be washed in fuel. Excessive oil in the starter may be traceable to a defective crankshaft oil seal or a main drive shaft oil seal.

Renew brushes by soldering the new leads into place one at a time. If the commutator is worn and out of round it can be skimmed in a lathe. Mount the shaft between centres and take light cuts with a keen tool. Do not reduce Bosch commutators below a diameter of 1.35 inches. After machining, or if the insulation stands proud between the copper segments, undercut the insulation about $\frac{1}{64}$

inch, using a ground down hacksaw blade as shown in **FIG 11:2**. Maximum permissible runout is .002 inch.

Test the field coils 1 (see **FIG 11:6**) for open circuit by using a 6-volt battery and a test lamp with prods. Place the prods at the ends of each coil. If the outer insulation is in order it is rare to find a shortcircuit. Tests for short-circuits need special equipment.

Test for earthed coils by using test prods and a 240-volt lamp. Put one prod on a coil end and the other to the frame or body. Make sure that electrical connections between the coils are sound.

An electrical test for earthed armature windings can be made with test prods and a 240-volt lamp. Put one prod on the armature laminations and the other to each commutator segment in turn. Check the condition of the soldered joints at the risers off each segment. Sometimes the solder becomes overheated and is flung off.

Check the bearing bushes for play. After protracted use it is always advisable to renew these bushes. Before fitting new ones, soak them in hot engine oil for some hours. Press into place using a mandrel the same diameter as the armature shaft.

Check the solenoid connections by testing to earth with a 240-volt lamp and test prods. It is possible for excessive tightening of the terminal nuts to damage the insulation. The pull-in and hold-in windings of the Bosch solenoid can be checked for power and consumption by an official Service Station. **If defective, a solenoid must be renewed complete.**

The VW solenoid should move the pinion .240 inch. If less than this, the reason may lie in worn linkages or excessive end float of the armature. The permissible end float of .004 to .012 inch can be obtained by shimming. If, when holding the VW armature, the pinion cannot be turned anticlockwise, the overrunning clutch is tight on the shaft. The clutch must be renewed as a unit. If the pinion does not spring right back to rest it may be due to sticking of the solenoid core or linkage, or the pressure spring in the overrunning clutch may not be engaging.

To test a 6-volt VW solenoid use a 6-volt battery and an ammeter reading to 50 amps. Insert the ammeter in a lead from the positive battery terminal to terminal 50. Connect the negative battery terminal to the pull-in winding terminal, when the meter should record a drain of 35 to 40 amps. To check the hold-in winding connect the negative battery terminal to the coverplate, when the meter should record a drain of 10 to 12 amps. Renew a defective solenoid.

11:9 Starter motor assembling

If the solenoid on a recent Bosch starter has been renewed, check the dimension indicated in **FIG 11:7**. When the core is drawn right in the distance from the face of the solenoid body to the outer end of the operating slot must be .748 ± .004 inch. Loosen the locknut and turn the rod to adjust.

Assembling Bosch starters:

Refer to **FIG 11:8** for details of the places where effective sealing is necessary to prevent the entry of water and road grit.

Assemble the armature and drive pinion to the intermediate bracket. Fit the stop ring and circlip, locking the stop ring in place by peening with a small chisel. Lubricate all moving parts and the shift lever with universal grease. Check that the support washer and seal between the starter body and the intermediate bracket are correctly fitted and assemble the parts together, using VW sealing compound D1a. Apply a touch of special Bosch grease to the shaft at the commutator end. Excessive lubricant at this point is liable to cause trouble with an oily commutator.

Fit the brushes and, on recent models, the brush holder. Apply sealing compound VW/D1a as indicated and fit the end cover. Apply sealer to the long through-bolts and fit them. Before fitting the cover on early models, check the armature end float and adjust with shims if necessary. The float should lie between .004 and .012 inch. On later models, fit the shims and lockwasher to the end of the shaft and check the end float, which should be the same as that just given. Fit the end cap with seal and put sealer under the screw heads.

To fit the solenoid, apply a strip of VW sealing compound D14 to the outer edge of the end face. Pull on the drive pinion and hook the solenoid operating slot over the lever. Put sealer on the solenoid fixing screws. Connect the field coil connector to the solenoid.

To install the starter motor, first put universal grease in the bush in the transmission casing. Apply VW sealing compound D1a between the intermediate bracket and the transmission. Insert the long screw in the bracket and fit the starter to the transmission. Connect the leads, making sure the terminals are clean and tightened securely but not excessively.

Assembling VW starters:

The steel balls of the drive assembly can be held in place with high-melting point grease. Lightly grease all moving parts. Push the overrunning clutch into place by jerking slightly to ensure that the inner spring passes over the shoulder of the pinion and engages the groove. Pull the clutch forward to check the engagement of the spring. Fitting the circlip is easier if a tapered mandrel is available.

Fit the linkage and solenoid core to the shift collar and insert the driving end of the armature in the intermediate bracket. Turn the solenoid contact plate through 90 deg. and insert the insulating plate above it, and up to the stop. Fit the two pivot pins and secure with the spring clips. Fit the thrust ring and brake washer in the commutator end plate. Fit the body to the end plate so that the nose enters the groove in the plate. Connect the field coil lead to the positive brush holder. Insert the armature assembly and fit the through-bolts, making sure the washers and shims are correctly positioned. Install the solenoid with the terminal in perfect contact and the profiled rubber seal seated properly.

Make sure all parts are sealed against the ingress of water and dirt, including the brush inspection covers and the end cap. Renew parts which do not seat properly. Use **FIG 11:8** for reference.

Fit the starter motor to the transmission casing in the manner described for the Bosch starter.

Transporter starters:

From June 1960 three types of starter were fitted intermittently. The earlier Bosch was type EED which closely resembled its predecessor. This was followed by

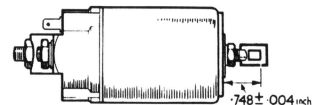

FIG 11:7 Correct setting of solenoid actuating rod on Bosch starter motor

·748 ± ·004 inch

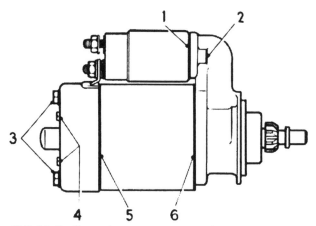

FIG 11:8 To seal starter motor against water and grit, use sealing compound at points indicated. Use compound D14 at point 1, and compound D1a under screw heads at 2, 3 and 4, and at joints 5 and 6

type EEF which was shorter and parts were not interchangeable with type EED. The VW starter, type 113/911/021A was fitted with a tab connector for cable 50 and the positive battery cable was repositioned. The starters are all interchangeable because the cables were lengthened to suit. The two Bosch starters can be service installed in earlier vehicles, and the cables do not need lengthening.

11:10 Headlamp servicing and adjustment

All vehicles were originally fitted with headlamps incorporating parking lights and renewable bulbs with twin filaments to give main and dipped beams. Latest models are now fitted with sealed-beam headlamps in which the front glass and reflector are sealed and form the bulb with the filaments inside. Failure of a filament in this type means that the complete unit must be renewed.

On the earlier type with separate bulb it is essential to handle the bulb with a piece of cloth or paper and not the bare fingers. Never attempt to clean the reflecting surface and do not touch it with the fingers. If the reflector loses its shine it must be renewed.

Renewing headlamp bulb:

1 Loosen the screw at the bottom of the rim. Take out the light unit by lifting the bottom to unhook the rim at the top.
2 From the back of the reflector, remove the bulb holder by turning to the left, as shown in **FIG 11:9**. Pull the connector off the base of the bulb.
3 Fit the new bulb, holding it with a piece of cloth or paper. When installing, the lug in the bulb holder must engage the notch in the reflector. The contact strip must press firmly on the base of the parking light bulb.

FIG 11:9 Removing the headlamp bulb (earlier non-sealed beam type)

Renewing headlamp glass:

1 Remove the light unit as just described. Take out both bulbs.

2 Note the long springs holding the reflector in the rim. Hold down one end of a spring firmly and release the other end. Be careful when doing this, as a flying spring might cause an accident.

3 Clean up the threaded ends of the adjusting screws and remove them. Take out the retaining ring with reflector, glass and seal. Do not finger the reflecting surface.

4 Fit the new glass and sealing ring with the 'TOP' mark correctly positioned. Fit the reflector and retaining ring with the sealing ring between the rim and the retainer.

5 Fit the adjusting screws and peen the ends. Fit the retaining springs. Fit the light unit and adjust the beam as instructed later. Do not fit headlamps of one make with parts of another make.

Renewing sealed-beam light unit:

1 Remove the light unit as described in the preceding instructions. The sealed-beam unit is recognizable by the three flat pins on the back, which fit into a socket. Pull off the socket and disconnect the two leads from the parking light socket.

2 Unscrew the parking light socket. Remove the retaining springs inside the rim, using the technique suggested in the preceding operation 2 on the renewable-bulb type of headlamp. Withdraw the retaining ring and sealed-beam unit.

3 The new unit can be located correctly by the tabs and slots in the retaining ring. Connect the leads correctly. Make sure the sealing ring between the front rim and the wing is properly seated.

Renewing sealed-beam headlamp glass:

1 Remove the unit and detach the leads. Take out the glass-retaining springs from inside the rim. Unscrew the adjusting screws as far as possible and detach the long spring clip.

2 Lift the retainer and light unit away from the rim until it is possible to remove the glass and sealing ring.

3 Put the seal on the new glass and insert in the rim with the VW sign upright and the arrow pointing down.

4 Fit the light unit and retainer with the seal between rim and retainer properly seated. Insert the retaining springs and after fitting the unit, adjust the beam settings as instructed later.

Headlamp beam setting:

This must be done in accordance with the Lighting Regulations of the country concerned. Basic setting on righthand drive vehicles is done as follows:

FIG 11:10 shows the layout of aiming points on a vertical surface which is symmetrical about the centre line of the vehicle and at right angles to the centre line. The vehicle must be standing on level ground 16 feet 5 inches away from the aiming surface, or 25 feet for sealed-beam lamps. Tyre pressures must be correct.

Dim the headlamps and cover one. Aim the other by turning the two adjusting screws indicated in FIG 11:11. The screw B is used for vertical aiming and screw A for horizontal aiming. On renewable-bulb headlamps the object is to get the horizontal borderline between light and dark to coincide with the horizontal line marked by the crosses. The point of the angle between light and dark should coincide with the cross. On sealed-beam headlamps use the lower diagram in FIG 11:10 and get the top edge of the high-intensity zone on the horizontal line and the righthand edge 2 inches to the left of the vertical line.

The setting of headlamp beams is so important in the interests of all road users that it is recommended to entrust the work to a Service Station equipped with the

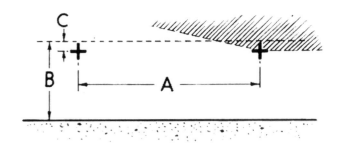

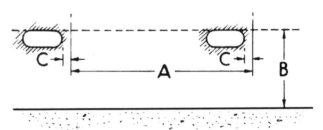

FIG 11:10 Headlamp beam setting on renewable bulb type (top), and on sealed beam type (bottom). A is distance between lamp centres, B is height of lamp centres above ground level, and C is 2 inches

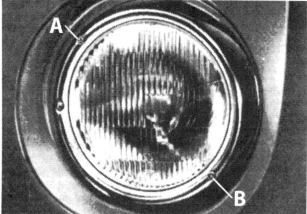

FIG 11:11 Adjusting headlamps, sealed-beam unit shown in the upper view and the renewable bulb type in the lower view. For both types turn screw A for horizontal setting and screw B for vertical setting

necessary devices, unless the greatest care is taken to ensure accurate results which conform to the Regulations.

11:11 Fuses and warning lights

There are so many variations in the disposition and use of fuses that it will be impossible to illustrate every one. Those given are typical. Early vehicles from 1954 had a four-way set of fuses on the back of the instrument panel and a two-way set for the headlamps, beside the fuel tank. Soon after this the two-way set was replaced by a four-way set to give protection to the low-beam headlamp circuits. This arrangement is shown in **FIG 11:12**. Later, this was superseded by a row of eight fuses under the parcel shelf in Transporters. The arrangement of wiring to this is shown in **FIG 11:13**. Some earlier vehicles had slightly different wiring along the bottom. From August 1966 ten fuses are fitted as shown in **FIG 11:14**. The lefthand fuse protecting the horn, flashers and stop-lights is for 16 amps but the rest are 8 amp fuses, although some righthand fuses are also 16 amp. Always carry spares and never substitute a blown fuse with a piece of wire or tinfoil. **Before renewing a fuse find the reason for blowing, otherwise the replacement may also fail.**

The warning lights and instrument lights have bulbs which can be reached from under the instrument panel. To renew bulbs it is a simple matter to pull the holders out of their sockets.

11:12 Direction indicators and flashers

Arm-type direction indicators should be cleaned with a brush and a little fuel if they become sluggish. It does no harm to prise the arm out if it refuses to work. Lubricate with thin anti-corrosion chassis oil. Thick engine oil or grease must not be used. After cleaning, check the connections and lamp contacts. Hold the indicator arm out to renew the bulb.

Flashing direction indicators :

Before renewing an apparently defective flasher unit, check that it is making a good earth connection with the vehicle body. The flasher unit is behind the lefthand front trim panel.

Failure of the flashers may be due to a blown fuse. The warning light on the dash will flash faster than usual if one of the flasher bulbs has failed. If both flashers on one side fail, the warning light will not operate, but do not forget that it is possible for the warning light to have burned out.

Before removing a flasher unit, take the earthing strap off the battery. Then remove the three leads, noting how they are connected. Screw the unit out of the mounting bracket or slide it free on later models where it is clipped in place.

Defective units cannot be repaired. When refitting a unit make quite sure that it is correctly connected and is effectively earthed to the frame.

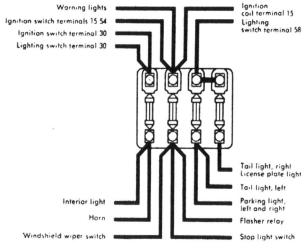

Fuse box on the back of the instrument panel

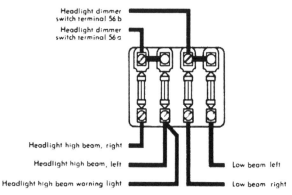

Fuse box adjacent to the fuel tank

FIG 11:12 Early fuse arrangement. Preceding this, only the two lefthand fuses on the lower block were fitted

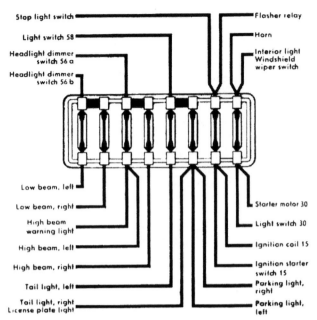

FIG 11:13 Later fuse arrangements for the 1960–64 Transporter

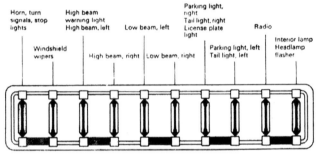

FIG 11:14 Latest 10-fuse arrangement

Self-cancelling indicator switch:

Below the cables leaving the switch under the steering wheel hub is a screw which clamps the switch to the column. To set the switch so that it cancels correctly, slacken the clamping screw and turn the switch in the required direction. If the wheel is removed at any time, set the front wheels straight-ahead and fit the brass washer so that its recess points to the right. Fit the steering wheel with the spokes horizontal and the spoke recesses for the horn ring towards the driver's seat. The tongue on the cancelling ring must then engage with the brass washer.

The self-cancelling switch must be fitted so that the distance between the lower face of the steering wheel hub and the upper face of the switch is .4 to .8 inch. Failure to cancel correctly can be cured by turning the switch on the column.

11:13 Horn and windscreen wipers

The horn is mounted under the lefthand wing. If a horn does not operate or has a poor note, check the security of the mounting and see that the horn does not touch the body. Also check the earthing and current supply from the horn button or ring. High resistance of dirty contacts and connections will be a contributory cause of trouble with the horn.

An attempt to adjust the horn must be made with great care. If the vibrating contacts inside the horn are kept in

contact for too long with current passing, they will be damaged and the fuse will be likely to blow.

The adjusting screw is on the back of the horn. Turn it fractionally in either direction and test with a quick operation of the horn button or ring. Continue until the best note is achieved. If it is impossible to find a position which gives a loud clear note, the horn must be renewed. After adjustment, the adjusting screw must be sealed with paint or shellac to prevent the ingress of water.

Before removing the horn, take out the fuse on the extreme left. Make sure the horn is properly earthed, and that it does not touch the body.

Horn controls can be examined by prising off the cap. Make sure all contact parts are clean and bright, and any spring correctly located.

The windscreen wipers:

These are operated by a linkage connected to a motor mounted under the panel between the warm air ducts to the screen.

The automatic parking action cannot work if the blades stop outside the area at the end of the return stroke, where switching takes place. If the blades are frozen to the screen or obstructed by piled snow it is possible for the motor to be burnt out. If the battery is flat and the arms have stopped midway, it is essential to move them to the parked position.

Apart from the renewal of wiper blades, there are several points which need lubrication after long service and the wiper motor brushes and commutator will also need cleaning and checking.

To remove the motor and linkage, lift off the righthand connecting rod and disconnect the lefthand ball joint from the wiper shaft, under the dash. Remove the two motor securing screws, pull out the motor slightly and disconnect the cable. Remove the motor together with the lefthand rod.

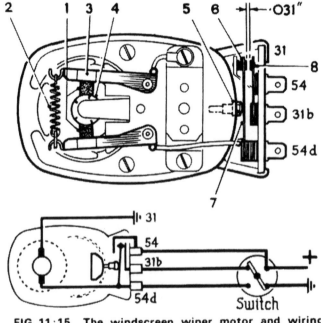

FIG 11:15 The windscreen wiper motor and wiring diagram. Note contact clearance

Key to Fig 11:15 1 Carbon brushes 2 Brush tension spring 3 Brush-holder 4 Commutator 5 Self-parking plunger 6 Moving contact 7 Moving contact spring blade 8 Fixed contact

Servicing wiper motor:

Refer to **FIG 11:15** and take off the cap by releasing the clip or removing a screw. Unhook the brush holder spring 2 and swing the holders 3 outwards. Use long-nosed pliers to remove and insert brushes 1. Clean the commutator 4 with a fuel-moistened cloth. When the brush holders are restored to the working position, make sure that the brushes bear on the commutator. Before reassembling, lubricate all linkage joints, shaft bearings and wiper arm joints. Note that plunger 5 is operated by a cam on the large gear at the other end of the motor and movement of the plunger operates the contacts 6 and 8 which form part of the parking switch. On early vehicles the mechanical details of the parking switch are different, but not in principle.

Installation of wiper assembly:

Before fitting the assembly, check that the driving link is fitted with its angled end towards the righthand wiper bearing. The inner seal on the wiper arm bearing must be fitted so that the shoulder of the rubber moulding faces the wiper arm when installed. Move the wiper frame on its elongated hole so that the wiper spindles are at right angles to the windscreen. The earthing cable on the securing screw must make good electrical contact.

11:14 Fault diagnosis

(a) Battery discharged

1 Terminals loose or dirty
2 Battery internally defective
3 Shortcircuits
4 Generator not charging
5 Regulator defective

(b) Insufficient charging current

1 Check 1 and 4 in (a)
2 Generator driving belt slipping

(c) Battery will not hold charge

1 Low level of electrolyte
2 Battery plates sulphated
3 Electrolyte leaking from cracked casing or top seal
4 Plate separators ineffective

(d) Battery overcharged

1 Regulator defective

(e) Generator output low or nil

1 Belt broken or slipping
2 Faulty regulator unit
3 Shaft bent, worn bearings, loose polepieces
4 Commutator insulation proud, segments worn, burned or shorted
5 Brushes sticking, springs broken or weak
6 Field coils faulty

(f) Warning lamp not lighting with ignition on

1 Battery faults
2 Defective ignition switch
3 Bulb burned out
4 Generator brushes not contacting commutator

(g) Warning lamp stays on or brightens with engine speed

1 Driving belt loose, generator faulty
2 Regulator faulty, charging cables loose or broken

(h) Warning lamp goes out only at high speed

1 Generator or regulator faulty

(j) Warning lamps stays on with ignition off

1 Contact points in regulator stuck

(k) Starter motor lacks power or will not operate

1 Battery discharged, loose connections
2 Solenoid switch contacts worn or dirty
3 Brushes worn or sticking, springs weak or broken
4 Commutator, armature or field coils defective
5 Armature shaft bent, engine abnormally stiff

(l) Starter motor runs but does not turn engine

1 Drive gear or flywheel gear defective

(m) Drive pinion stays in mesh

1 Armature shaft bent or dirty
2 Solenoid switch faulty

(n) Lamps inoperative or erratic

1 Battery low, bulbs burned out
2 Switch faulty, poor earthing, loose connections, broken wiring

(o) Wiper motor inoperative

1 Armature touching polepieces, windings faulty
2 Brush or commutator trouble
3 On early models, brake band not clearing armature
4 Tight bearings, bent linkage
5 Switch faulty, terminals 1 and 2 not connected. Wiring fault from terminal 1 to motor terminal 54

(p) Wiper motor runs with switch off, does not park blades

1 On early models, brake band broken or ineffective
2 Contacts damaged, insulation broken
3 Contact 31b not touching contact 54d
4 Poor earthing of terminal 31b through wiper switch

(q) Wiper motor slow, armature burns out, squeaky operation

1 Lack of lubrication to linkage
2 Armature spindle presses on stop of brush holder
3 Cover incorrectly positioned
4 Armature touches polepiece

CHAPTER 12

THE BODYWORK

12:1 Body finish

The high standard of paintwork on VW vehicles is obtained by skilful application of special primers and finishing coats. These are exclusively available to VW Service Stations so that the repair and painting of anything but minor damage must be left to them. Small scratches and tiny blemishes can be retouched by the owner, using the special touch-up paint which is supplied by VW. Before applying the paint it is essential to remove all traces of polish. This is done with white spirit, but in the case of silicone finishes, very gentle abrasion with the finest 'wet-or-dry' paper will be needed. If it is intended to retouch a small rusty spot or scratch, the rust must be removed with a gentle abrasive or a piece of wood. Leave each application of paint to dry before adding another coat and restore the brilliance of the abraded areas with a mild cutting compound. Repolish in the usual way.

12:2 Maintenance of bodywork

Apart from the normal cleaning and polishing there are a few places where lubrication is needed. The door hinges should have a spot of general-purpose oil applied after dirt has been wiped away. On the edge of the door above the lock is a small hole through which a little oil should be injected to lubricate the lock. Lock cylinders must not be oiled, but graphite powder can be applied to the key, which is then inserted and operated a few times.

A tiny smear of universal grease should be applied to the door lock striker plates on the body to the sliding prop stays, collapsible brackets and lid locks or panel locks. In the case of door locks be sparing with grease as it might otherwise come off on clothing.

Clean the seat runners of adhering dust and apply a thin smear of grease.

Other useful attention is to dust the rubber sealing strips round doors with French chalk. This helps to keep the seals flexible and prevents squeaks. Use the same technique on rubber buffers to eliminate noise.

Use universal grease on other contact surfaces such as door locks.

12:3 Removing and installing cab doors

To remove the cab doors, loosen the four cross-head screws securing the hinges to the body with a hammer and impact screwdriver as shown in **FIG 12:1**. Support the door and remove the screws, starting with the lower ones.

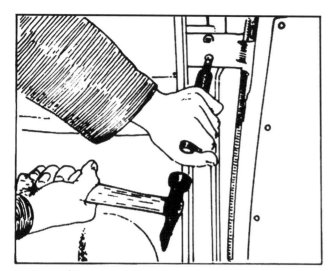

FIG 12:1 Remove door hinge securing screws using a hammer and impact screwdriver

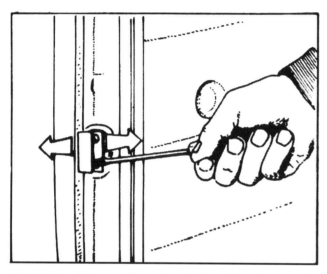

FIG 12:2 Adjust striker plate in direction of arrows by loosening screws

Check the weathstrips on the door and body and replace if they have deteriorated. Coat the new weatherstrips with a suitable adhesive before fitting.

Install the door, ensuring that it is aligned correctly before tightening the hinge screws. The door should open and close smoothly and make contact all round. If the door rattles, adjust the striker plate by loosening the screws (see FIG 12:2) and tapping the plate until the play is eliminated. Before doing this on vehicles which have seen much service, check the rubber buffer wedges as they may be worn. Fit new or oversize wedges as necessary. Finally, oil the hinges and apply a smear of grease to the sliding surfaces of the lock. Do not oil the lock cylinder but put graphite powder on the key, insert it and operate the lock a few times.

12:4 Removing and installing cab door ventilator

Press in the remote control escutcheon plate, drive out the pin as shown in FIG 12:3 and remove the handle and escutcheon. Remove screws and take off trim panel, then lift off the spring and rubber insert from the door handle spindle.

Refer to FIG 12:4, knock down ears of tabwasher 4, unscrew pivot nut 5 and remove tabwasher, spring 3, washer 1 and friction washer 2. Chisel off the rivet head at the upper pivot point and drive out rivet. Lift out the ventilator and remove friction washer 2 and washer 1 from inside the lower bracket.

Check the condition of the weatherstrip on the ventilator and renew if necessary. Refit the ventilator, fitting the friction washer 2 and washer 1 on the lower pivot point inside the bracket. Attach at the top pivot point using a new rivet. Fit the washers, spring, tabwasher and nut in the order shown in FIG 12:4. Tighten the nut until the ventilator is stiff enough not to be closed by wind pressure. Bend down the tabwasher to lock the nut.

12:5 Removing and installing window frame

Remove inner door handle and trim panel as described in **Section 12:3**. Take out the rubber plugs from hinge side of door frame and remove two screws (see FIG 12:5). Remove two window frame securing screws at top of

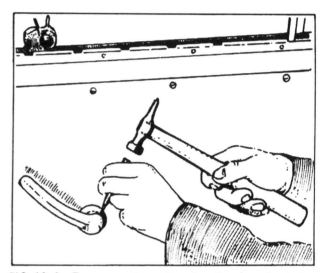

FIG 12:3 To remove inner door handle, press back the escutcheon plate and drive out retaining pin

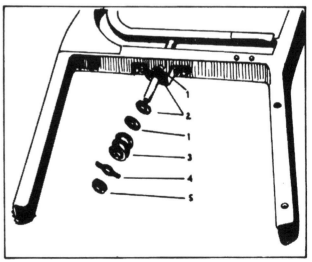

FIG 12:4 Ventilator lower pivot point

Key to Fig 12:4   1 Washer   2 Friction washer
3 Spring   4 Tabwasher   5 Nut

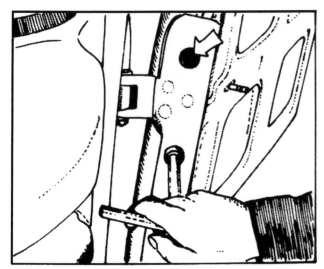

FIG 12:5 Fixing points for front leg of door window frame

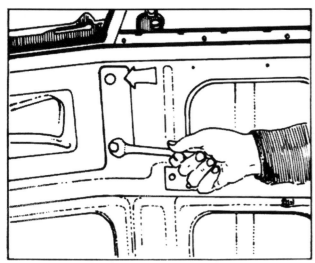

FIG 12:6 Fixing points for centre leg of door window frame

door inner panel, as shown in **FIG 12:6**. Unscrew two countersunk head screws at lock side of door. Remove two nuts between inner and outer door panels, arrowed in **FIG 12:7**. Lift window frame up and out of door.

Inspect weatherstrip between window frame and door for signs of deterioration and renew if necessary. Install window frame in the door, ensuring that the weatherstrip seals correctly. Fit the screws in the reverse order to that given for removal.

12:6 Removing and installing cab door lock

Remove inner door handle and trim panel as described in **Section 12:3**. Remove four screws at door lock side. Lift out outer handle and seal. Remove two lock securing screws and two remote control securing screws. Withdraw lock and remote control gear as shown in **FIG 12:8**.

Inspect remote control gear and renew any worn components. If the rivets at the ends of the operating rod are loose, peen them over. Clean the lock and lubricate moving parts lightly with grease. Align rubber sleeve on connecting rod with the projection on the door inner panel

and lightly preload rod. Lubricate rubbing surfaces with grease.

12:7 Servicing hinged side doors

If the original doors are to be removed and refitted, simply drive out the hinge pins, unless the hinges themselves are worn. First open the door and lift the check strap pin. Disconnect the strap. Remove the check strap retainer (two cross-head screws) and take off both retainer and strap. Take out the rubber plugs and remove the cross-head hinge screws. If necessary, renew the weatherstrips, sticking the new ones in place with adhesive. Clean and oil the hinges and put a little universal grease on the lock mechanism. Refit the door and align it properly before fully tightening the screws.

Side door locks:

To remove these, undo the door handle securing screw and take off the handle, gasket, escutcheon plate and rubber packing. In the case of the rear side door remove the two door lock screws and lift away the lock. On front

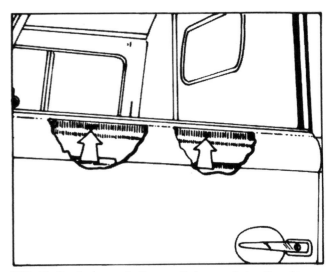

FIG 12:7 Arrows indicate fixing points for lower frame of door window

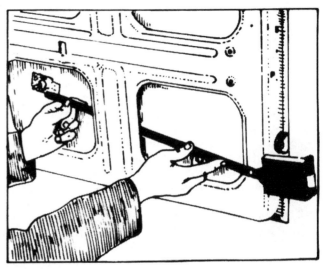

FIG 12:8 Remove door lock and remote control as shown

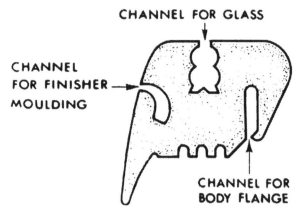

FIG 12:9 Section of windscreen moulding, showing channels for glass, finisher moulding and body flange

doors remove the link screws from the upper and lower lock bars and the four screws from the lock. On both assemblies, mark the upper and lower bars and then remove them by sliding up or down. The bars are not interchangeable.

Clean all parts and oil the lock. Use universal grease on the bars. When replacing the bars in rear door locks, make sure the tongues in the lock engage correctly in the notches in the bars.

12:8 Removing and installing engine compartment lid

Disconnect battery and licence plate lamp cable. Remove lamp lens and pull out lamp holder. Unscrew four screws securing lock and remove lock. Remove lid stay screw. Unscrew eight hinge securing screws and lift out lid.

Inspect lid seal for signs of deterioration, renew if necessary. Cement the new seal in position using suitable adhesive. Refit the lid and check that it fits evenly

all round. Connect lamp and battery. Apply a few drops of oil to the lid hinges and support stay hinge points.

12:9 Removing and installing windscreen

These instructions apply also to the renewal of other fixed glass windows. It is important to know whether the glass is laminated, of the safety type or simply plate glass as fitted to early models. Safety glass can be removed and refitted with blows of the fist or a rubber hammer, but it is dangerous to use this method with the other two types of glass. For these, hand pressure must suffice, and in all cases it is wise to protect the hands with cloth.

1 Remove the wiper arms. With laminated glass, use a wooden wedge to loosen the weatherstrip from the body. Start at one of the upper corners and push the screen and weatherstrip outwards.

2 The decorative finisher moulding fitted to the outer face of the rubber surround is secured by two sleeves. Drive these off and remove the moulding halves, followed by the rubber weatherstrip.

3 Remove old sealing compound from the body aperture and check the flange edges. These must be flat and smooth to ensure a leaktight seal.

4 Work the weatherstrip round the edge of the new glass, letting the ends meet halfway along the top edge. Prepare to fit the finisher moulding by inserting some strong cord in the slot in the weatherstrip shown in FIG 12:9. This is most readily done by using two or three inches of $\frac{5}{16}$ inch tubing flattened at one end for insertion into the slot. The cord is fed through the tube, which is then drawn round the slot, leaving the cord in position. Cross the cord ends in the centre of the lower edge and leave enough hanging out for handholds.

5 Push one half of the moulding into the slot, followed by the other. Slowly pull on the cord while pushing the moulding into place, until the operation is completed. Fit the two cover sleeves over the joins.

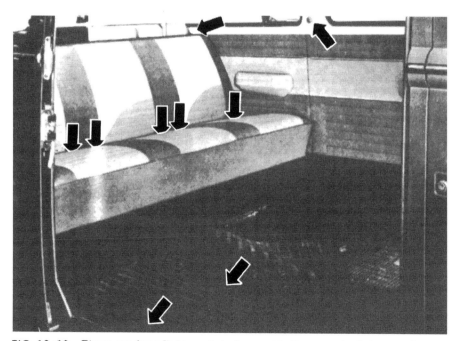

FIG 12:10 There are four fixing points for seat belts at each of the two front seats, as indicated by arrows in righthand view. The seat belt fixing points for the rear seat are indicated by arrows in lefthand view

6 Fit the cord into the slot in the weatherstrip which fits the body aperture, in the manner just described. Apply sealing compound to the outer surface of the weatherstrip and to the bottom corners of the aperture. Secure the services of an assistant.

7 Offer the screen to the outside of the frame with the cord ends inside. Press on the glass and pull at one end of the cable, keeping parallel to the glass. This should draw the lip of the weatherstrip over the body aperture. Continue pulling and pressing until the screen is in place. Safety-glass screens can be helped into place with modest blows from the fist. At all times avoid concentrated pressure in one place.

8 When the glass is properly seated, clean away all surplus sealing compound with petrol or white spirit.

12:10 Trim and headlining

To remove the partition panel on Delivery Vans, remove the five screws and the two rubber seals at the top corners. Slide the panel downwards, pulling it away from the spare wheel housing. If required, remove the rear view window. Check the rubber strip which seals on the fresh air regulator and the felt seal on the bottom half of the partition panel. The channels can be straightened to improve the fit of the panel. Use adhesive to secure the two rubber seals.

The cable trim panel can be removed by taking out the top half of the partition panel and removing the three securing screws. Withdraw the panel to the rear. Straighten the channels to improve the fit of the roof trim panel.

To remove the headlining of the Micro Bus, remove the three securing screws and the sun visor. With a screwdriver, bend up the retaining strip at the windscreen and pull out the lining. Remove the self-tapping screws and take off the trim panel. Remove the rear seat backrest. Remove the interior light in the passenger's compartment and the fresh air outlet to the rear of the roof ventilator. Remove both luggage compartment side trim panels and the upper trim panels on both sides at the rear. Carefully detach the parts of the headlining which are stuck in place. Prise up the metal tabs on the roof and remove the lining. The headlining is detached from the rails on both sides as far as the partition panel by lifting the cardboard strip sewn to the lining edges. Loosen the edges of the lining glued to the front panel. Bend up the tabs above the cab doors and pull out the headlining. Also bend up the retainers at the roof ventilator and release the glued parts of the lining. Disconnect the headlining bows from the side rails and remove the complete headlining. Clean and restore any damaged parts of the headlining. Examine the rubber end to the bows as these wear through and may cause rattling by metal-to-metal contact. Secure the lining with adhesive, to the body at the front and rear.

12:11 Seat belts

These are obtainable from VW Dealers. All seats can be fitted with lap belts. The drivers and front passengers seats and the outer seats in the rear compartment can be fitted with combined lap and shoulder belts. The anchor points for the seat belts are shown arrowed in **FIG 12:10**. There are four anchor points for each of the two front seats and a total of sixteen in the rear compartment. The tapped holes are fitted with plastic plugs to keep out dirt.

Inches		Decimals	Milli-metres	Inches to Millimetres		Millimetres to Inches	
				Inches	mm	mm	Inches
	1/64	.015625	.3969	.001	.0254	.01	.00039
1/32		.03125	.7937	.002	.0508	.02	.00079
	3/64	.046875	1.1906	.003	.0762	.03	.00118
1/16		.0625	1.5875	.004	.1016	.04	.00157
	5/64	.078125	1.9844	.005	.1270	.05	.00197
3/32		.09375	2.3812	.006	.1524	.06	.00236
	7/64	.109375	2.7781	.007	.1778	.07	.00276
1/8		.125	3.1750	.008	.2032	.08	.00315
	9/64	.140625	3.5719	.009	.2286	.09	.00354
5/32		.15625	3.9687	.01	.254	.1	.00394
	11/64	.171875	4.3656	.02	.508	.2	.00787
3/16		.1875	4.7625	.03	.762	.3	.01181
	13/64	.203125	5·1594	.04	1.016	.4	.01575
7/32		.21875	5.5562	.05	1.270	.5	.01969
	15/64	.234375	5.9531	.06	1.524	.6	.02362
1/4		.25	6.3500	.07	1.778	.7	.02756
	17/64	.265625	6.7469	.08	2.032	.8	.03150
9/32		.28125	7.1437	.09	2.286	.9	.03543
	19/64	.296875	7.5406	.1	2.54	1	.03937
5/16		.3125	7.9375	.2	5.08	2	.07874
	21/64	.328125	8.3344	.3	7.62	3	.11811
11/32		.34375	8.7312	.4	10.16	4	.15748
	23/64	.359375	9.1281	.5	12.70	5	.19685
3/8		.375	9.5250	.6	15.24	6	.23622
	25/64	.390625	9.9219	.7	17.78	7	.27559
13/32		.40625	10.3187	.8	20.32	8	.31496
	27/64	.421875	10.7156	.9	22.86	9	.35433
7/16		.4375	11.1125	1	25.4	10	.39370
	29/64	.453125	11.5094	2	50.8	11	.43307
15/32		.46875	11.9062	3	76.2	12	.47244
	31/64	.484375	12.3031	4	101.6	13	.51181
1/2		.5	12.7000	5	127.0	14	.55118
	33/64	.515625	13.0969	6	152.4	15	.59055
17/32		.53125	13.4937	7	177.8	16	.62992
	35/64	.546875	13.8906	8	203.2	17	.66929
9/16		.5625	14.2875	9	228.6	18	.70866
	37/64	.578125	14.6844	10	254.0	19	.74803
19/32		.59375	15.0812	11	279.4	20	.78740
	39/64	.609375	15.4781	12	304.8	21	.82677
5/8		.625	15.8750	13	330.2	22	.86614
	41/64	.640625	16.2719	14	355.6	23	.90551
21/32		.65625	16.6687	15	381.0	24	.94488
	43/64	.671875	17.0656	16	406.4	25	.98425
11/16		.6875	17.4625	17	431.8	26	1.02362
	45/64	.703125	17.8594	18	457.2	27	1.06299
23/32		.71875	18.2562	19	482.6	28	1.10236
	47/64	.734375	18.6531	20	508.0	29	1.14173
3/4		.75	19.0500	21	533.4	30	1.18110
	49/64	.765625	19.4469	22	558.8	31	1.22047
25/32		.78125	19.8437	23	584.2	32	1.25984
	51/64	.796875	20.2406	24	609.6	33	1.29921
13/16		.8125	20.6375	25	635.0	34	1.33858
	53/64	.828125	21.0344	26	660.4	35	1.37795
27/32		.84375	21.4312	27	685.8	36	1.41732
	55/64	.859375	21.8281	28	711.2	37	1.4567
7/8		.875	22.2250	29	736.6	38	1.4961
	57/64	.890625	22.6219	30	762.0	39	1.5354
29/32		.90625	23.0187	31	787.4	40	1.5748
	59/64	.921875	23.4156	32	812.8	41	1.6142
15/16		.9375	23.8125	33	838.2	42	1.6535
	61/64	.953125	24.2094	34	863.6	43	1.6929
31/32		.96875	24.6062	35	889.0	44	1.7323
	63/64	.984375	25.0031	36	914.4	45	1.7717

UNITS	Pints to Litres	Gallons to Litres	Litres to Pints	Litres to Gallons	Miles to Kilometres	Kilometres to Miles	Lbs. per sq. In. to Kg. per sq. Cm.	Kg. per sq. Cm. to Lbs. per sq. In.
1	.57	4.55	1.76	.22	1.61	.62	.07	14.22
2	1.14	9.09	3.52	.44	3.22	1.24	.14	28.50
3	1.70	13.64	5.28	.66	4.83	1.86	.21	42.67
4	2.27	18.18	7.04	.88	6.44	2.49	.28	56.89
5	2.84	22.73	8.80	1.10	8.05	3.11	.35	71.12
6	3.41	27.28	10.56	1.32	9.66	3.73	.42	85.34
7	3.98	31.82	12.32	1.54	11.27	4.35	.49	99.56
8	4.55	36.37	14.08	1.76	12.88	4.97	.56	113.79
9		40.91	15.84	1.98	14.48	5.59	.63	128.00
10		45.46	17.60	2.20	16.09	6.21	.70	142.23
20				4.40	32.19	12.43	1.41	284.47
30				6.60	48.28	18.64	2.11	426.70
40				8.80	64.37	24.85		
50					80.47	31.07		
60					96.56	37.28		
70					112.65	43.50		
80					128.75	49.71		
90					144.84	55.92		
100					160.93	62.14		

UNITS	Lb ft to kgm	Kgm to lb ft	UNITS	Lb ft to kgm	Kgm to lb ft
1	.138	7.233	7	.967	50.631
2	.276	14.466	8	1.106	57.864
3	.414	21.699	9	1.244	65.097
4	.553	28.932	10	1.382	72.330
5	.691	36.165	20	2.765	144.660
6	.829	43.398	30	4.147	216.990

CHAPTER 13
TECHNICAL DATA
Dimensions are in inches unless otherwise stated
The word 'limit' indicates the maximum permissible wear or clearance

ENGINE

Bore and stroke:
1192 cc	77 x 64 mm
1285 cc	77 x 69 mm
1493 cc	83 x 69 mm

Compression ratio:
1192 cc (to August 1955)	6.6 : 1
1192 cc (from August 1955)	7.0 : 1
1285 cc	7.3 : 1
1493 cc	7.5 : 1

Crankshaft (all models):

Main journal diameters:
Nos. 1, 2 and 3	2.1654
No. 4	1.5748

Main bearings:
Nos. 1, 3 and 4	Sleeve type, aluminium alloy
No. 2	Split shells, aluminium alloy

Main bearing running clearance:
Nos. 1, 2 and 3	.0016 to .004 (limit .0072)
No. 4	.002 to .004 (limit .0075)
Regrind undersizes	—.25, —.50 and —.75 mm
End float	.0027 to .005 (limit .006)
Crankpin diameter	2.1654
Crankpin regrind undersizes	—.25, —.50 and —.75 mm

Connecting rods (all models):
Running clearance, big-end	.0008 to .003 (limit .006)
End float, big-end	.004 to .016 (limit .028)
Maximum permissible weight variation	.18 oz

Pistons (all models):
Type	Aluminium alloy with steel strut
Running clearance (½ inch below crown at right angles to gudgeon pin)	.0015 to .002 (.0024 on '1500') (limit .008)
Weight tolerance, maximum	.18 oz
Piston rings (all models)	2 compression, 1 oil scraper
Side clearance, top compression	.0027 to .0035 (limit .005)
Side clearance, second compression	.002 to .0027 (limit .004)
Side clearance, oil control	.0012 to .002 (limit .004)
Compression ring gap	.012 to .018 (limit .035)
Oil control ring gap	.010 to .016 (limit .037)
Gudgeon pin type	Fully floating, located by circlips
Gudgeon pin bush	Bronze, pressed into connecting rod
Gudgeon pin clearance in bush	.0004 to .0008 (limit .0016)

Camshaft:
Type (all models)	Cast iron, three bearings

Bearings:
1192 cc up to August 1965	Direct in crankcase
1192 cc from August 1965, 1285 cc and 1493 cc	Split steel-backed, whitemetal lined
Running clearance (all models)	.0008 to .002 (limit .0047)
End float up to Engine No. 5067817 ..	.0012 to .0033 (limit .004)
End float from Engine No. 5067817 ..	.0024 to .0045 (limit .0056)
Backlash between timing gears	.0000 to .002

Tappets:
    Diameter (early)   ..   ..   .5893 to .5899
    Diameter (later)   ..   ..   .7466 to .7472 (limit .7452)
    Working clearance (early)   ..   ..   .0006 to .002
    Working clearance (later)   ..   ..   .0008 to .0024 (limit .0047)

Rocker shaft:
    Diameter (early)   ..   ..   .6285 to .6293
    Diameter (later)   ..   ..   .7073 to .7080 (limit .7069)
    Running clearance of rocker (early)   ..   ..   .0002 to .002
    Running clearance of rocker (later) ..   ..   ..   .0006 to .002 (limit .0031)

Valves:
    Head diameter, inlet:
        1192 cc (early) 1.181
        1192 cc (later) 1.24
        1285 cc 1.3
        1493 cc 1.4
    Head diameter, exhaust:
        1192 cc (early) 1.102
        1192 cc (later) 1.18
        1285 cc 1.18
        1493 cc 1.26
    Seat angle (all models)   ..   ..   45 deg.
    Stem diameter, inlet:
        1192 cc (early)   ..   ..   .2738 to .2742
        1192 cc (later), 1285 cc and 1493 cc   ..   .3126 to .3130
    Stem diameter, exhaust:
        1192 cc (early)   ..   ..   .2734 to .2738
        1192 cc (later), 1285 cc and 1493 cc   ..   .3114 to .3118
    Stem to guide clearance, inlet:
        1192 cc (early)   ..   ..   .0017 to .0027
        1192 cc (later) and 1285 cc   ..   ..   .0020 to .0030
        1493 cc   ..   ..   .008 to .009
    Stem to guide clearance, exhaust:
        1192 cc (early)   ..   ..   .0027 to .0037
        1192 cc (later) and 1285 cc   ..   ..   .0031 to .0041
        1493 cc   ..   ..   .011 to .012

Valve springs:
    Free length:
        1192 cc (early) 1.70
        1192 cc (later) and 1285 cc 1.89
    Loaded length:
        1192 cc (early)   ..   ..   1.10 at 73.5 lb
        1192 cc (later)   ..   ..   1.35 at 94$\pm$7 lb
        1285 cc and 1493 cc   ..   ..   ..   1.32 at 95$\pm$6 lb

Valve timing (with rocker clearance of .040):
    Inlet opens and closes:
        1192 cc (before Engine No. 5/000/001)..   .. $2\frac{1}{2}$ deg. BTDC, $37\frac{1}{2}$ deg. ABDC
        1192 cc (Engine Nos. 5/000/001 to 5/009/663)   2 deg. BTDC, 24 deg. ABDC
        1192 cc (later)   ..   ..   6 deg. BTDC, $35\frac{1}{2}$ deg. ABDC
        1285 cc and 1493 cc   ..   ..   .. $7\frac{1}{2}$ deg. BTDC, 37 deg. ABDC
    Exhaust opens and closes:
        1192 cc (before Engine No. 5/000/001)   .. $37\frac{1}{2}$ deg. BBDC, $2\frac{1}{2}$ deg. ATDC
        1192 cc (Engine Nos. 5/000/001 to 5/009/663)   32 deg. BBDC, 9 deg. ATDC
        1192 cc (later)   ..   .. $42\frac{1}{2}$ deg. BBDC, 3 deg. ATDC
        1285 cc and 1493 cc   ..   ..   .. $44\frac{1}{2}$ deg. BBDC, 4 deg. ATDC

Rocker clearance (cold):
    Inlet and exhaust:
        1192 cc (early, with sticker on fan housing)   .004
        1192 cc (with no sticker)   Inlet .008, exhaust .012
        1192 cc (after Engine No. 5/000/001)   .008 (Transporter exhaust .012)
        1285 cc   .004
        1493 cc   Inlet .008, exhaust .012

Oil pump:
    End float in housing (with gasket)   .003 to .007
    Backlash between gears   .001 to .003
    Pressure (hot, with SAE.20 oil)   7 lb/sq in (idling)
    Pressure (hot, with SAE.20 oil)   28 lb/sq in (at 2500 rev/min)
    Relief valve spring free length   2.480±.040
    Load when compressed to .930   17 lb
Fan—clearance between fan and fan housing   .065

FUEL SYSTEM

Carburetter:
    Type:
        Early '1200' Transporter (pre-1960)   Solex 28 PCI
        Later '1200' Transporter   Solex 28 PICT
        '1500' Transporter   Solex 28 PICT–1
    Venturi:
        '1200' Transporter (28 PCI)   21.5 mm
        Later Transporter ('1200' and '1500') (28 PICT) 22.5 mm
    Main jet:
        Early '1200' Transporter (28 PCI)   117.5 mm
        '1500' Transporter (28 PICT)   115 mm
    Air correction jet:
        '1200' Transporter (28 PCI)   180
        '1200' and '1500' Transporter (28 PICT)   145Y
    Pilot jet:
        Early '1200' Transporter (28 PCI)   50
        Later Transporter '1200' (PICT 28)   55g
    '1500' Transporter   45g
    Pilot jet air bleed:
        Early '1200' Transporter (28 PCI)   .80 mm
        Later '1200' Transporter (28 PICT, 28 PICT–1) 2.0 mm
        '1500' Transporter (28 PICT)   1.55 mm
    Emulsion tube:
        Early '1200' Transporter (28 PCI)   29
    Pump jet:
        '1200' Transporter (28 PICT)   1.0
        '1500' Transporter (28 PICT)   .50
    Power fuel jet:
        '1500' Transporter (28 PICT)   .7

IGNITION SYSTEM

Sparking plugs:
    Type:
        Bosch   W175 T1 (W145 T1, '1500' Car)
        Champion   L10, later L85, L87Y or L95Y
        KLG   F70
        AC   43L
        Lodge   H14
        Also any other make with similar values
        Gap   .025 to .028

Distributor:
Type:
Early '1200' Transporter (30 hp) .. Bosch VJR/4BR/25 or VW 211/905/205H
Later '1200' and '1500' Transporter Bosch ZV/PAU/4R/5mk or VW 113/905/205B
Contact breaker gap .. .. .016
Ignition timing:
All Transporters .. .. 10 deg. BTDC
Firing order 1–4–3–2

CLUTCH

Type .. .. Single plate, dry disc
Pressure plate springs (free length):
'1200' Transporter .. .. Inner 1.95, outer 1.95
Pressure plate springs (loaded length):
'1200' Transporter .. .. Inner 1.03, outer 1.16
Spring pressure (loaded):
'1200' Transporter .. .. Inner 35 to 40 lb, outer 108 to 144 lb
Pedal free play.. .. .. .40 to .80

TRANSMISSION

Gearbox casing:
Type (early '1200') .. .. 2-piece, split vertically
Type (all later models) .. .. .. 1-piece, tunnel
Gear selection:
Early '1200' .. .. 4-speed, 'crash' type or
                                      Synchromesh on 2nd, 3rd and Top
All subsequent models .. .. Synchromesh on all four forward gears
Gear ratios:
'Crash' type gearbox
1st 3.60:1
2nd 2.07:1
3rd 1.25:1
4th .. .. .80:1
Reverse 6.60:1
Early '1200':
1st 3.60:1
2nd 1.88:1
3rd 1.22:1
4th .. .. .79:1
Reverse 4.63:1
Later '1200' Transporter (30 hp):
1st 3.80:1
2nd 2.06:1
3rd 1.32:1
4th .. .. .89:1
Reverse 3.88:1
Transporter (from chassis 614/456), 34 hp:
1st 3.80:1
2nd 2.06:1
3rd 1.22:1
4th .. .. .82:1
Reverse 3.88:1
'1500':
1st 3.80:1
2nd 2.06:1
3rd 1.26:1
4th .. .. .82:1
Reverse 3.61:1

Differential ratio:
    '1200' and '1500' Transporter 4.125:1
    Reduction gear at axle end ('1200') 1.39:1
    Reduction gear at axle end ('1500') 1.26:1

STEERING

Type	Ross peg and cam
Steering wheel turns (lock to lock)	2.80
Wheel alignment (unladen):	
Camber angle	0° 40' ±30'
Kingpin inclination	4° 20'
Castor angle	0°
Toe-in	0 ±.040

FRONT SUSPENSION

Torsion bars:
    Number of leaves   9

REAR SUSPENSION

Spring type	One round torsion bar each side
Torsion bars:	
Length	23.2
Diameter	1.14
Inclination of spring plate:	
Transporter	20° ±30'
Transporter Ambulance	18° 40' ±20'
Transporter Fire Truck	21° 30' ±20'
Rear wheel toe-out	20' ±15'
Rear wheel camber angle:	
Transporter	4° 30' ±30'
Transporter Ambulance (from chassis 420/574)	1° 50' ±20'
Transporter Fire Truck (from chassis 425/460)	4° 30' ±20'

BRAKES

Type	Hydraulic front and rear
Handbrake	Cable operation on rear wheels only
Dual circuit braking	Later Transporters
Brake types:	
'1200'	Drum, 9 inch diameter
'1500'	Drum, 9.85 inch diameter
Lining width:	
Front:	
'1200'	1.97
'1500'	2.17
Rear:	
'1200'	1.58
'1500'	1.78
Lining thickness	.188 to .196

ELECTRICAL EQUIPMENT

Battery:
    '1500' during 1967 ..   ..   12V, 45 amp/hr
    Transporter pre 1967   ..   ..   6V, 77 amp/hr

Generator:
    Early '1200' (Bosch) LJ/REF–160/6/2500L4
    Later '1200' (Bosch) LJ/REG–180/6/2500L3
    Alternative (VW) 113/903/021C
    '1500' (12-volt) Bosch   ..   ..   G (L) 14V/30A/20
    Transporter (30 hp) Bosch LJ/REG/180/6L2
    Transporter (34 hp) VW 113/903/021A

Regulator:
    Early '1200' (Bosch) RS/TA–160/6/A1
    Later '1200' (Bosch) RS/TAA–180/6/4
    Alternative (VW) 113/903/801C
    Test voltage..   ..   ..   7.4 to 8.1 (1895 to 2220 engine rev/min at 68°F)
    '1500' 12-volt (Bosch) VA/14V/30A
    Transporter (30 hp) Bosch RS/TA180/6A3
    Test voltage (at 68°F)   ..   ..   7.2 to 8.2 at 1890 to 2160 engine rev/min
    Transporter (34 hp) VW 211/903/801
    Test voltage (at 68°F)   ..   ..   7.2 to 8.2 at 1890 to 2160 engine rev/min
(Generators and regulators must be of the same make when installed.)

Starter:
    Early '1200' (Bosch) EED–0.5/6–L4 (4-brush)
    Later '1200' (Bosch)   ..   ..   EED–0.5/6–L49 or EEF–0.5/6–L1
    Alternative (VW) 113/911/021A
    '1500' (12-volt), Bosch   ..   ..   EF (L) 12VO/7PS
    Transporter (30 hp), Bosch EED–0.5/6–L44
    Transporter (34 hp), Bosch ..   ..   EED–0.5/6–L49 or EEF–0.5/6–L1
    Alternative (VW)   ..   ..   113/911/021A or 111/911/021D

CAPACITIES

Fuel tank (all models) ..   ..   8.8 Imperial gallons
Engine sump   ..   ..   4.4 Imperial pints
Transmission   ..   ..   5.3 Imperial pints initially
                                                       (4.4 pints on refilling)
Oil bath air cleaner   ..   ..   .4 Imperial pints approx.
Brakes ..   ..   .5 Imperial pint
Reduction gear case   ..   ..   .4 Imperial pints
Steering box   ..   ..   .4 Imperial pint

TORQUE WRENCH SETTINGS
Figures are in lb ft unless otherwise specified

Engine:
Crankcase nuts (early '1200')	22
Crankcase nuts (8 mm)	14
Crankcase nuts (12 mm)	24 to 26
Cylinder head nuts	22 to 23
Flywheel gland nut	217
Connecting rod bolt	36
Fan nut	40 to 47
Generator pulley nut	40 to 47
Sparking plug	22 to 29
Oil drain plug	22
Copper-plated rocker shaft nuts	18

Transmission:
Bolts/nuts for casing	14
Nuts for differential side cover	22
Crownwheel bolts	43
Selector fork screws	18
Reverse selector fork screw	14
Drive pinion nut (early 'crash'-type transmission)	36 (tighten to 108, release and then to 36)
Drive pinion nut (2-piece casing)	80 to 87
Drive pinion nut (tunnel casing)	43 (tighten to 87, release and then to 43)
Main drive shaft nut (2-piece casing)	30 to 36
Main drive shaft nut (tunnel casing)	43 (tighten to 87, release and then to 43)
Rear axle shaft nut	217
Bolts/nuts for spring plate mounting	72 to 87

Brakes and wheels:
Backplate bolts	30
Hose and pipe unions (early)	11 to 18
Hose and pipe unions (later)	10 to 14
Wheel bolts (oiled)	65 to 79

Steering:
Steering wheel nut (except later Transporter)	36 to 43
Transporter after chassis 20/041712	18 to 22
Drop arm nut	58 to 72
Nuts for ball joints	18 to 25

Front axle:
Axle to frame	65 to 72
Steering knuckle ball joints	29 to 36 (10 mm) and 36 to 50 (12 mm)

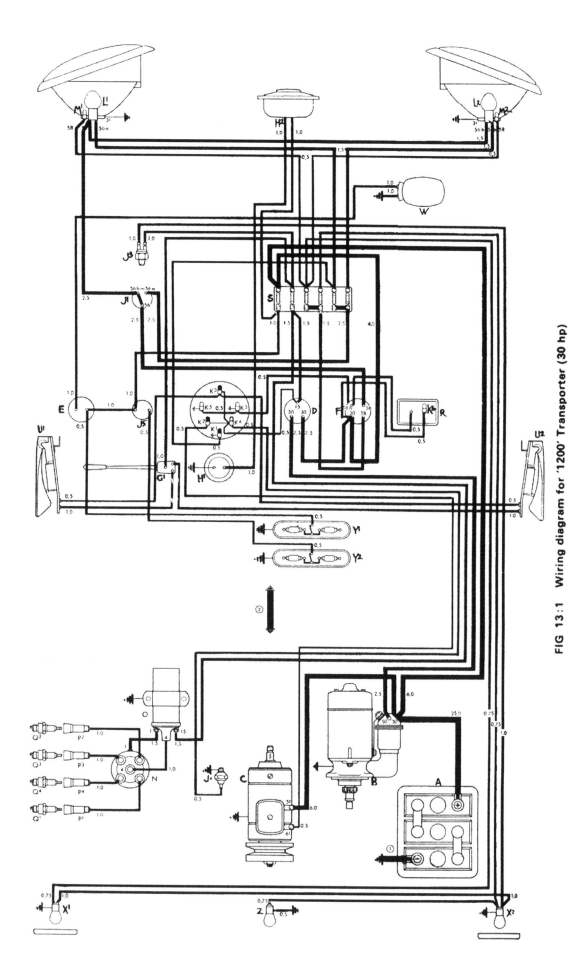

FIG 13:1   Wiring diagram for '1200' Transporter (30 hp)

Key to Fig 13:1   A Battery   B Starting motor   C Generator   D Ignition switch   E Windshield wiper switch   F Lighting switch
G1 Direction indicator switch   H1 Horn button   H2 Horn   J1 Dimmer switch   J3 Stoplight switch   J4 Oil pressure switch   J5 Switch for interior light
K1 Headlamp warning light   K2 Generator and cooling warning light   K3 Direction indicator warning light   K4 Oil pressure warning light   K5 Speedometer light
K6 Clock light   L1 Two-filament bulb (lefthand)   L2 Two-filament bulb (righthand)   M1 Parking light (lefthand)   M2 Parking light (righthand)
N Ignition distributor   O Ignition coil   p1 Spark plug connector (cylinder 1)   p2 Spark plug connector (cylinder 2)   p3 Spark plug connector (cylinder 3)
p4 Spark plug connector (cylinder 4)   Q1 Spark plug for cylinder 1   Q2 Spark plug for cylinder 2   Q3 Spark plug for cylinder 3   Q4 Spark plug for cylinder 4
R Clock   S Fuse box   U1 Direction indicator (lefthand)   U2 Direction indicator (righthand)   W Windshield wiper motor   X1 Stop tail light (lefthand)
X2 Stop tail light (righthand)   Y1 Interior light (front)   Y2 Interior light (rear)   Z Number plate light

137

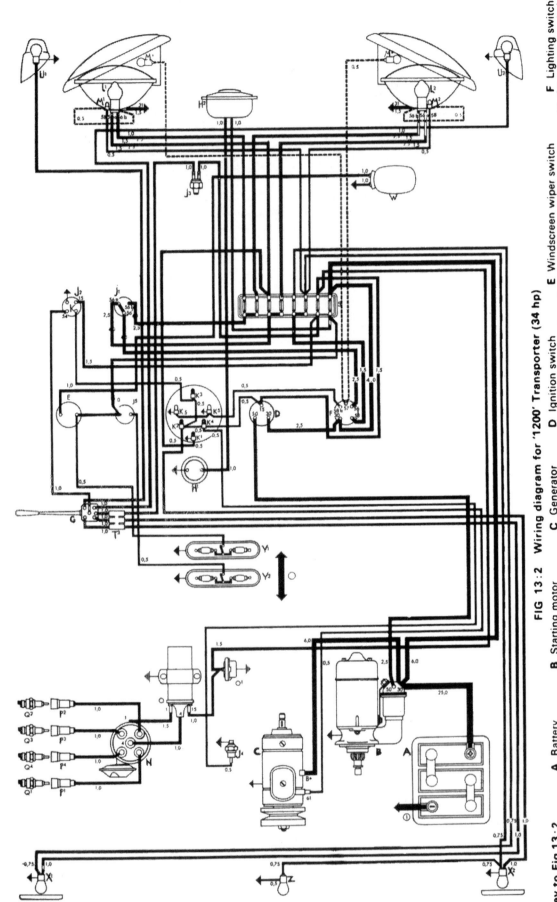

FIG 13 : 2   Wiring diagram for '1200' Transporter (34 hp)

Key to Fig 13 : 2   A Battery   B Starting motor   C Generator   D Ignition switch   E Windscreen wiper switch   F Lighting switch
G Direction indicator switch   H1 Horn button   H2 Horn   J1 Dimmer switch   J2 Indicator flasher relay   J3 Stoplight switch   J4 Oil pressure switch
J5 Switch for interior light   K1 Headlamp warning light   K2 Generator and cooling warning light   K3 Direction indicator warning light   K4 Oil pressure warning light
K5 Speedometer light   L1 Twin-filament bulb or sealed-beam unit (lefthand)   L2 Twin-filament bulb or sealed-beam unit (righthand)   M1 Parking light (lefthand)
M2 Parking light (righthand)   M3 Parking light sealed-beam headlight (lefthand)   M4 Parking light sealed-beam headlight (righthand)   N Ignition distributor
O Ignition coil   O1 Automatic choke   p1 Spark plug connector (cylinder 1)   p2 Spark plug connector (cylinder 2)   p3 Spark plug connector (cylinder 3)
p4 Spark plug connector (cylinder 4)   Q1 Spark plug for cylinder 1   Q2 Spark plug for cylinder 2   Q3 Spark plug for cylinder 3   Q4 Spark plug for cylinder 4
R Clock   S Fuse box   T Cable connector (3-point)   U1 Direction indicator (front lefthand)   U2 Direction indicator (front righthand)   W Windscreen wiper motor
X1 Stop tail/indicator light (lefthand)   X2 Stop tail/indicator light (righthand)   Y1 Interior light (front)   Y2 Interior light (rear)   Z Number plate light
1 Earth connection from battery to body   2 Earth connection from transmission to body

138

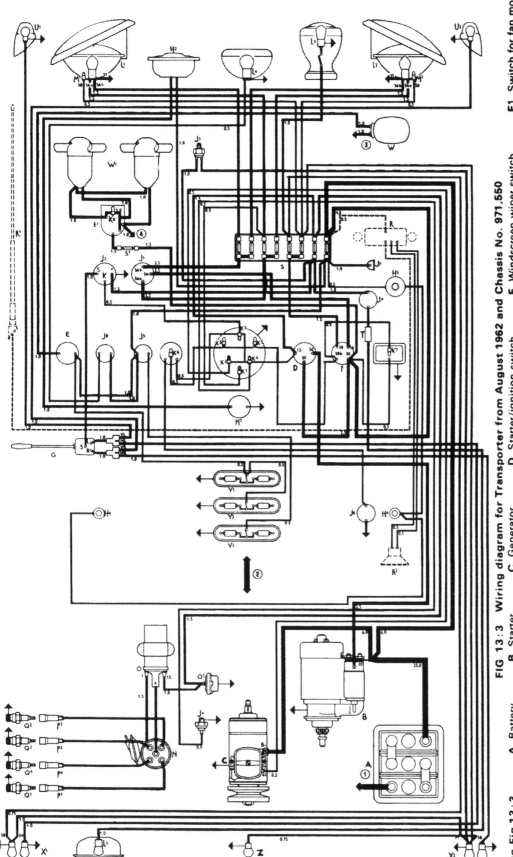

FIG 13:3 Wiring diagram for Transporter from August 1962 and Chassis No. 971,550

Key to Fig 13:3

A Battery B Starter C Generator D Starter/ignition switch E Windscreen wiper switch E1 Switch for fan motors*
F Lighting switch G Turn indicator switch H1 Horn button H2 Horn H3 Buzzer* H4 Buzzer button* J1 Dimmer switch*
J2 Flasher relay J3 Stoplight switch J4 Oil pressure switch J5 Switch for interior light J6 Fuel gauge sender unit J7 Socket*
J8 Switch for Red Cross Lamp* J9 Speedometer cable switch* K1 High beam warning light K2 Generator and cooling warning light
K3 Turn indicator warning light K4 Oil pressure warning light K5 Speedometer light K6 Fuel gauge light K7 Clock light K8 Ventilator fan warning light*
L1 Twin-filament bulb (lefthand) L2 Twin-filament bulb (righthand) L3 Spotlight bulb* L4 Red Cross light bulb* L5 Reversing light bulb*
M1 Parking light (lefthand) M2 Parking light (righthand) N Distributor O Coil O1 Automatic choke P1 Spark plug connector (cylinder 1)
P2 Spark plug connector (cylinder 2) P3 Spark plug connector (cylinder 3) P4 Spark plug connector (cylinder 4) Q1 Spark plug for cylinder 1
Q2 Spark plug for cylinder 2 Q3 Spark plug for cylinder 3 Q4 Spark plug for cylinder 4 R Radio R1 Aerial R2 Connector for rear
loudspeaker (only models 241-244 and 251) S Fuse box S1 Connector with fuse* T Cable connector U1 Turn indicator light (front lefthand)
indicator light (rear righthand) U2 Turn indicator light (front righthand) W Windscreen wiper motor X1 Stop, tail, indicator light (rear lefthand) X2 Stop, tail,
W1 Fan motors* Y1 Front interior light Y2 Ambulance compartment light* Y3 Rear interior light Z Number plate light
1 Earth strap from battery to body 2 Earth strap from transmission to body 3 Windscreen wiper motor earth cable 4 Fan motor earth cable
*For Ambulances only.

139

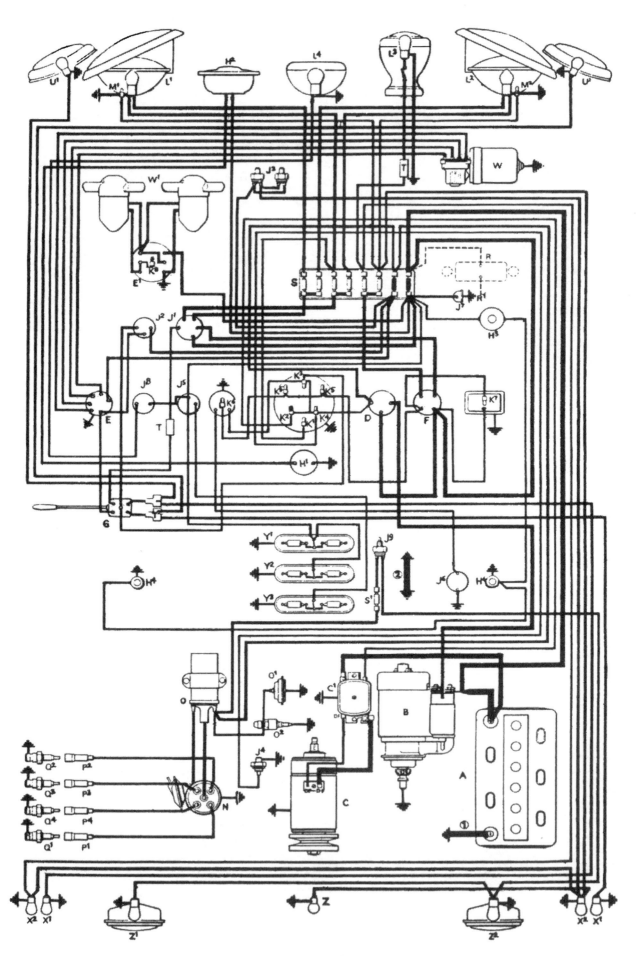

FIG 13:4 Wiring diagram for Transporter with 12-volt system (from August 1966 and Chassis No. 217,000,001)

Key to Fig 13:4

A Battery
B Starter
C Generator
C1 Regulator
D Ignition/starter switch
E Windscreen wiper switch
E1 Ventilator fan motor switch*
F Lighting switch
G Turn signal switch
H1 Horn button
H2 Horn
H3 Buzzer*
H4 Buzzer button*
J1 Headlamp flasher and dimmer relay
J2 Flasher unit
J3 Brake light switch
J4 Oil pressure switch
J5 Interior light switch
J6 Fuel gauge sender unit
J7 Socket*
J8 Red Cross light switch*
J9 Reversing light switch
K1 High beam warning light
K2 Generator and cooling fan warning light
K3 Turn signal warning light
K4 Oil pressure warning light
K5 Speedometer light bulb
K6 Fuel gauge light bulb
K7 Clock light bulb*
K8 Ventilator fan motor warning light*
L1 Twin-filament bulb (lefthand)
L2 Twin-filament bulb (righthand)
L3 Spotlight bulb*
L4 Red Cross light bulb*
M1 Parking light (lefthand)
M2 Parking light (righthand)
N Distributor
O Ignition coil
O1 Automatic choke
O2 Electro-magnetic pilot jet
P1 Spark plug connector (cylinder 1)
P2 Spark plug connector (cylinder 2)
P3 Spark plug connector (cylinder 3)
P4 Spark plug connector (cylinder 4)
Q1 Spark plug for cylinder 1
Q2 Spark plug for cylinder 2
Q3 Spark plug for cylinder 3
Q4 Spark plug for cylinder 4
R Radio
R1 Aerial connection
S Fuse box
S1 Connector and fuse
T Cable connector
T2 Cable adapter
U1 Turn signal (front lefthand)
U2 Turn signal (front righthand)
W Windshield wiper motor
W1 Ventilator fan motor*
X1 Turn signals (rear)
X2 Brake and tail lights (rear)
Y1 Interior light (front)
Y2 Ambulance compartment light*
Y3 Interior light (rear)
Z Number plate light
Z1 Reversing light (lefthand)
Z2 Reversing light (righthand)
1 Battery to body earthing strap
2 Transmission to body earthing strap

* For Ambulance only.

HINTS ON MAINTENANCE AND OVERHAUL

There are few things more rewarding than the restoration of a vehicle's original peak of efficiency and smooth performance.

The following notes are intended to help the owner to reach that state of perfection. Providing that he possesses the basic manual skills he should have no difficulty in performing most of the operations detailed in this manual. It must be stressed, however, that where recommended in the manual, highly-skilled operations ought to be entrusted to experts, who have the necessary equipment, to carry out the work satisfactorily.

Quality of workmanship:

The hazardous driving conditions on the roads to-day demand that vehicles should be as nearly perfect, mechanically, as possible. It is therefore most important that amateur work be carried out with care, bearing in mind the often inadequate working conditions, and also the inferior tools which may have to be used. It is easy to counsel perfection in all things, and we recognise that it may be setting an impossibly high standard. We do, however, suggest that every care should be taken to ensure that a vehicle is as safe to take on the road as it is humanly possible to make it.

Safe working conditions:

Even though a vehicle may be stationary, it is still potentially dangerous if certain sensible precautions are not taken when working on it while it is supported on jacks or blocks. It is indeed preferable not to use jacks alone, but to supplement them with carefully placed blocks, so that there will be plenty of support if the car rolls off the jacks during a strenuous manoeuvre. Axle stands are an excellent way of providing a rigid base which is not readily disturbed. Piles of bricks are a dangerous substitute. Be careful not to get under heavy loads on lifting tackle, the load could fall. It is preferable not to work alone when lifting an engine, or when working underneath a vehicle which is supported well off the ground. To be trapped, particularly under the vehicle, may have unpleasant results if help is not quickly forthcoming. Make some provision, however humble, to deal with fires. Always disconnect a battery if there is a likelihood of electrical shorts. These may start a fire if there is leaking fuel about. This applies particularly to leads which can carry a heavy current, like those in the starter circuit. While on the subject of electricity, we must also stress the danger of using equipment which is run off the mains and which has no earth or has faulty wiring or connections. So many workshops have damp floors, and electrical shocks are of such a nature that it is sometimes impossible to let go of a live lead or piece of equipment due to the muscular spasms which take place.

Work demanding special care:

This involves the servicing of braking, steering and suspension systems. On the road, failure of the braking system may be disastrous. Make quite sure that there can be no possibility of failure through the bursting of rusty brake pipes or rotten hoses, nor to a sudden loss of pressure due to defective seals or valves.

Problems:

The chief problems which may face an operator are:
1 External dirt.
2 Difficulty in undoing tight fixings.
3 Dismantling unfamiliar mechanisms.
4 Deciding in what respect parts are defective.
5 Confusion about the correct order for reassembly.
6 Adjusting running clearance.
7 Road testing.
8 Final tuning.

Practical suggestions to solve the problems:

1 Preliminary cleaning of large parts – engines, transmissions, steering, suspensions, etc, – should be carried out before removal from the car. Where road dirt and mud alone are present, wash clean with a high-pressure water jet, brushing to remove stubborn adhesions, and allow to drain and dry. Where oil or grease is also present, wash down with a proprietary compound (Gunk, Teepol etc,) applying with a stiff brush – an old paint brush is suitable – into all crevices. Cover the distributor and ignition coils with a polythene bag and then apply a strong water jet to clear the loosened deposits. Allow to drain and dry. The assemblies will then be sufficiently clean to remove and transfer to the bench for the next stage.

On the bench, further cleaning can be carried out, first wiping the parts as free as possible from grease with old newspaper. Avoid using rag or cotton waste which can leave clogging fibres behind. Any remaining grease can be removed with a brush dipped in paraffin. Avoid using paraffin or petrol in large quantities for cleaning in enclosed areas, such as garages, on account of the high fire risk.

When all exteriors have been cleaned, and not before, dismantling can be commenced. This ensures that dirt will not enter into interiors and orifices revealed by dismantling. In the next phases, where components have to be cleaned, use a special solvent or petrol and keep the containers covered except when in use. After the components have been cleaned, plug small holes with tapered hard wood plugs cut to size and blank off larger orifices with greaseproof paper and masking tape. Do not use soft wood plugs or matchsticks as they may break.

2 It is not advisable to hammer on the end of a screw thread, but if it must be done, first screw on a nut to protect the thread, and use a lead hammer. This applies particularly to the removal of tapered cotters. Nuts and bolts seem to 'grow' together, especially in exhaust systems. If penetrating oil does not work, try the judicious application of heat, but be careful of starting a fire. Asbestos sheet or cloth is useful to isolate heat.

Tight bushes or pieces of tail-pipe rusted into a silencer can be removed by splitting them with an open-ended hacksaw. Tight screws can sometimes be started by a tap from a hammer on the end of a suitable screwdriver. Many tight fittings will yield to the judicious use of a hammer, but it must be a soft-faced hammer, if damage is to be avoided, use a heavy block on the opposite side to absorb shock. Any parts of the steering system which have been damaged should be renewed, as attempts to repair them may lead to cracking and subsequent failure, and steering ball joints should be disconnected using a recommended tool to prevent damage.

3 It often happens that an owner is baffled when trying to dismantle an unfamiliar piece of equipment. So many modern devices are pressed together or assembled by spinning-over flanges, that they must be sawn apart. The intention is that the whole assembly must be renewed. However, parts which appear to be in one piece to the naked eye may reveal close-fitting joint lines when inspected with a magnifying glass, and this may provide the necessary clue to dismantling. Lefthanded screw threads are used where rotational forces would tend to unscrew a righthanded screw thread.

Be very careful when dismantling mechanisms which may come apart suddenly. Work in an enclosed space where the parts will be contained, and drape a piece of cloth over the device if springs are likely to fly in all directions. Mark everything which might be reassembled in the wrong position, scratched symbols may be used on unstressed parts, or a sequence of tiny dots from a centre punch can be useful. Stressed parts should never be scratched or centre-popped as this may lead to cracking under working conditions. Store parts which look alike in the correct order for reassembly. Never rely upon memory to assist in the assembly of complicated mechanisms, especially when they will be dismantled for a long time, but make notes, and drawings to supplement the diagrams in the manual, and put labels on detached wires. Rust stains may indicate unlubricated wear. This can sometimes be seen round the outside edge of a bearing cup in a universal joint. Look for bright rubbing marks on parts which normally should not make heavy contact. These might prove that something is bent or running out of truth. For example, there might be bright marks on one side of a piston, at the top near the ring grooves, and others at the bottom of the skirt on the other side. This could well be the clue to a bent connecting rod. Suspected cracks can be proved by heating the component in a light oil to approximately 100°C, removing, drying off, and dusting with french chalk. If a crack is present the oil retained in the crack will stain the french chalk.

4 In determining wear, and the degree, against the permissible limits set in the manual, accurate measurement can only be achieved by the use of a micrometer. In many cases, the wear is given to the fourth place of decimals; that is in ten-thousandths of an inch. This can be read by the vernier scale on the barrel of a good micrometer. Bore diameters are more difficult to determine. If, however, the matching shaft is accurately measured, the degree of play in the bore can be felt as a guide to its suitability. In other cases, the shank of a twist drill of known diameter is a handy check.

Many methods have been devised for determining the clearance between bearing surfaces. To-day the best and simplest is by the use of Plastigage, obtainable from most garages. A thin plastic thread is laid between the two surfaces and the bearing is tightened, flattening the thread. On removal, the width of the thread is compared with the scale supplied with the thread and the clearance is read off directly. Sometimes joint faces leak persistently, even after gasket renewal. The fault will then be traceable to distortion, dirt or burrs. Studs which are screwed into soft metal frequently raise burrs at the point of entry. A quick cure for this is to chamfer the edge of the hole in the part which fits over the stud.

5 **Always check a replacement part with the original one before it is fitted.**

If parts are not marked, and the order for reassembly is not known, a little detective work will help. Look for marks which are due to wear to see if they can be mated. Joint faces may not be identical due to manufacturing errors, and parts which overlap may be stained, giving a clue to the correct position. Most fixings leave identifying marks especially if they were painted over on assembly. It is then easier to decide whether a nut, for instance, has a plain, a spring, or a shakeproof washer under it. All running surfaces become 'bedded' together after long spells of work and tiny imperfections on one part will be found to have left corresponding marks on the other. This is particularly true of shafts and bearings and even a score on a cylinder wall will show on the piston.

6 Checking end float rocker clearances by feeler gauge may not always give accurate results because of wear. For instance, the rocker tip which bears on a valve stem may be deeply pitted, in which case the feeler will simply be bridging a depression. Thrust washers may also wear depressions in opposing faces to make accurate measurement difficult. End float is then easier to check by using a dial gauge. It is common practice to adjust end play in bearing assemblies, like front hubs with taper rollers, by doing up the axle nut until the hub becomes stiff to turn and then backing it off a little. Do not use this method with ballbearing hubs as the assembly is often preloaded by tightening the axle nut to its fullest extent. If the splitpin hole will not line up, file the base of the nut a little.

Steering assemblies often wear in the straight-ahead position. If any part is adjusted, make sure that it remains free when moved from lock to lock. Do not be surprised if an assembly like a steering gearbox, which is known to be carefully adjusted outside the car, becomes stiff when it is bolted into place. This will be due to distortion of the case by the pull of the mounting bolts, particularly if the mounting points are not all touching together. This problem may be met in other equipment and is cured by careful attention to the alignment of mounting points.

When a spanner is stamped with a size and A/F it means that the dimension is the width between the jaws and has no connection with ANF, which is the designation for the American National Fine thread. Coarse threads like Whitworth are rarely used on cars to-day except for studs which screw into soft aluminium or cast iron. For this reason it might be found that the top end of a cylinder head stud has a fine thread and the lower end a coarse thread to screw into the cylinder block. If the car has mainly UNF threads then it is likely that any coarse threads will be UNC, which are not the same as Whitworth. Small sizes have the same number of threads in Whitworth and UNC, but in the $\frac{1}{2}$ in size for example, there are twelve threads to the inch in the former and thirteen in the latter.

7 After a major overhaul, particularly if a great deal of work has been done on the braking, steering and suspension systems, it is advisable to approach the problem of testing with care. If the braking system has been overhauled, apply heavy pressure to the brake pedal and get a second operator to check every possible source of leakage. The brakes may work extremely well, but a leak could cause complete failure after a few miles.

Do not fit the hub caps until every wheel nut has been checked for tightness, and make sure that the tyre pressures are correct. Check the levels of coolant, lubricants and hydraulic fluids. Being satisfied that all is well, take the car on the road and test the brakes at once. Check the steering and the action of the handbrake. Do all this at moderate speeds on quiet roads, and make sure there is no other vehicle behind you when you try a rapid stop.

Finally, remember that many parts settle down after a time, so check for tightness of all fixings after the car has been on the road a hundred miles or so.

8 It is useless to tune an engine which has not reached its normal running temperature. In the same way, the tune of an engine which is stiff after a rebore will be different when the engine is again running free. Remember too, that rocker clearances on pushrod operated valve gear will change when the cylinder head nuts are tightened after an initial period of running with a new head gasket.

Trouble may not always be due to what seems the obvious cause. Ignition, carburation and mechanical condition are interdependent and spitting back through the carburetter, which might be attributed to a weak mixture, can be caused by a sticking inlet valve.

For one final hint on tuning, never adjust more than one thing at a time or it will be impossible to tell which adjustment produced the desired result.

WARNING

If, during any overhaul or service, it is necessary to extract any roll pins and/or circlips they MUST be discarded.

New pins and/or circlips MUST be fitted on reassembly. The refitting of used roll pins and/or circlips could result in failure of a component and possibly create a safety hazard.

GLOSSARY OF TERMS

Allen key Cranked wrench of hexagonal section for use with socket head screws.

Alternator Electrical generator producing alternating current. Rectified to direct current for battery charging.

Ambient temperature Surrounding atmospheric temperature.

Annulus Used in engineering to indicate the outer ring gear of an epicyclic gear train.

Armature The shaft carrying the windings, which rotates in the magnetic field of a generator or starter motor. That part of a solenoid or relay which is activated by the magnetic field.

Axial In line with, or pertaining to, an axis.

Backlash Play in meshing gears.

Balance lever A bar where force applied at the centre is equally divided between connections at the ends.

Banjo axle Axle casing with large diameter housing for the crownwheel and differential.

Bar Standard unit of pressure equal to 14.5lb/sq in.

Bendix pinion A self-engaging and self-disengaging drive on a starter motor shaft.

Bevel pinion A conical shaped gearwheel, designed to mesh with a similar gear with an axis usually at 90° to its own.

bhp Brake horse power. Now superseded by kW.

bmep Brake mean effective pressure. Average pressure on a piston during the working stroke.

Brake cylinder Cylinder with hydraulically operated piston(s) acting on brake shoes or pads.

Brake regulator Control valve fitted in hydraulic braking system which limits brake pressure to rear brakes during heavy braking to prevent rear wheel locking.

Camber Angle at which a wheel is tilted from the vertical.

Capacitor Modern term for an electrical condenser. Part of distributor assembly, connected across contact breaker points, acts as an interference suppressor.

Castellated Top face of a nut, slotted across the flats to take a locking splitpin.

Castor Angle at which the kingpin or swivel pin is tilted when viewed from the side.

cc or cm³ Cubic centimetres. Engine capacity is arrived at by multiplying the area of the bore in sq cm by the stroke in cm by the number of cylinders.

Clevis U-shaped forked connector used with a clevis pin, usually at handbrake connections.

Collet A type of collar, usually split and located in a groove in a shaft, and held in place by a retainer. The arrangement used to retain the spring(s) on a valve stem in most cases.

Commutator Rotating segmented current distributor between armature windings and brushes.

Compression ratio The ratio, or quantitative relation, of the total volume (piston at bottom of stroke) to the unswept volume (piston at top of stroke) in an engine cylinder.

Condenser See 'Capacitor'.

Core plug Plug for blanking off a manufacturing hole.

Crownwheel Large bevel gear in rear axle, driven by a bevel pinion attached to the propeller shaft.

'C'-spanner Like a 'C' with a handle. For use on screwed collars without flats, but with slots or holes.

Damper Modern term for shock absorber, used in vehicle suspension systems to damp out spring oscillations.

Depression The lowering of atmospheric pressure as in the inlet manifold and carburetter.

Dowel Close tolerance pin, peg, tube or bolt, which accurately locates mating parts.

Drag link Rod connecting steering box drop arm (pitman arm) to nearest front wheel steering arm in certain types of steering systems.

Dry liner Thinwall tube pressed into cylinder bore.

Dry sump Lubrication system where all oil is scavenged from the sump, and returned to a separate tank.

Dynamo Electrical generator producing direct current.

Electrode Terminal part of an electrical component, such as the points or 'Electrodes' of a sparking plug.

Electrolyte In lead-acid car batteries a solution of sulphuric acid and distilled water.

End float The axial movement between associated parts, end play.

EP Extreme pressure. In lubricants, special grades for heavily loaded bearing surfaces, such as gear teeth in a gearbox, or crownwheel and pinion in a rear axle.

Fade Of brakes. Reduced efficiency due to overheating.

Field coils Windings on the polepieces of motors and generators.

Fillets Narrow finishing strips usually applied to interior bodywork.

First motion shaft Input shaft from clutch to gearbox.

Fullflow filter Filters in which all the oil is pumped to the engine. If the element becomes clogged, a bypass valve operates to pass unfiltered oil to the engine.

FWD Front wheel drive.

Gear pump Two meshing gears in a close fitting casing. Oil is carried from the inlet round the outside of both gears in the spaces between the gear teeth and casing to the outlet, the meshing gear teeth prevent oil passing back to the inlet, and the oil is forced through the outlet port.

Generator An alternator or a dynamo.

Grommet A ring of protective or sealing material. Can be used to protect pipes or leads passing through bulkheads.

Grubscrew Fully threaded headless screw with screwdriver slot. Used for locking or alignment purposes.

Gudgeon pin Shaft which connects a piston to its connecting rod. Sometimes called 'wrist pin' or 'piston pin'.

Halfshaft One of a pair transmitting drive from the differential.

Helical In spiral form. The teeth of helical gears are cut at a spiral angle to the side faces of the gearwheel.

Hot spot Hot area that assists vapourisation of fuel on its way to cylinders. Often provided by close contact between inlet and exhaust manifolds.

HT High Tension. Applied to electrical current produced by the ignition coil for the sparking plugs.

Hydrometer A device for checking specific gravity of liquids. Used to check specific gravity of electrolyte.

Hypoid bevel gears A form of bevel gear used in the rear axle drive gears. The bevel pinion meshes below the centre line of the crownwheel, giving a lower propeller shaft line.

Idler A device for passing on movement. A free running gear between driving and driven gears. A lever transmitting track rod movement to a side rod in steering gear.

Impeller A centrifugal pumping element. Used in water pumps to stimulate flow.

Journals Those parts of a shaft that are in contact with the bearings.

kW Standard unit of power, equal to 1.34102hp

Kingpin The main vertical pin which carries the front wheel spindle, and permits steering movement. May be called 'steering pin' or 'swivel pin'.

Layshaft The shaft which carries the laygear in the gearbox. The laygear is driven by the first motion shaft and drives the third motion shaft according to the gear selected. Sometimes called the 'countershaft' or 'second motion shaft'.

lbf ft A measure of twist or torque. A pull of 10lb at a radius of 1ft is a torque of 10lbf ft.

lb/sq in Pounds per square inch.

Little-end The small, or piston end of a connecting rod. Sometimes called the 'small-end'.

LT Low Tension. The current output from the battery.

Mandrel Accurately manufactured bar or rod used for test or centring purposes.

Manifold A pipe, duct or chamber, with several branches.

Nm Standard unit of torque equal to 0.738lbf ft.

Needle rollers Bearing rollers with a length many times their diameter.

Oil bath Reservoir which lubricates parts by immersion. In air filters, a separate oil supply for wetting a wire mesh element to hold the dust.

Oil wetted In air filters, a wire mesh element lightly oiled to trap and hold airborne dust.

Overlap Period during which inlet and exhaust valves are open together.

Panhard rod Bar connected between fixed point on chassis and another on axle to control sideways movement.

Pawl Pivoted catch which engages in the teeth of a ratchet to permit movement in one direction only.

Peg spanner Tool with pegs, or pins, to engage in holes or slots in the part to be turned.

Pendant pedals Pedals with levers pivoted at the top.

Phillips screwdriver A cross-point screwdriver for use with the cross-slotted heads of Phillips screws.

Pinion A small gear, usually in relation to another gear.

Piston-type damper Shock absorber in which damping is controlled by a piston working in a closed oil-filled cylinder.

Preloading Preset static pressure on ball or roller bearings not due to working loads.

Radial Radiating from a centre, like the spokes of a wheel.

Radius rod Pivoted arm confining movement of a part to an arc of fixed radius.

Ratchet Toothed wheel or rack which can move in one direction only, movement in the other being prevented by a pawl.

Ring gear A gear tooth ring attached to outer periphery of flywheel. Starter pinion engages with it during starting.

Runout Amount by which rotating part is out of true.

Semi-floating axle Outer end of rear axle halfshaft is carried on bearing inside axle casing. Wheel hub is secured to end of shaft.

Servo A hydraulic or pneumatic system for assisting, or, augmenting a physical effort. See 'Vacuum Servo'.

Setscrew Fastener threaded the full length of the shank.

Shackle A coupling link, used in the form of two parallel pins connected by side plates to secure the end of the master suspension spring and absorb the effects of deflection.

Shell bearing Thinwalled steel shell lined with antifriction metal. Usually semi-circular and used in pairs for main and big-end bearings.

Shock absorber See 'Damper'.

Silentbloc Rubber bush bonded to inner and outer metal sleeves.

Socket-head screw Screw with hexagonal socket for an Allen key.

Solenoid A coil of wire creating a magnetic field when electric current passes through it. Used with a soft iron core to operate contacts or a mechanical device.

Spur gear A gear with teeth cut axially.

Stub axle Short axle fixed at one end only.

Tachometer An instrument for accurate measurement of rotating speed. Usually indicates in revolutions per minute.

TDC Top Dead Centre. The highest point reached by a piston in a cylinder, with the crank and connecting rod in line.

Thermostat Automatic device for regulating temperature. Used in vehicle coolant systems to open a valve which restricts circulation at low temperature.

Third motion shaft Output shaft of gearbox.

Threequarter floating axle Outer end of rear axle halfshaft flanged and bolted to wheel hub, which runs on bearing mounted on outside of axle casing. Vehicle weight is not carried by the axle shaft.

Thrust bearing or washer Used to reduce friction in rotating parts subject to axial loads.

Torque Turning or twisting effort. See 'lbf ft'.

Track rod The bar(s) across the vehicle which connect the steering arms and maintain the front wheel alignment.

UJ Universal joint. A coupling between shafts which permits angular movement.

UNF Unified National Fine screw thread.

Vacuum servo Device used in brake system, using difference between atmospheric pressure and inlet manifold depression to operate a piston which acts to augment brake pressure as required. See 'Servo'.

Venturi A restriction or 'choke' in a tube, as in a carburetter, used to increase velocity to obtain a reduction in pressure.

Vernier A sliding scale for obtaining fractional readings of the graduations of an adjacent scale.

Welch plug A domed thin metal disc which is partially flattened to lock in a recess. Used to plug core holes in castings.

Wet liner Removable cylinder barrel, sealed against coolant leakage, where the coolant is in direct contact with the outer surface.

Wet sump A reservoir attached to the crankcase to hold the lubricating oil.

INDEX

Other titles on VW Transporter

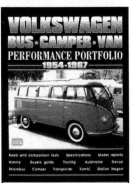

Printed in Great Britain
by Amazon